CHAPTER 31

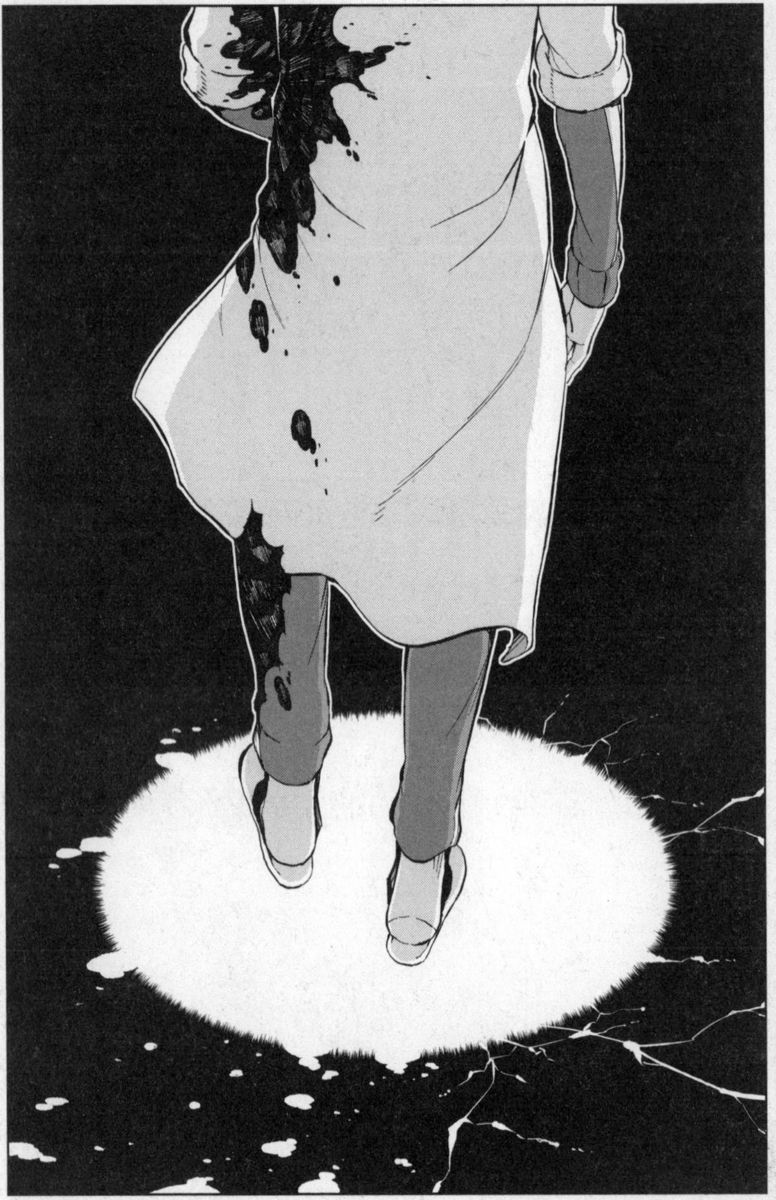

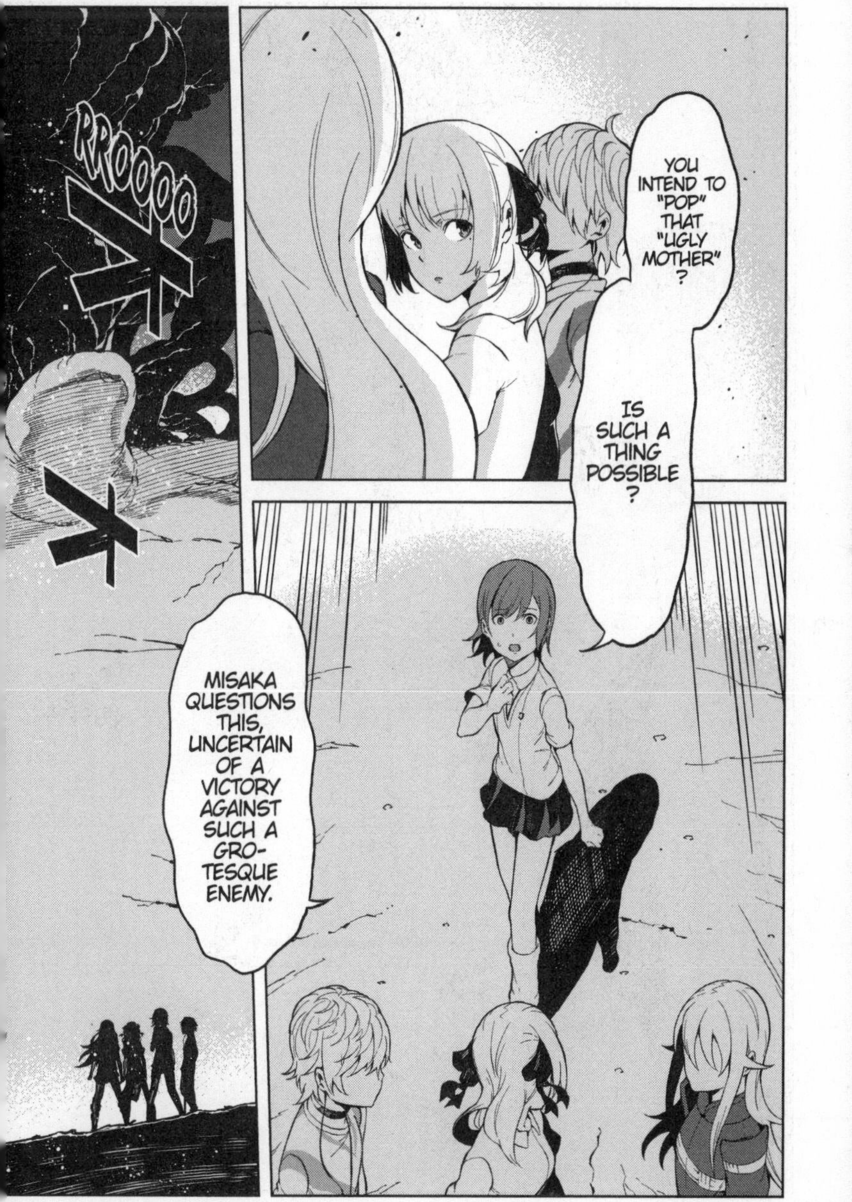
YOU INTEND TO "POP" THAT "UGLY MOTHER" ?
IS SUCH A THING POSSIBLE ?
MISAKA QUESTIONS THIS, UNCERTAIN OF A VICTORY AGAINST SUCH A GRO-TESQUE ENEMY.
RROOOO

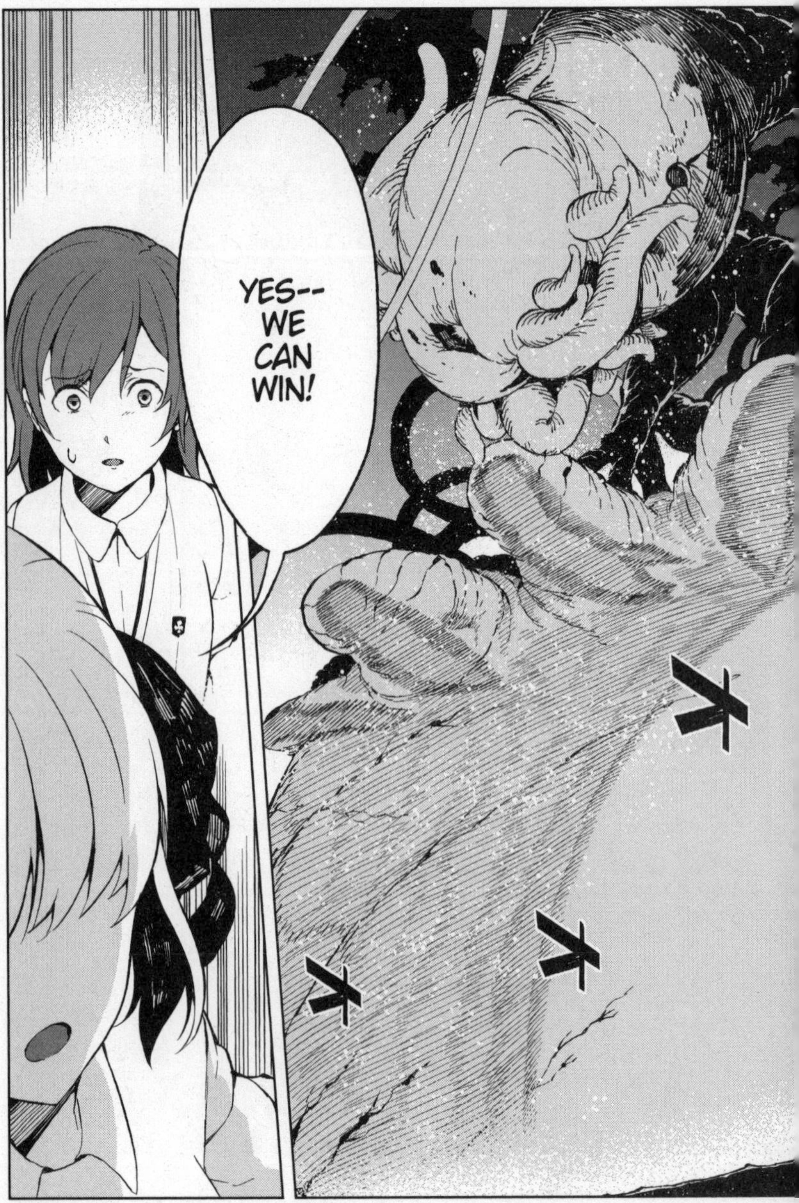
YES-- WE CAN WIN!

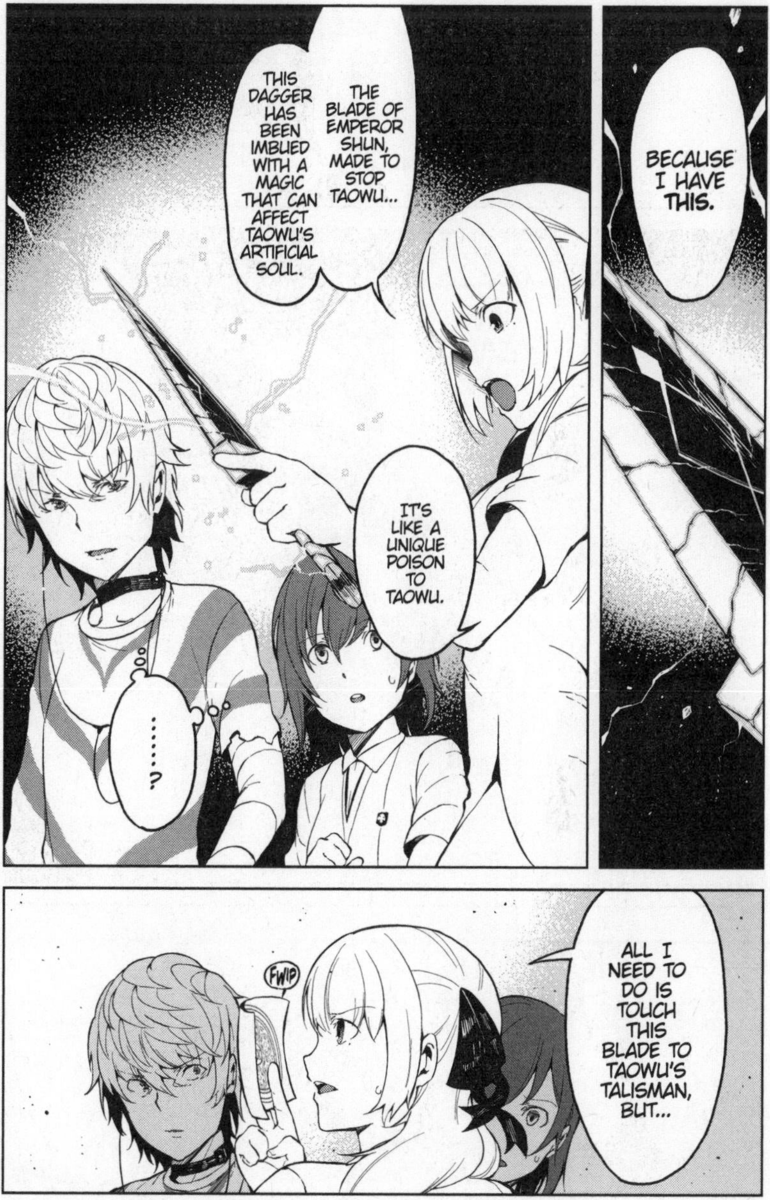
BECAUSE I HAVE THIS.
THE BLADE OF EMPEROR SHUN, MADE TO STOP TAOWU...
THIS DAGGER HAS BEEN IMBUED WITH A MAGIC THAT CAN AFFECT TAOWU'S ARTIFICIAL SOUL.
IT'S LIKE A UNIQUE POISON TO TAOWU.
......?
ALL I NEED TO DO IS TOUCH THIS BLADE TO TAOWU'S TALISMAN, BUT...
FWIP

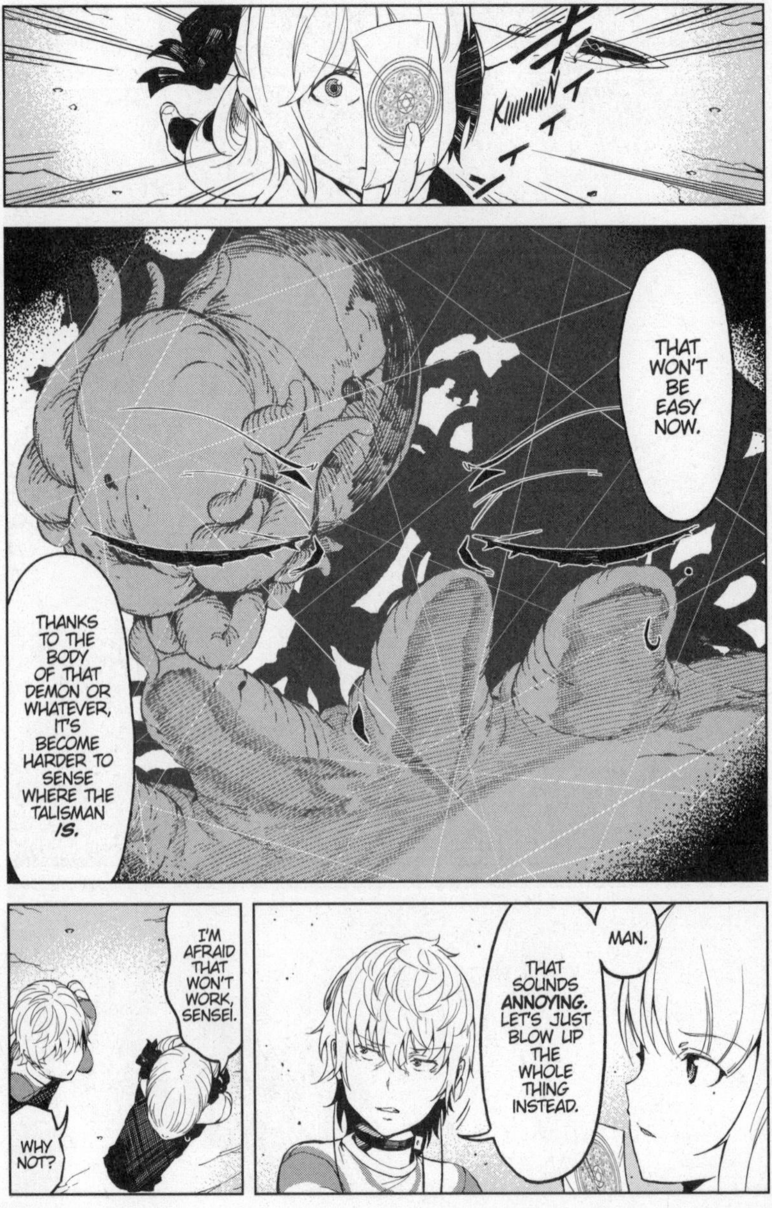
KIIIIIIIIN
THAT WON'T BE EASY NOW.
THANKS TO THE BODY OF THAT DEMON OR WHATEVER, IT'S BECOME HARDER TO SENSE WHERE THE TALISMAN *IS.*
MAN.
THAT SOUNDS **ANNOYING.** LET'S JUST BLOW UP THE WHOLE THING INSTEAD.
I'M AFRAID THAT WON'T WORK, SENSEI.
WHY NOT?

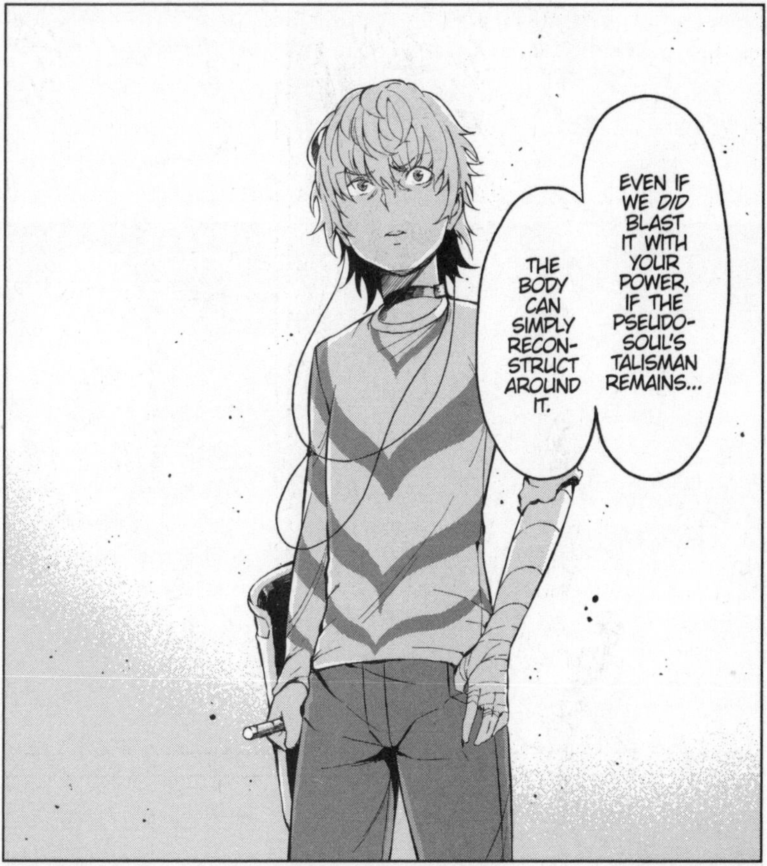
EVEN IF WE *DID* BLAST IT WITH YOUR POWER, IF THE PSEUDO-SOUL'S TALISMAN REMAINS...
THE BODY CAN SIMPLY RECON-STRUCT AROUND IT.
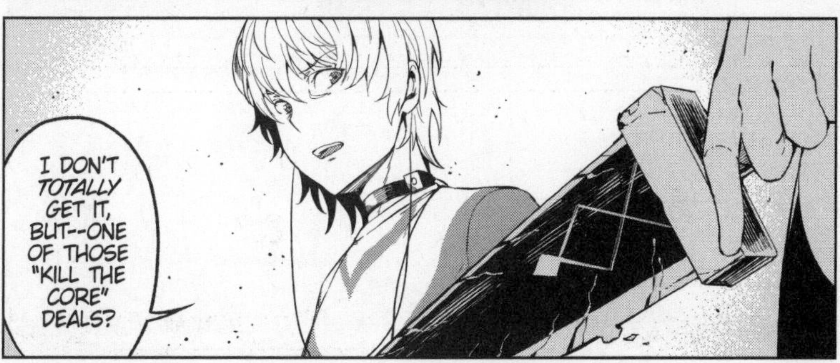
I DON'T *TOTALLY* GET IT, BUT--ONE OF THOSE "KILL THE CORE" DEALS?

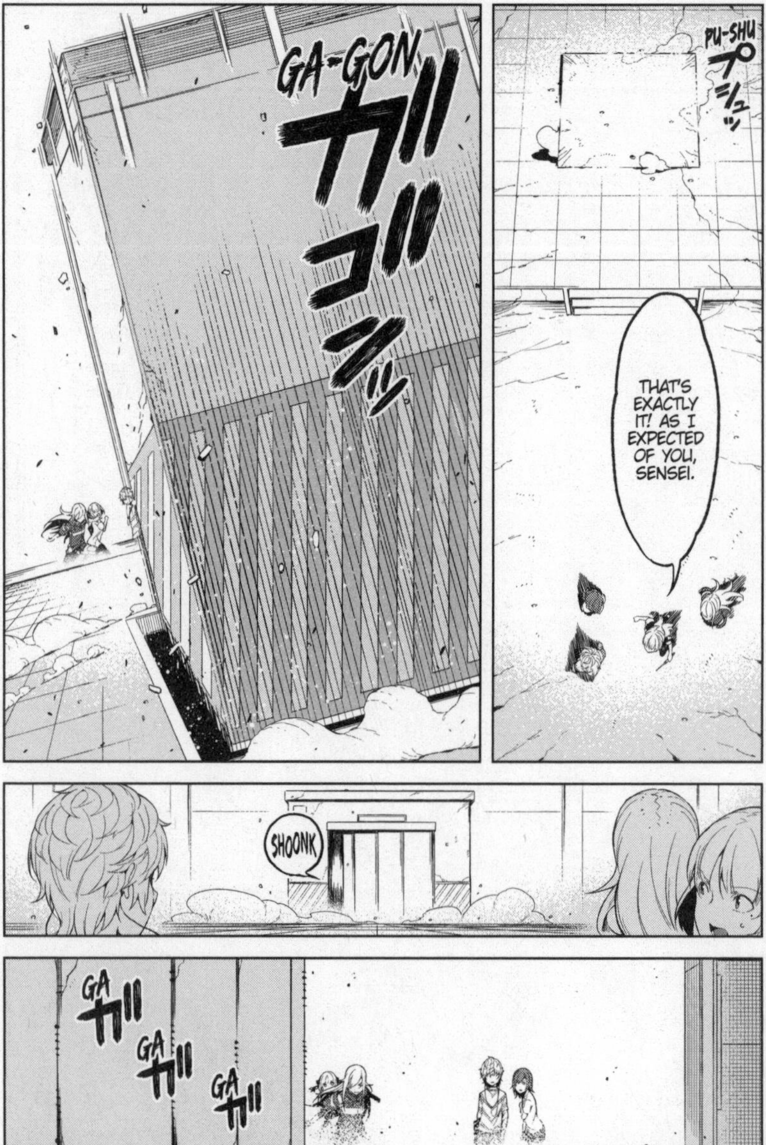
PU-SHU
THAT'S EXACTLY IT! AS I EXPECTED OF YOU, SENSEI.
GA-GON
SHOONK
GA
GA
GA

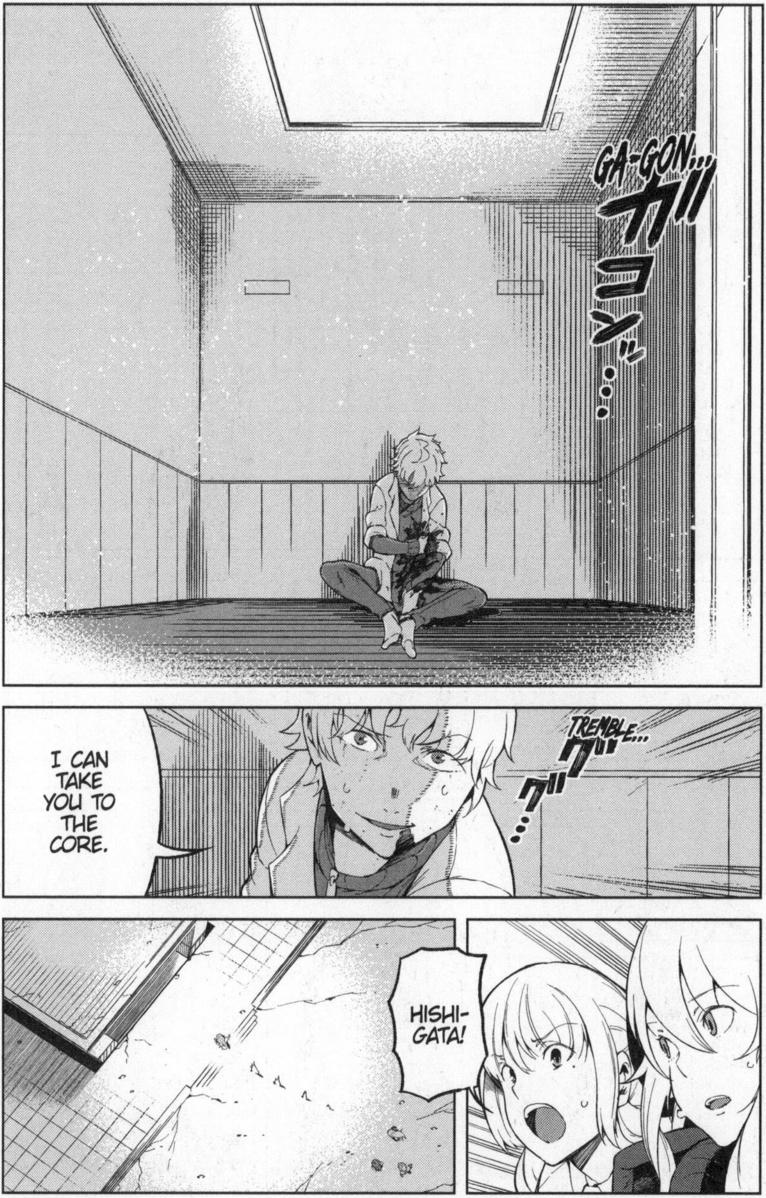
GA-GON...
ガコン…
TREMBLE...
ググ…
I CAN TAKE YOU TO THE CORE.
HISHI-GATA!

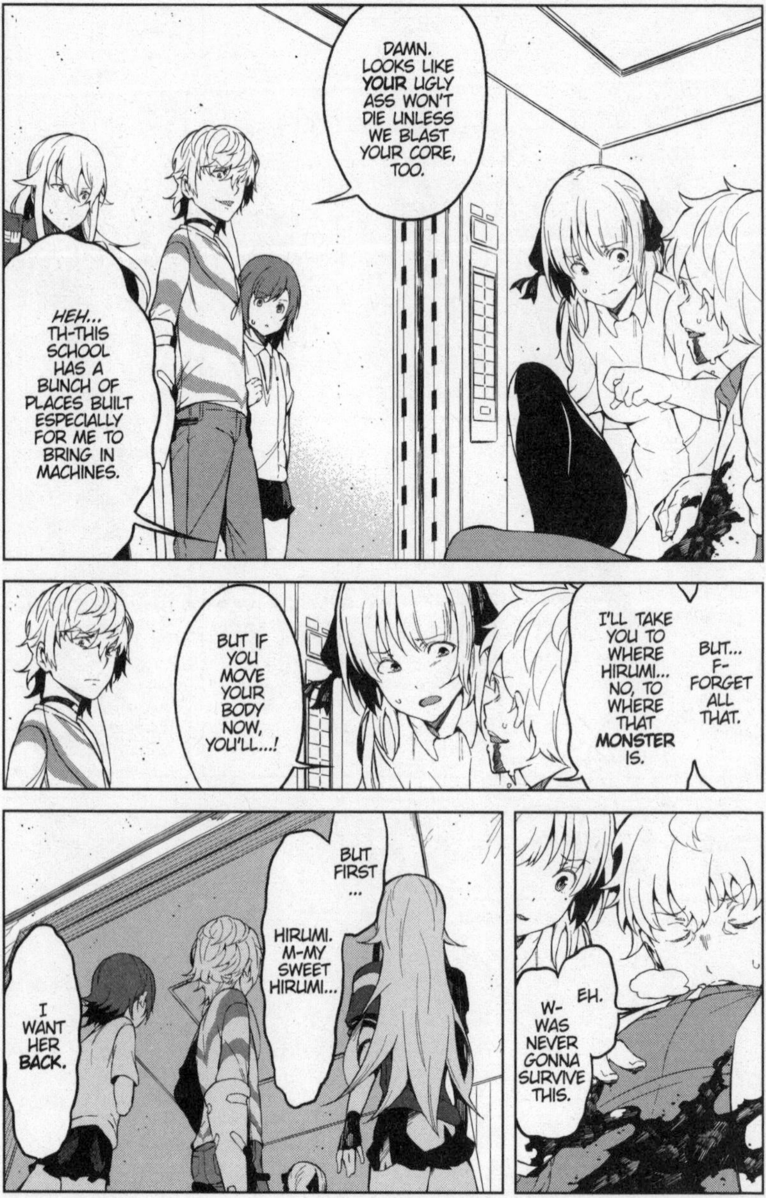
DAMN. LOOKS LIKE YOUR UGLY ASS WON'T DIE UNLESS WE BLAST YOUR CORE, TOO.
HEH... TH-THIS SCHOOL HAS A BUNCH OF PLACES BUILT ESPECIALLY FOR ME TO BRING IN MACHINES.
BUT... F-FORGET ALL THAT.
I'LL TAKE YOU TO WHERE HIRUMI... NO, TO WHERE THAT MONSTER IS.
BUT IF YOU MOVE YOUR BODY NOW, YOU'LL...!
EH.
W-WAS NEVER GONNA SURVIVE THIS.
BUT FIRST ...
HIRUMI. M-MY SWEET HIRUMI...
I WANT HER BACK.

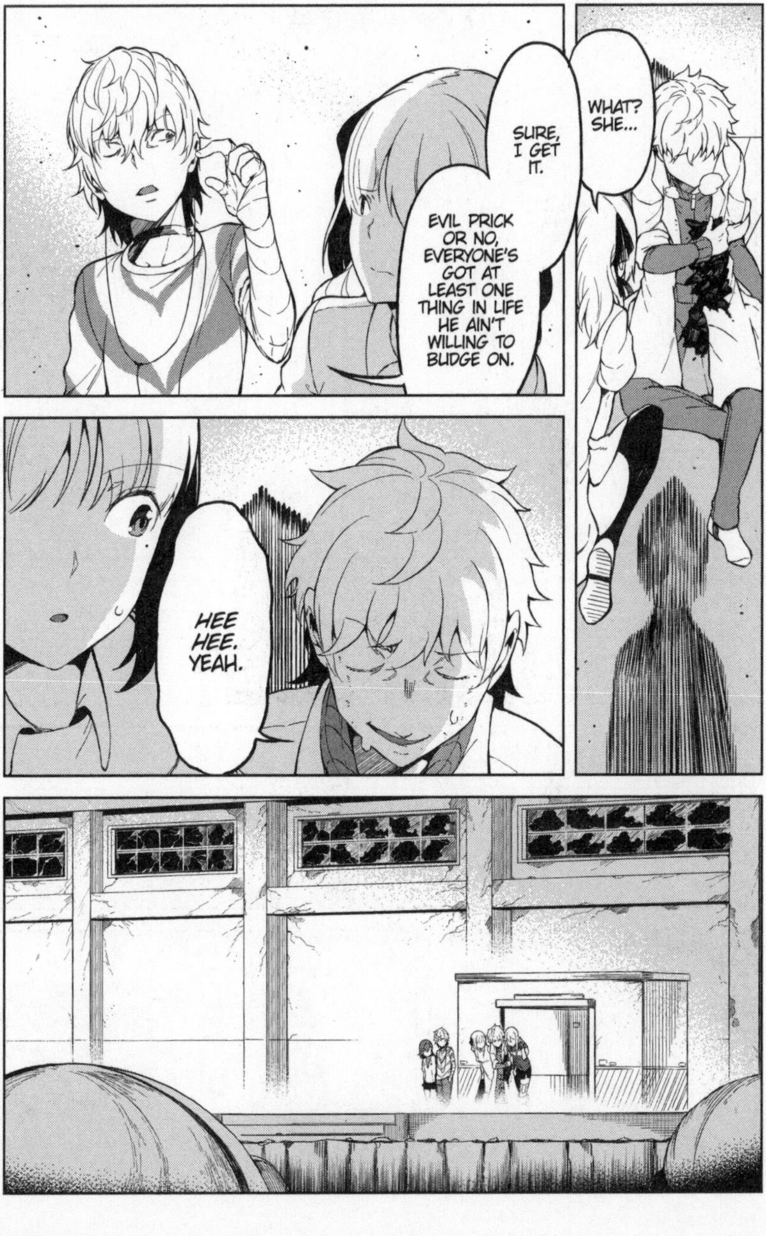
WHAT? SHE...
SURE, I GET IT.
EVIL PRICK OR NO, EVERYONE'S GOT AT LEAST ONE THING IN LIFE HE AIN'T WILLING TO BUDGE ON.
HEE HEE. YEAH.

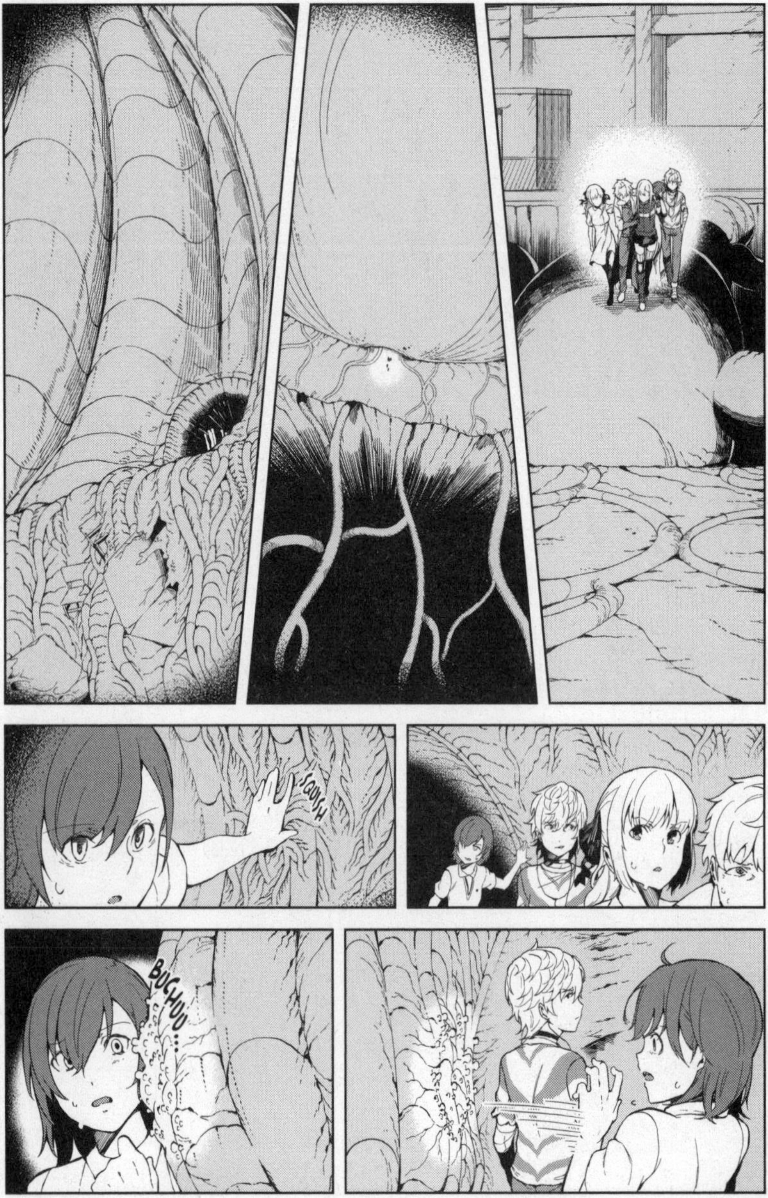
SQUISH
BUCHUU...

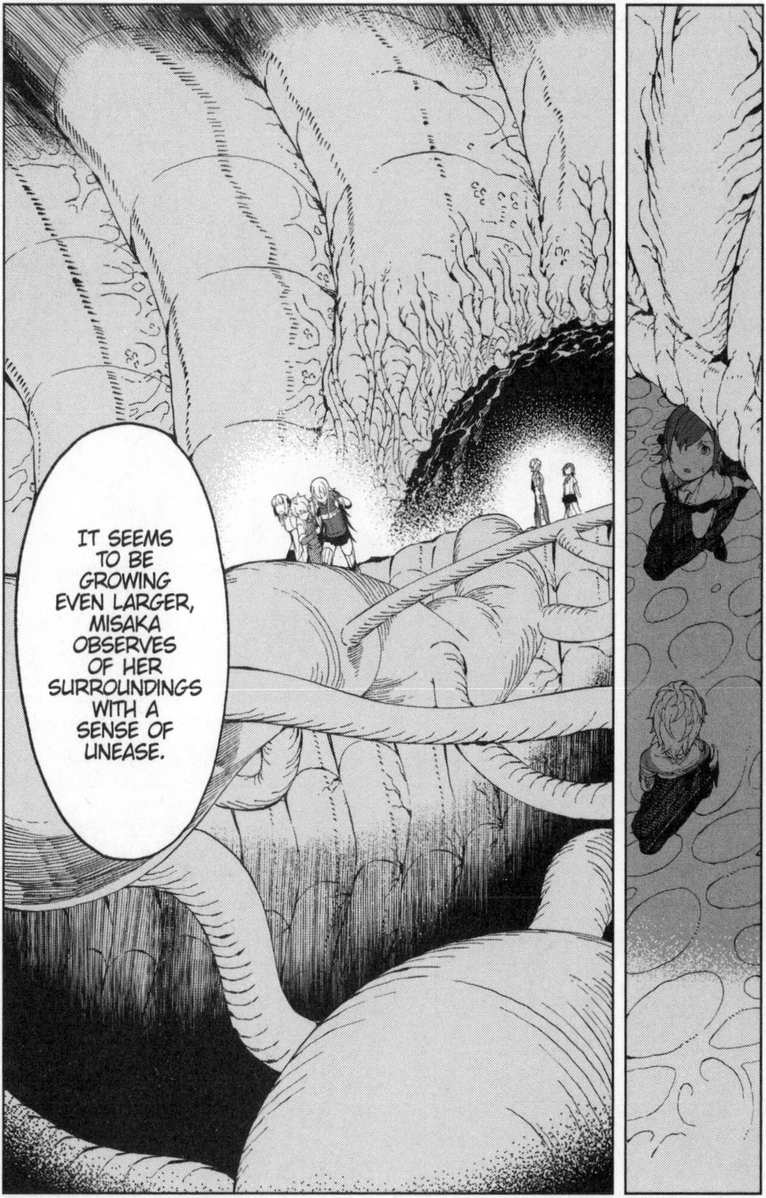
IT SEEMS TO BE GROWING EVEN LARGER, MISAKA OBSERVES OF HER SURROUNDINGS WITH A SENSE OF UNEASE.

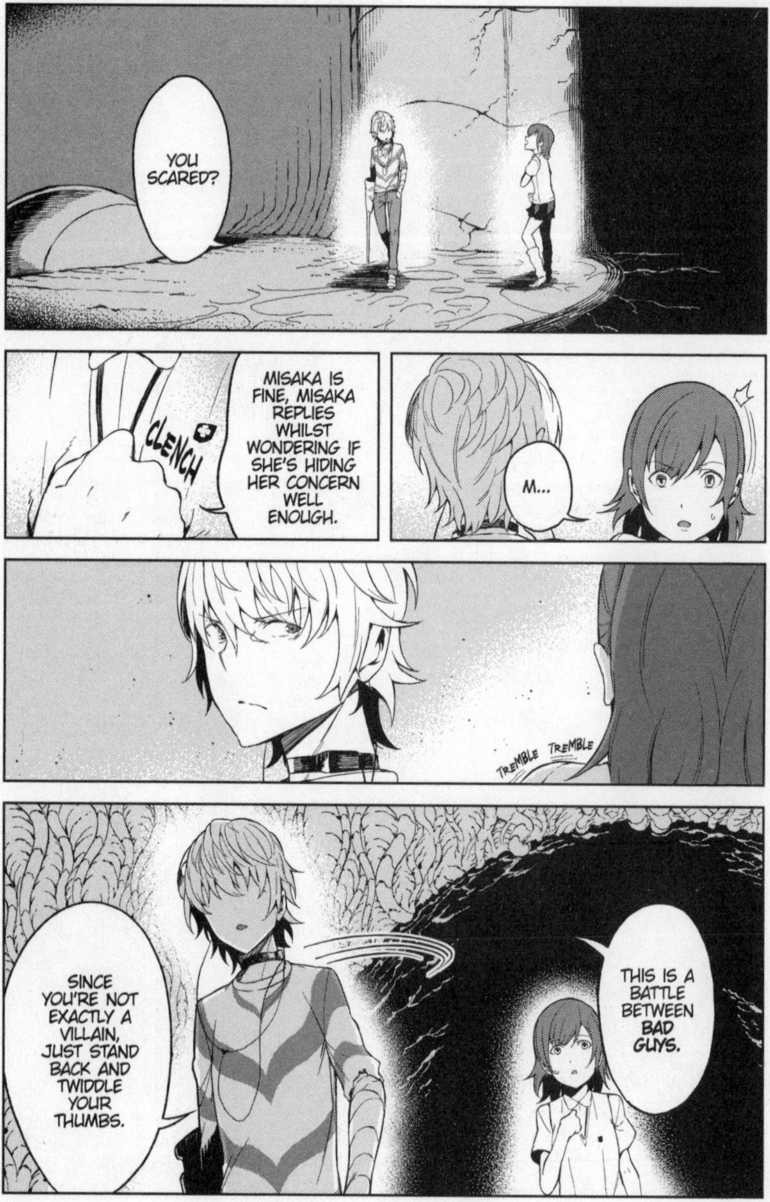
YOU SCARED?
M...
MISAKA IS FINE, MISAKA REPLIES WHILST WONDERING IF SHE'S HIDING HER CONCERN WELL ENOUGH.
CLENCH
TREMBLE TREMBLE
THIS IS A BATTLE BETWEEN BAD GUYS.
SINCE YOU'RE NOT EXACTLY A VILLAIN, JUST STAND BACK AND TWIDDLE YOUR THUMBS.

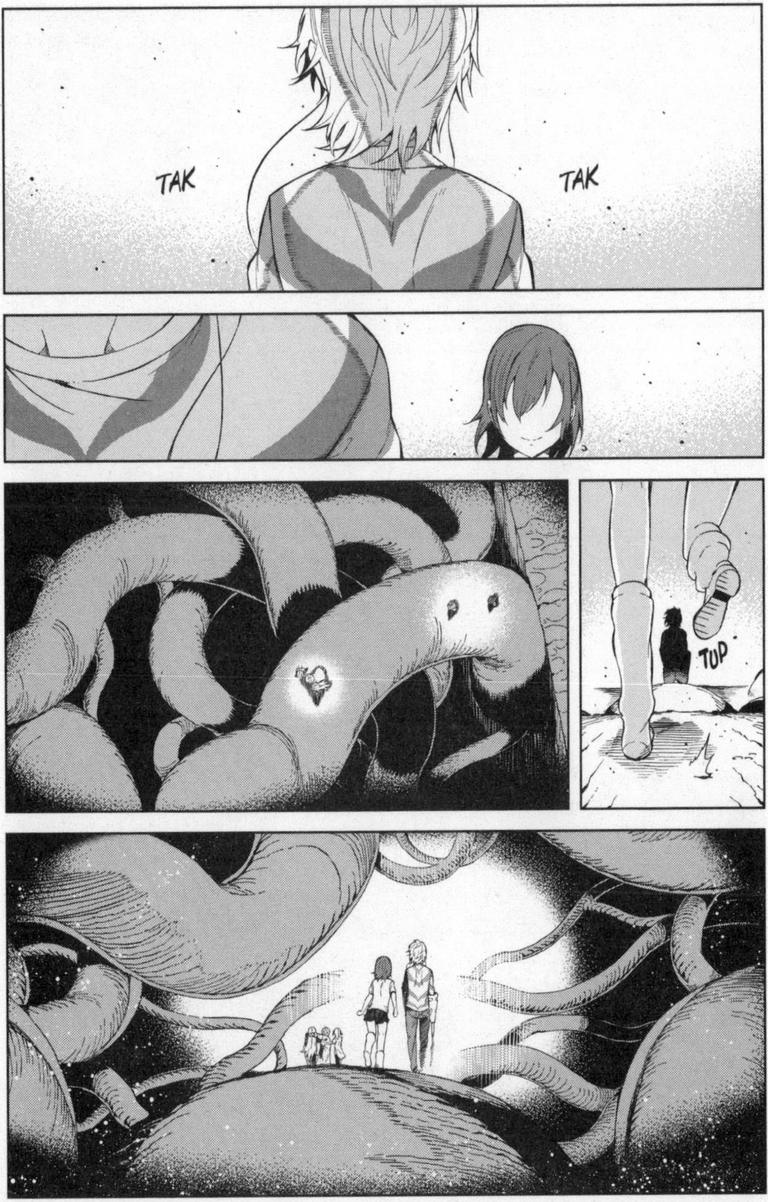
TAK
TAK
TUP

CHAPTER 32

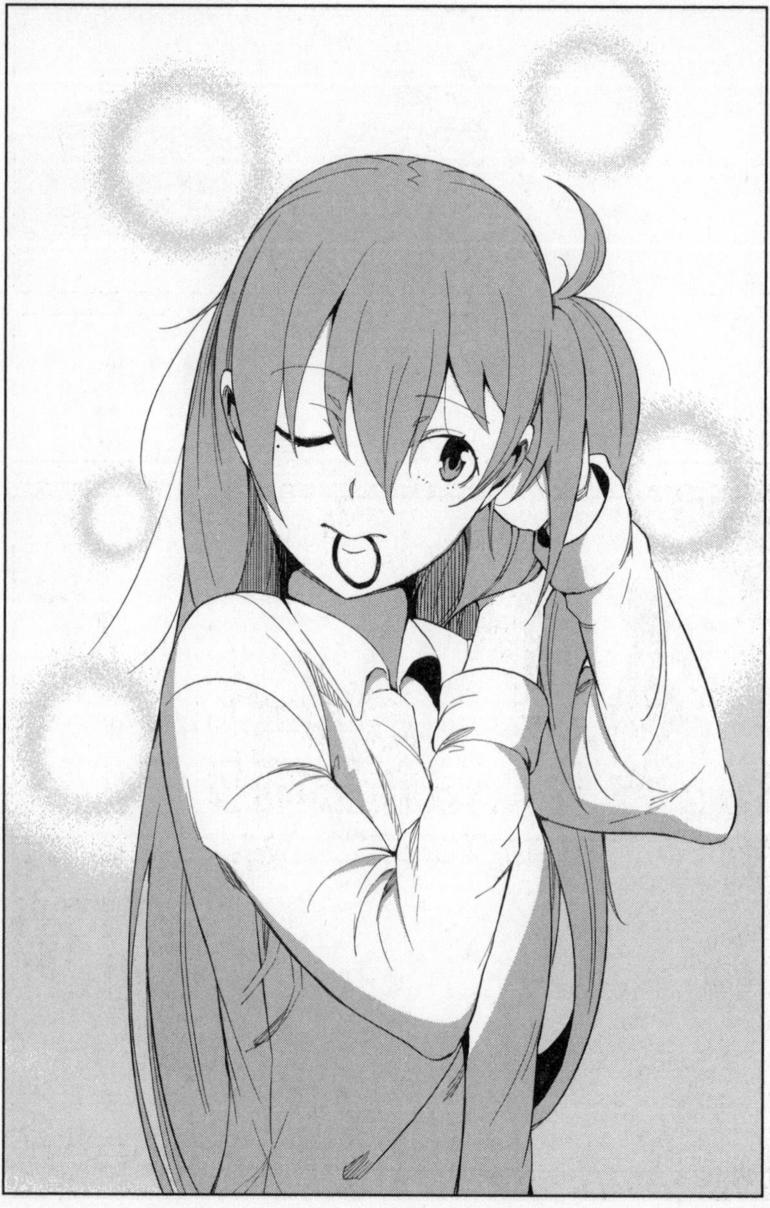

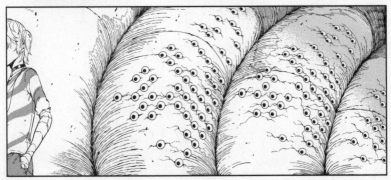

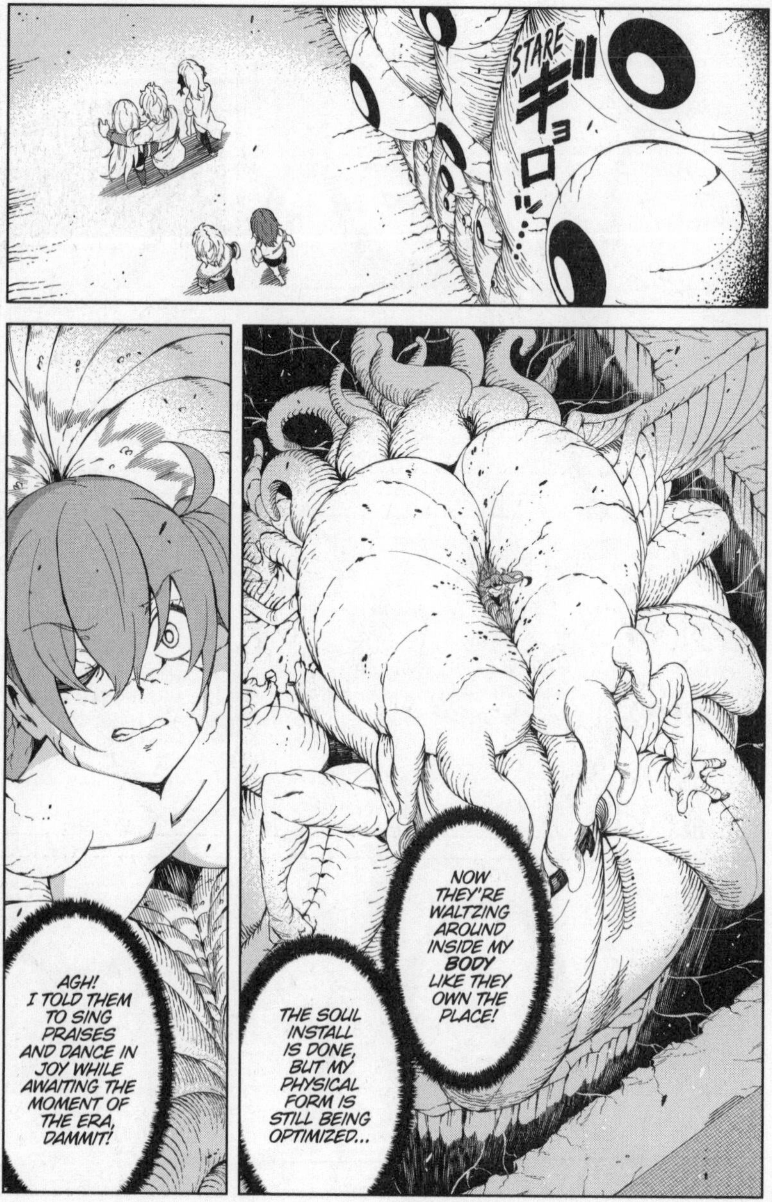
STARE
ギョロッ…
NOW THEY'RE WALTZING AROUND INSIDE MY BODY LIKE THEY OWN THE PLACE!
THE SOUL INSTALL IS DONE, BUT MY PHYSICAL FORM IS STILL BEING OPTIMIZED...
AGH! I TOLD THEM TO SING PRAISES AND DANCE IN JOY WHILE AWAITING THE MOMENT OF THE ERA, DAMMIT!

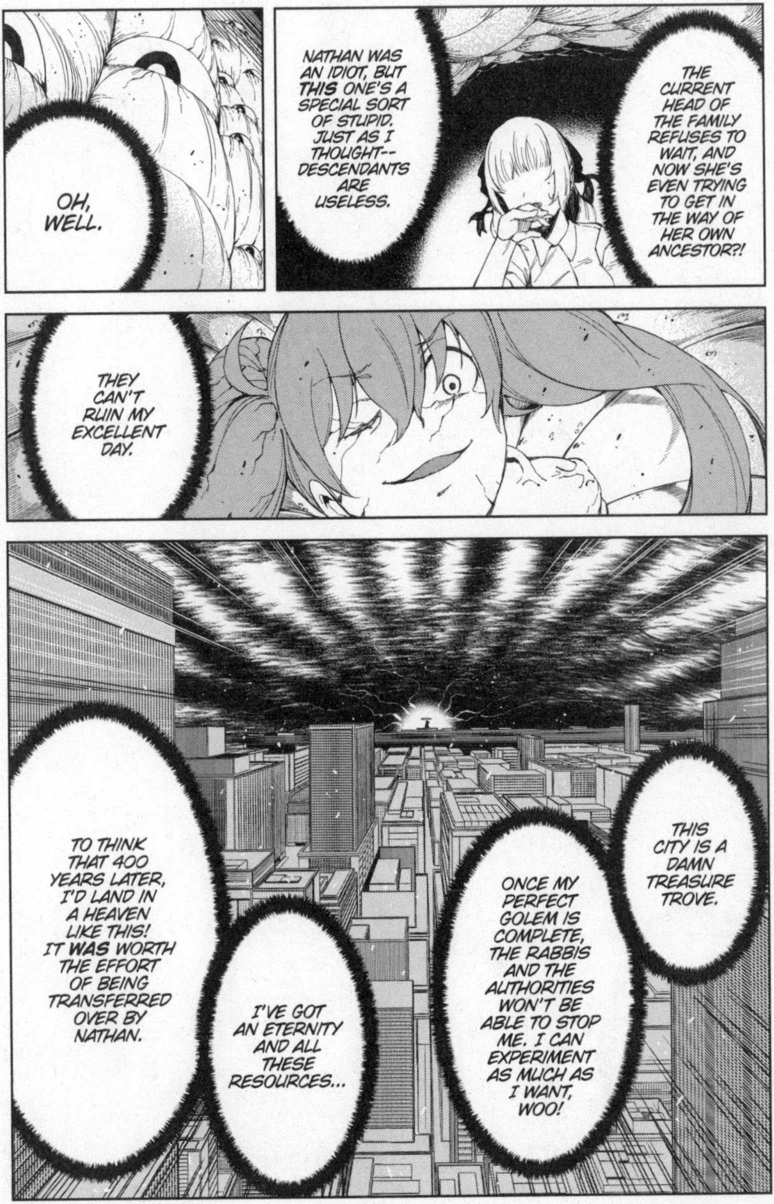
THE CURRENT HEAD OF THE FAMILY REFUSES TO WAIT, AND NOW SHE'S EVEN TRYING TO GET IN THE WAY OF HER OWN ANCESTOR?!
NATHAN WAS AN IDIOT, BUT THIS ONE'S A SPECIAL SORT OF STUPID. JUST AS I THOUGHT-- DESCENDANTS ARE USELESS.
OH, WELL.
THEY CAN'T RUIN MY EXCELLENT DAY.
THIS CITY IS A DAMN TREASURE TROVE.
ONCE MY PERFECT GOLEM IS COMPLETE, THE RABBIS AND THE AUTHORITIES WON'T BE ABLE TO STOP ME. I CAN EXPERIMENT AS MUCH AS I WANT, WOO!
I'VE GOT AN ETERNITY AND ALL THESE RESOURCES...
TO THINK THAT 400 YEARS LATER, I'D LAND IN A HEAVEN LIKE THIS! IT WAS WORTH THE EFFORT OF BEING TRANSFERRED OVER BY NATHAN.

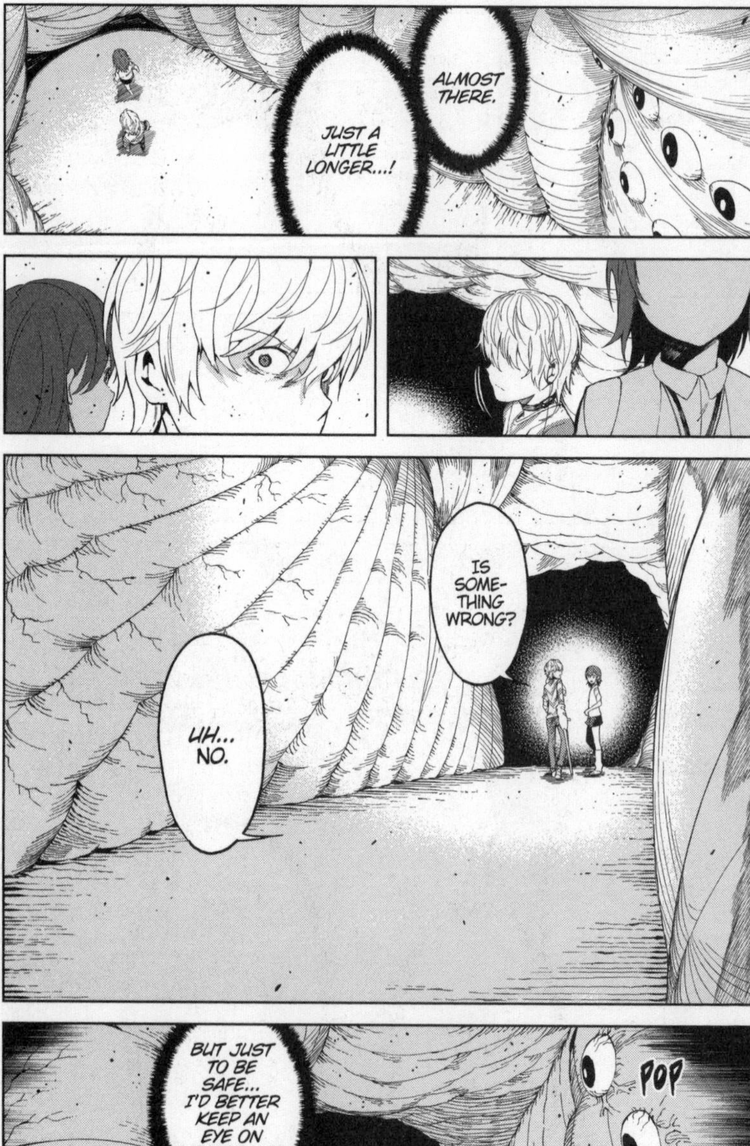
ALMOST THERE.
JUST A LITTLE LONGER...!
IS SOME-THING WRONG?
UH... NO.
POP
BUT JUST TO BE SAFE... I'D BETTER KEEP AN EYE ON THAT PALE GUY.

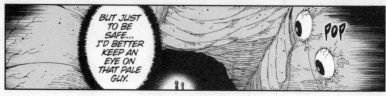

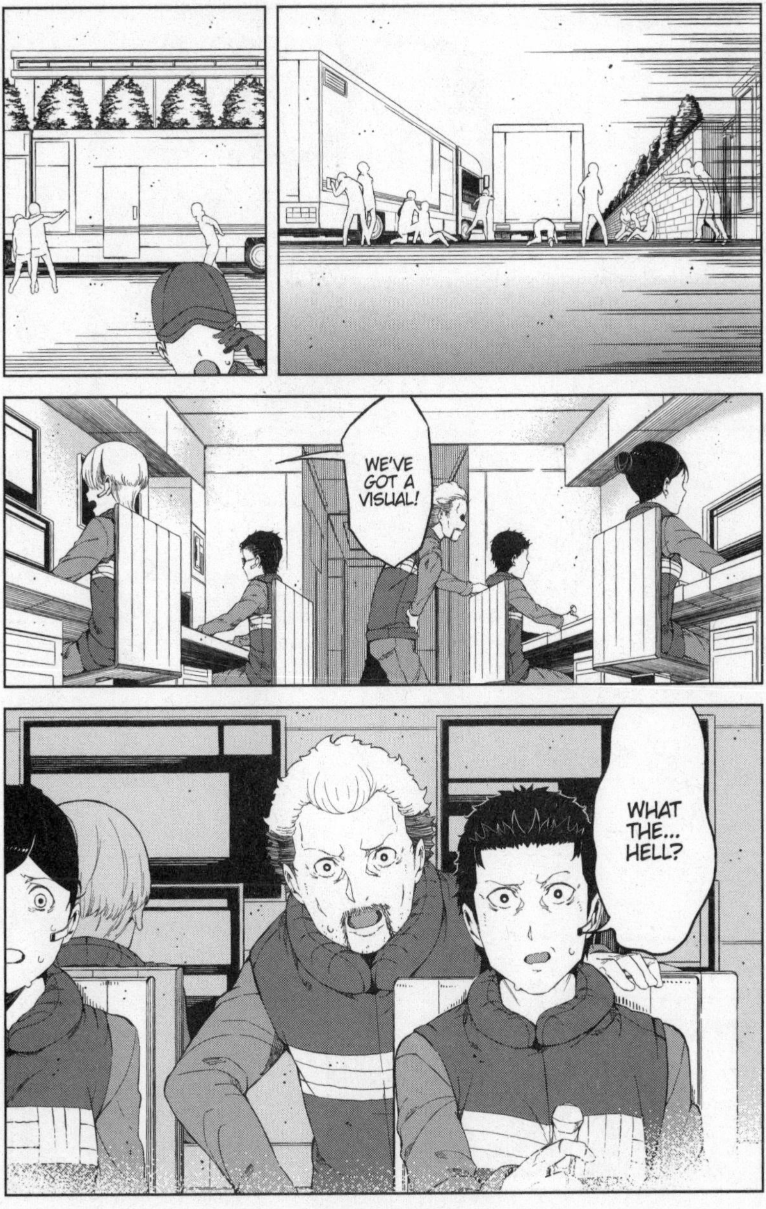
WE'VE GOT A VISUAL!
WHAT THE... HELL?

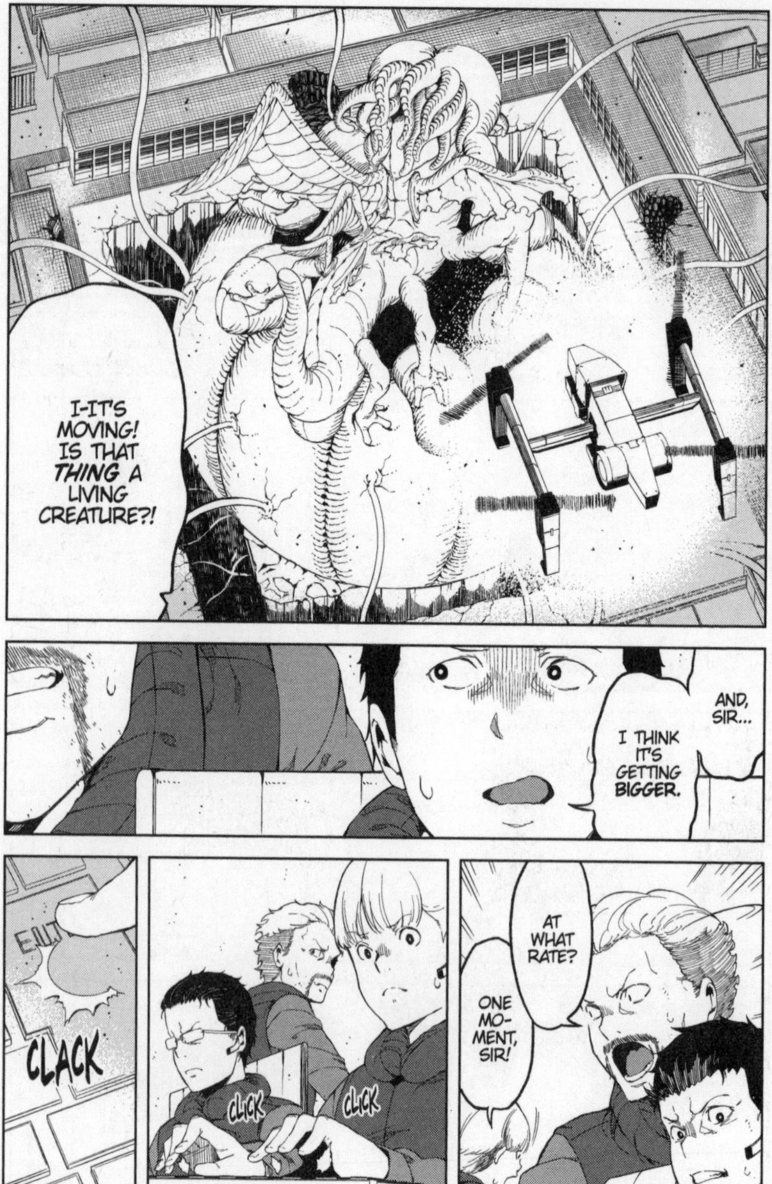
I-IT'S MOVING! IS THAT *THING* A LIVING CREATURE?!
AND, SIR...
I THINK IT'S GETTING BIGGER.
AT WHAT RATE?
ONE MO-MENT, SIR!
CLICK
CLICK
CLACK

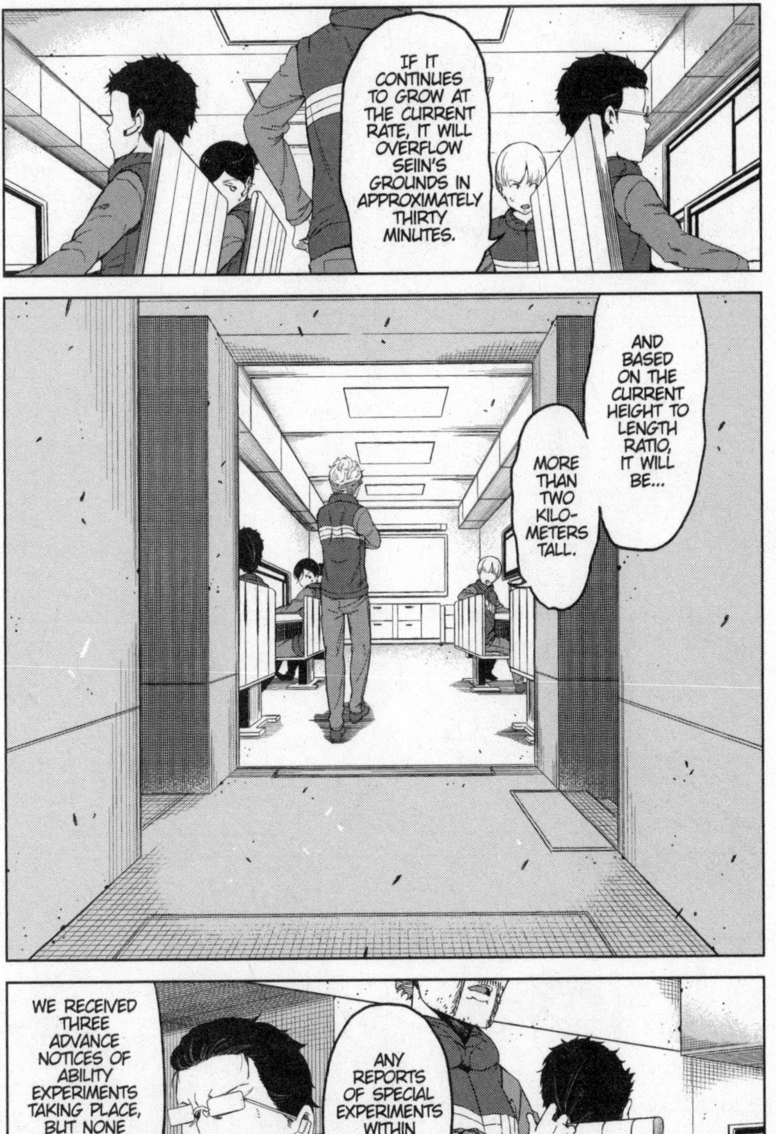
IF IT CONTINUES TO GROW AT THE CURRENT RATE, IT WILL OVERFLOW SEIIN'S GROUNDS IN APPROXIMATELY THIRTY MINUTES.
AND BASED ON THE CURRENT HEIGHT TO LENGTH RATIO, IT WILL BE...
MORE THAN TWO KILO-METERS TALL.
ANY REPORTS OF SPECIAL EXPERIMENTS WITHIN SEIIN?
WE RECEIVED THREE ADVANCE NOTICES OF ABILITY EXPERIMENTS TAKING PLACE, BUT NONE THAT COULD RESULT IN **THIS.**

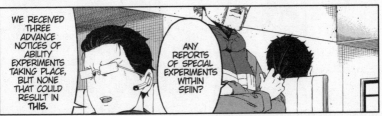

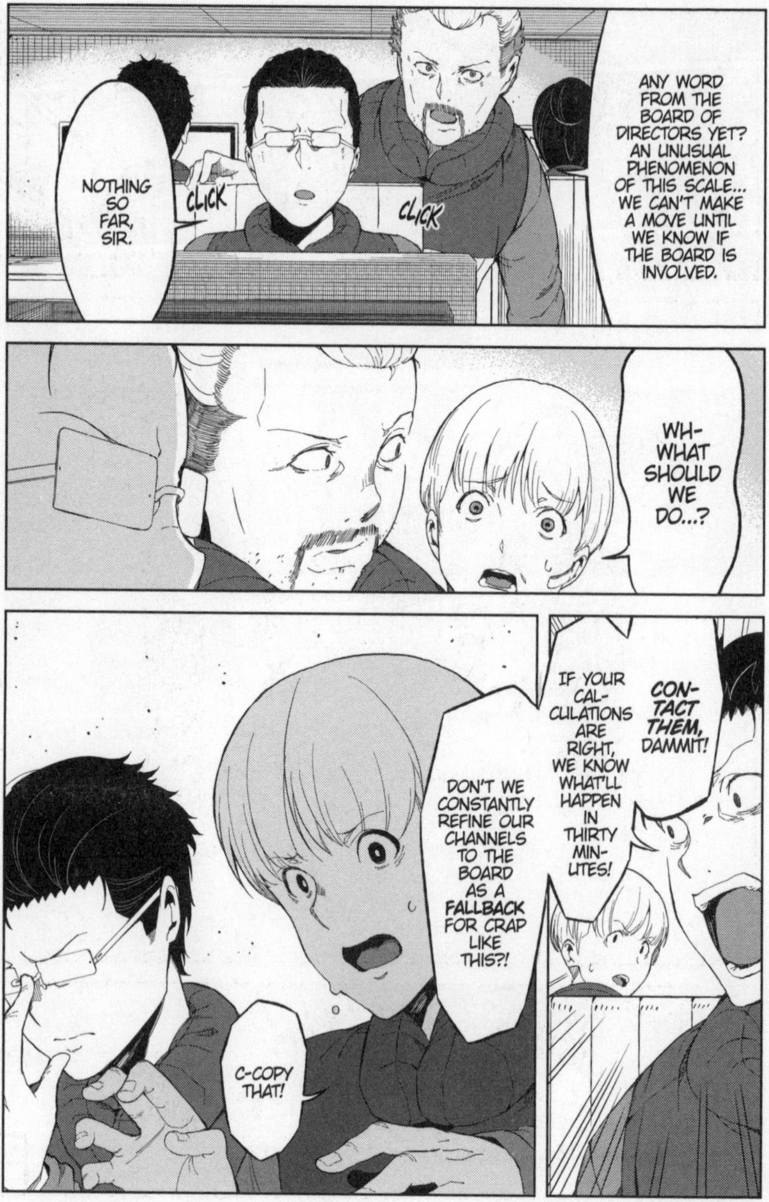
ANY WORD FROM THE BOARD OF DIRECTORS YET? AN UNUSUAL PHENOMENON OF THIS SCALE... WE CAN'T MAKE A MOVE UNTIL WE KNOW IF THE BOARD IS INVOLVED.
CLICK
CLICK
NOTHING SO FAR, SIR.
WH- WHAT SHOULD WE DO...?
CONTACT THEM, DAMMIT!
IF YOUR CALCULATIONS ARE RIGHT, WE KNOW WHAT'LL HAPPEN IN THIRTY MINUTES!
DON'T WE CONSTANTLY REFINE OUR CHANNELS TO THE BOARD AS A FALLBACK FOR CRAP LIKE THIS?!
C-COPY THAT!

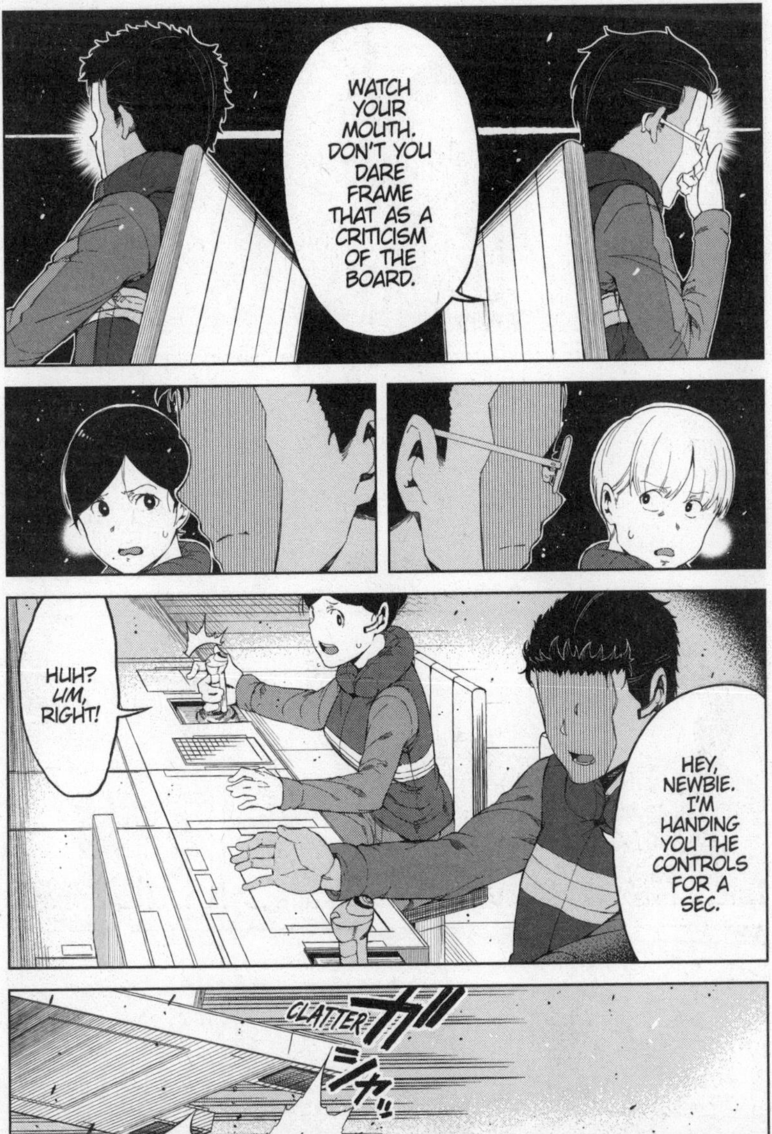
WATCH YOUR MOUTH. DON'T YOU DARE FRAME THAT AS A CRITICISM OF THE BOARD.
HEY, NEWBIE. I'M HANDING YOU THE CONTROLS FOR A SEC.
HUH? UM, RIGHT!
CLATTER

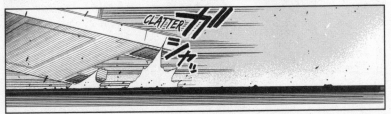

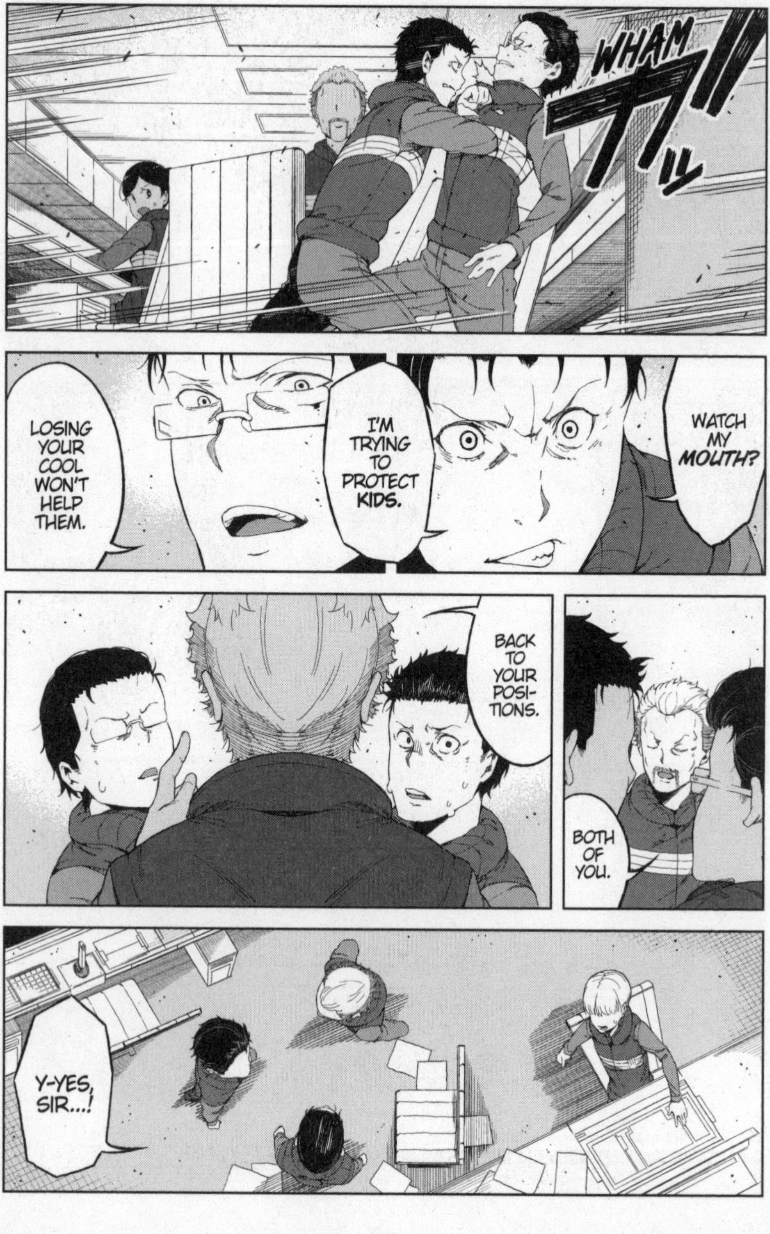
WHAM
WATCH MY MOUTH?
I'M TRYING TO PROTECT KIDS.
LOSING YOUR COOL WON'T HELP THEM.
BOTH OF YOU.
BACK TO YOUR POSI-TIONS.
Y-YES, SIR...!

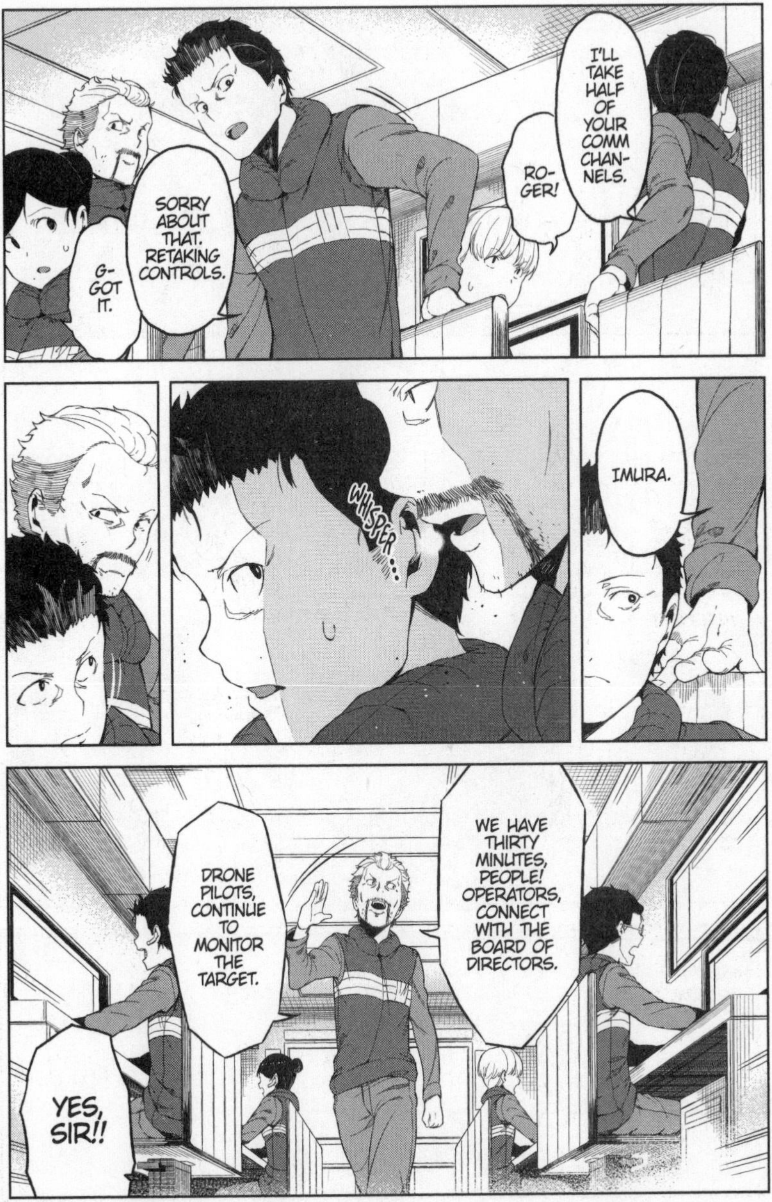
I'LL TAKE HALF OF YOUR COMM CHANNELS.
RO-GER!
SORRY ABOUT THAT. RETAKING CONTROLS.
G-GOT IT.
IMURA.
WHISPER...
WE HAVE THIRTY MINUTES, PEOPLE! OPERATORS, CONNECT WITH THE BOARD OF DIRECTORS.
DRONE PILOTS, CONTINUE TO MONITOR THE TARGET.
YES, SIR!!

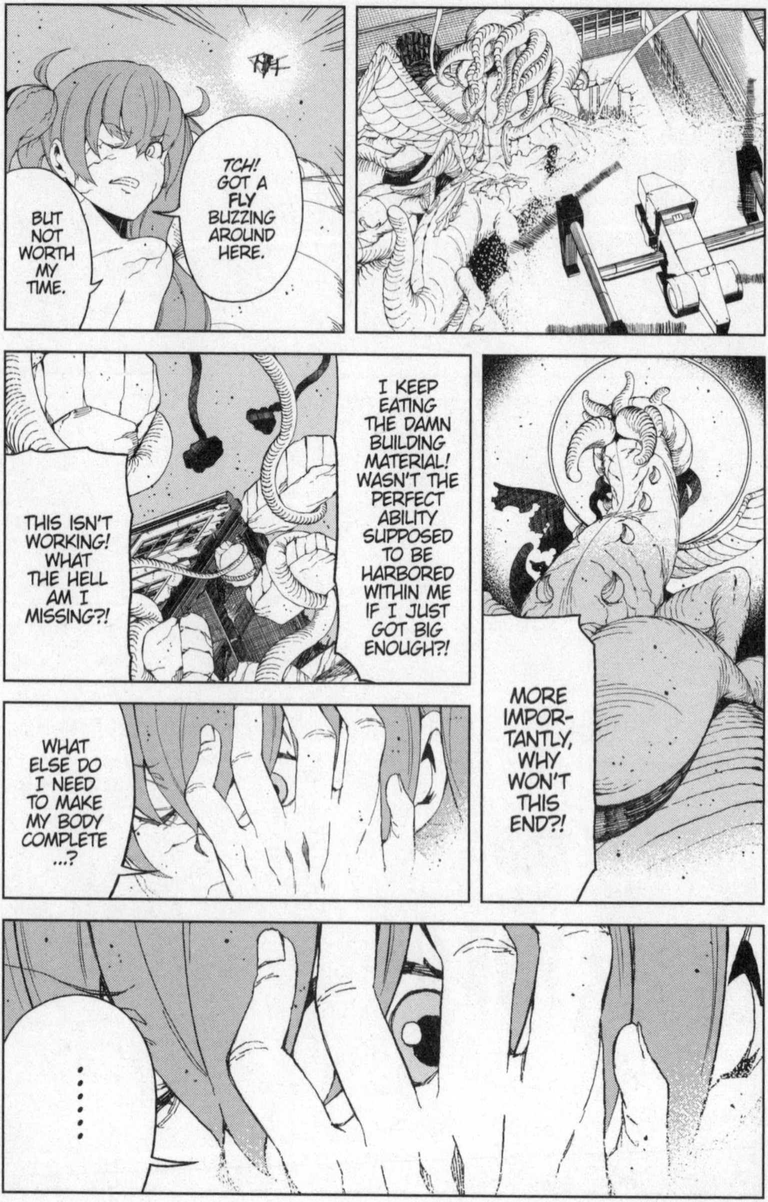
TCH! GOT A FLY BUZZING AROUND HERE.
BUT NOT WORTH MY TIME.
I KEEP EATING THE DAMN BUILDING MATERIAL! WASN'T THE PERFECT ABILITY SUPPOSED TO BE HARBORED WITHIN ME IF I JUST GOT BIG ENOUGH?!
THIS ISN'T WORKING! WHAT THE HELL AM I MISSING?!
MORE IMPORTANTLY, WHY WON'T THIS END?!
WHAT ELSE DO I NEED TO MAKE MY BODY COMPLETE ...?
......

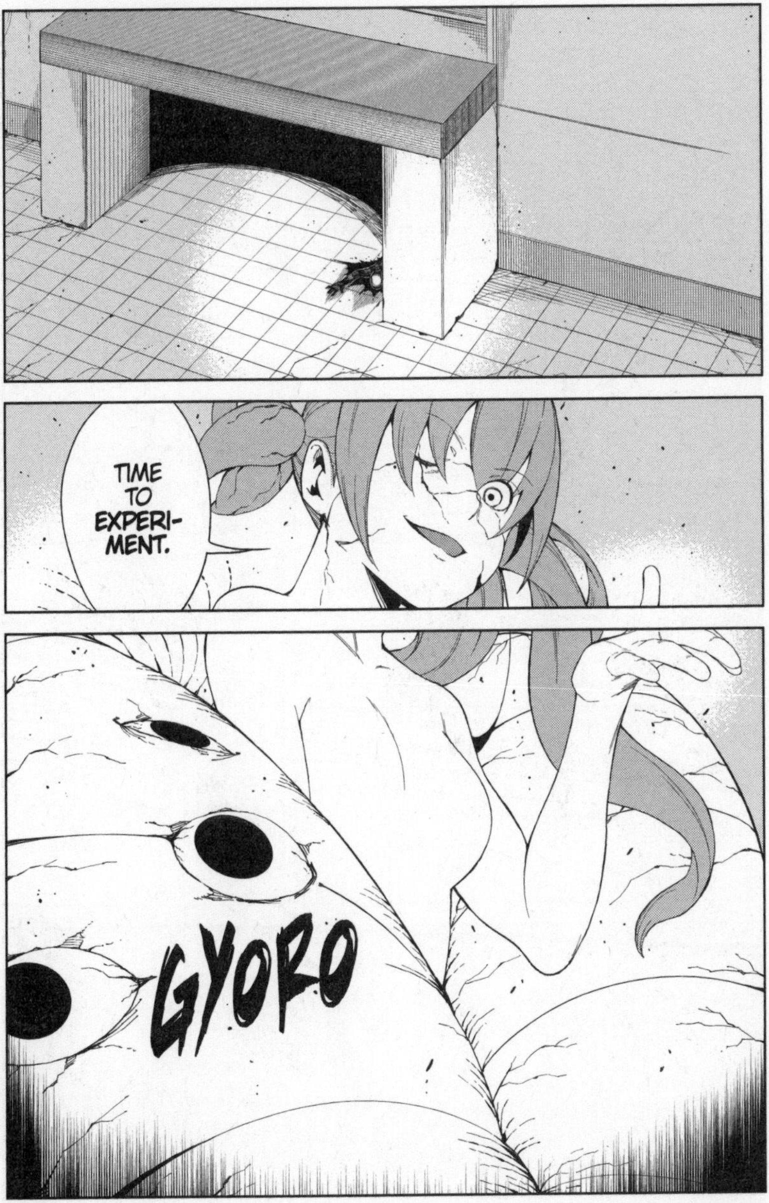
TIME TO EXPERIMENT.
GYORO

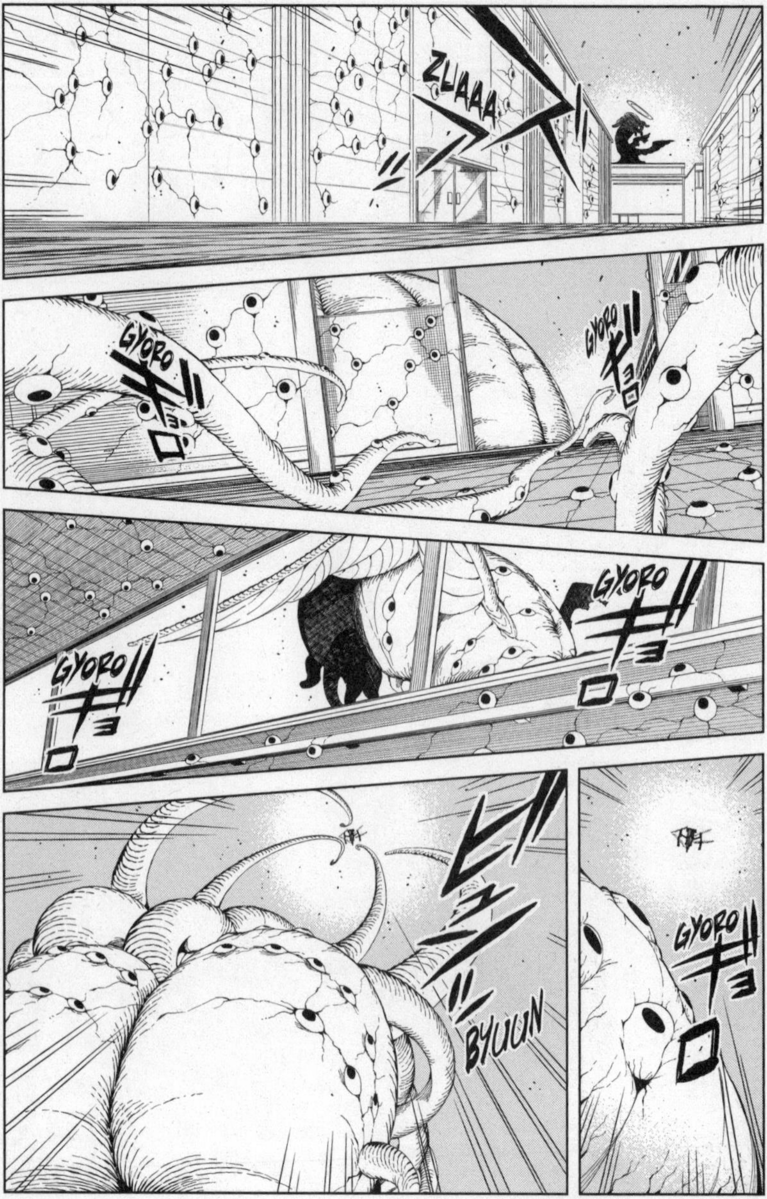
ZUAAA
GYORO
ギョロ
GYORO
ギョロ
GYORO
ギョロ
GYORO
ギョロ
GYORO
ギョロ
BYUUN

SIR, THE DRONE'S SIGNAL JUST WENT DEAD.

THUNK THUNK

BEEEP

HERE ARE THE LAST IMAGES IT GOT.

HUNH.

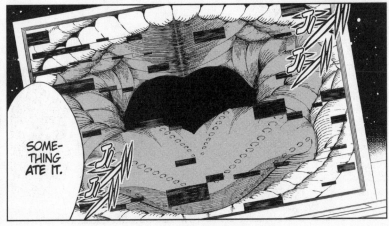

SOME-THING ATE IT.

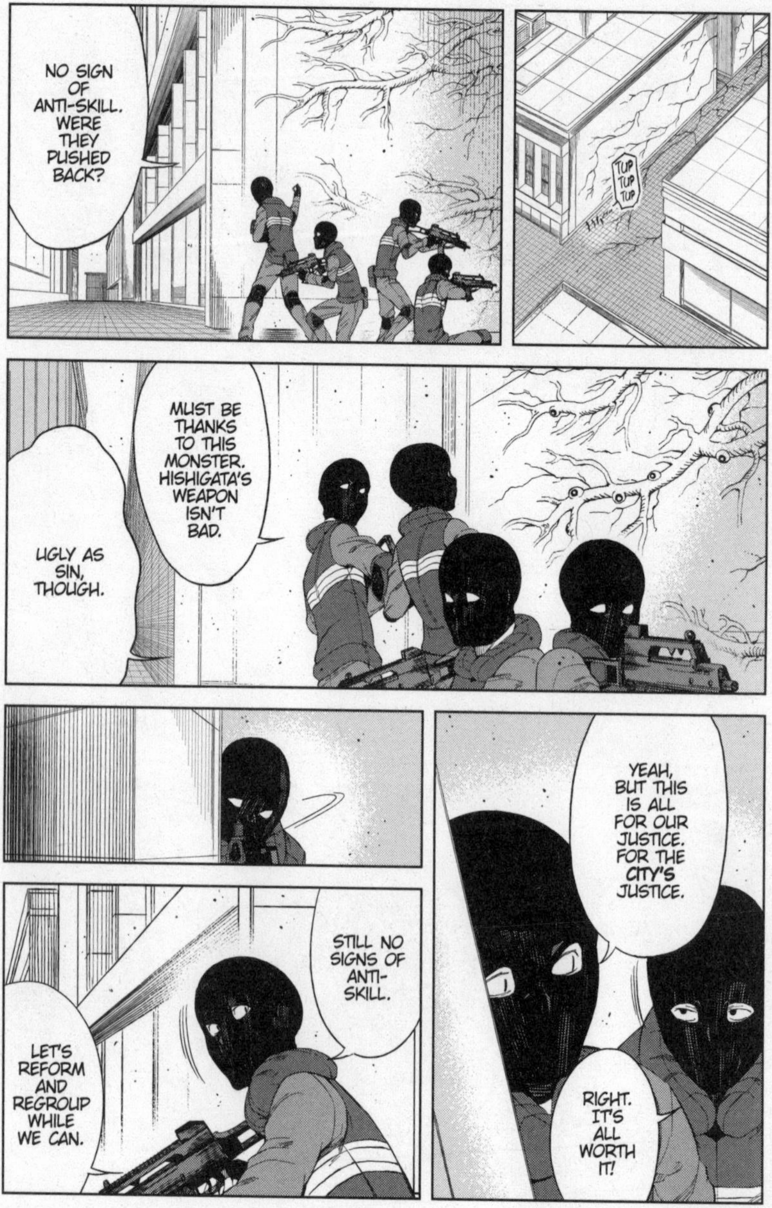
TUP TUP TUP
NO SIGN OF ANTI-SKILL. WERE THEY PUSHED BACK?
MUST BE THANKS TO THIS MONSTER. HISHIGATA'S WEAPON ISN'T BAD.
UGLY AS SIN, THOUGH.
YEAH, BUT THIS IS ALL FOR OUR JUSTICE. FOR THE CITY'S JUSTICE.
RIGHT. IT'S ALL WORTH IT!
STILL NO SIGNS OF ANTI-SKILL.
LET'S REFORM AND REGROUP WHILE WE CAN.

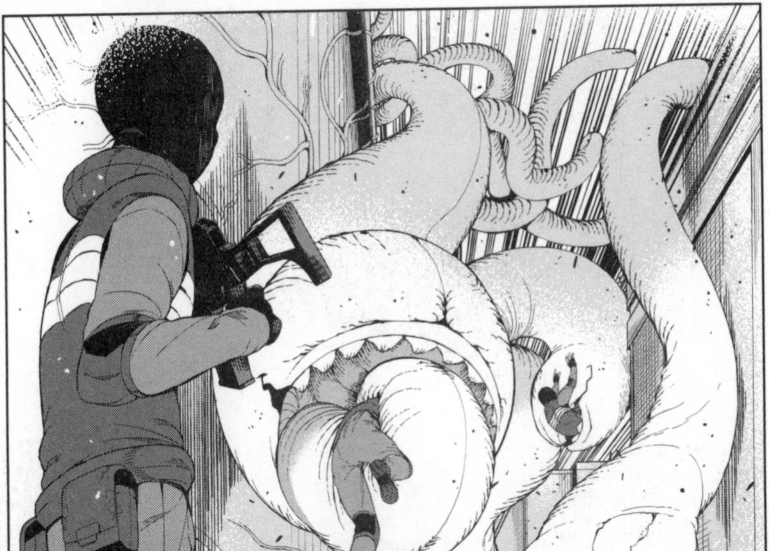

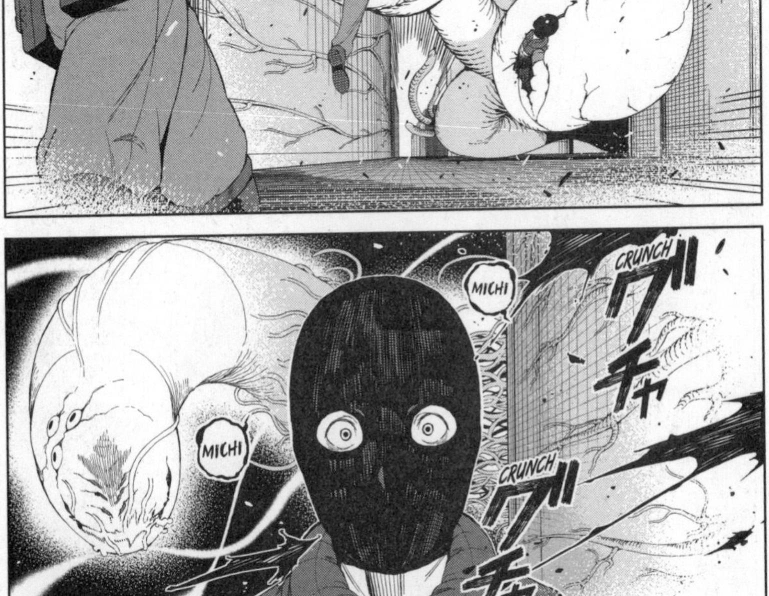
CRUNCH
グチャ
MICHI
CRUNCH
グチャ
MICHI

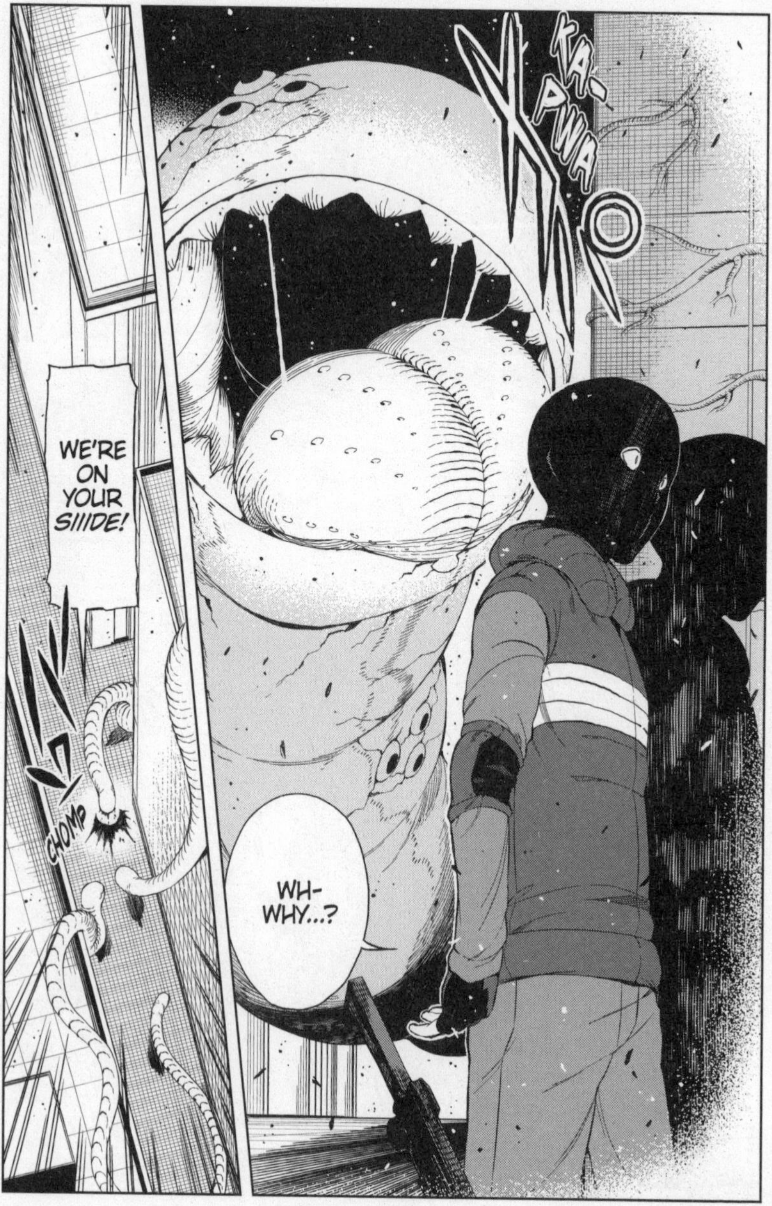
KA-PWAO
WH-WHY...?
WE'RE ON YOUR SIIIDE!
CHOMP

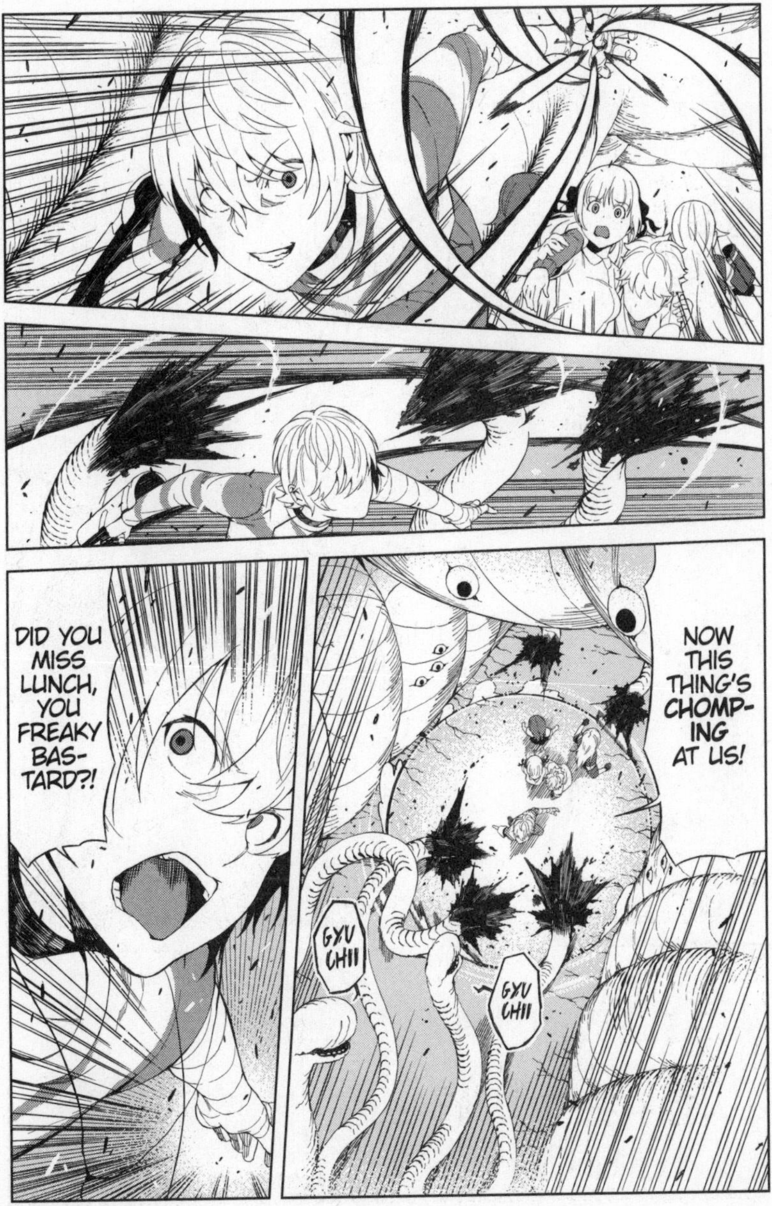
NOW THIS THING'S CHOMPING AT US!
GYU CHII
GYU CHII
DID YOU MISS LUNCH, YOU FREAKY BASTARD?!

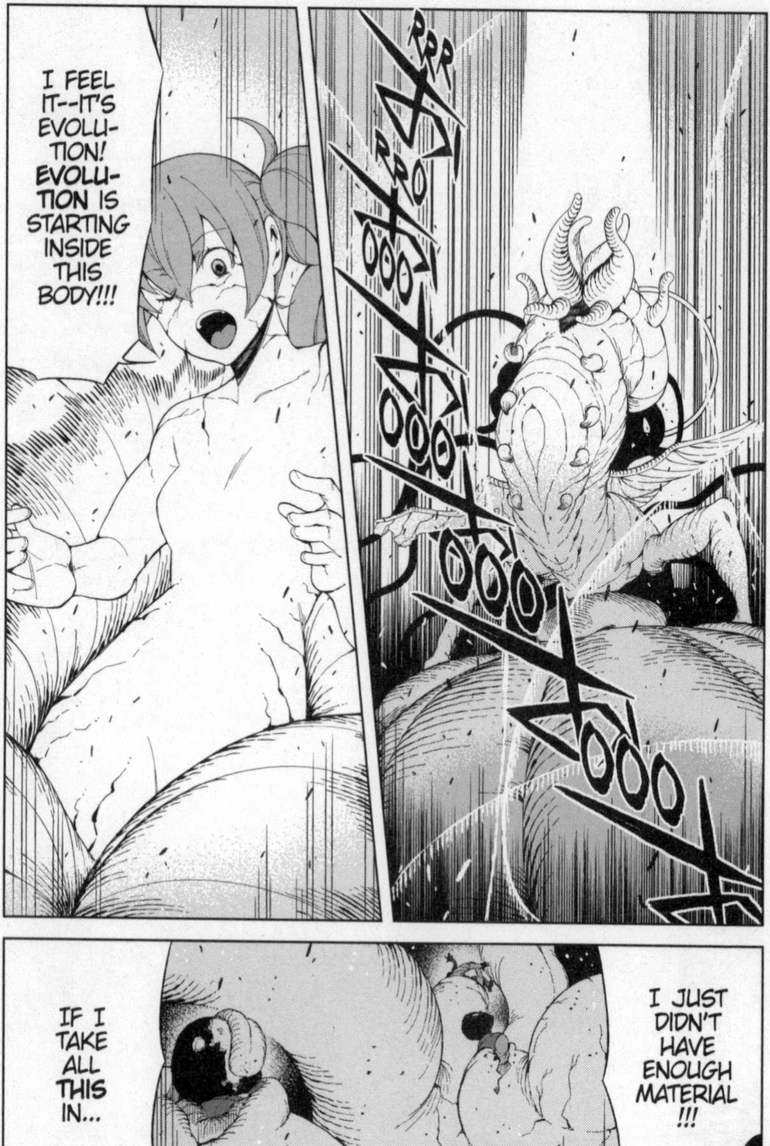
I FEEL IT--IT'S EVOLUTION! EVOLUTION IS STARTING INSIDE THIS BODY!!!
I JUST DIDN'T HAVE ENOUGH MATERIAL!!!
IF I TAKE ALL THIS IN...

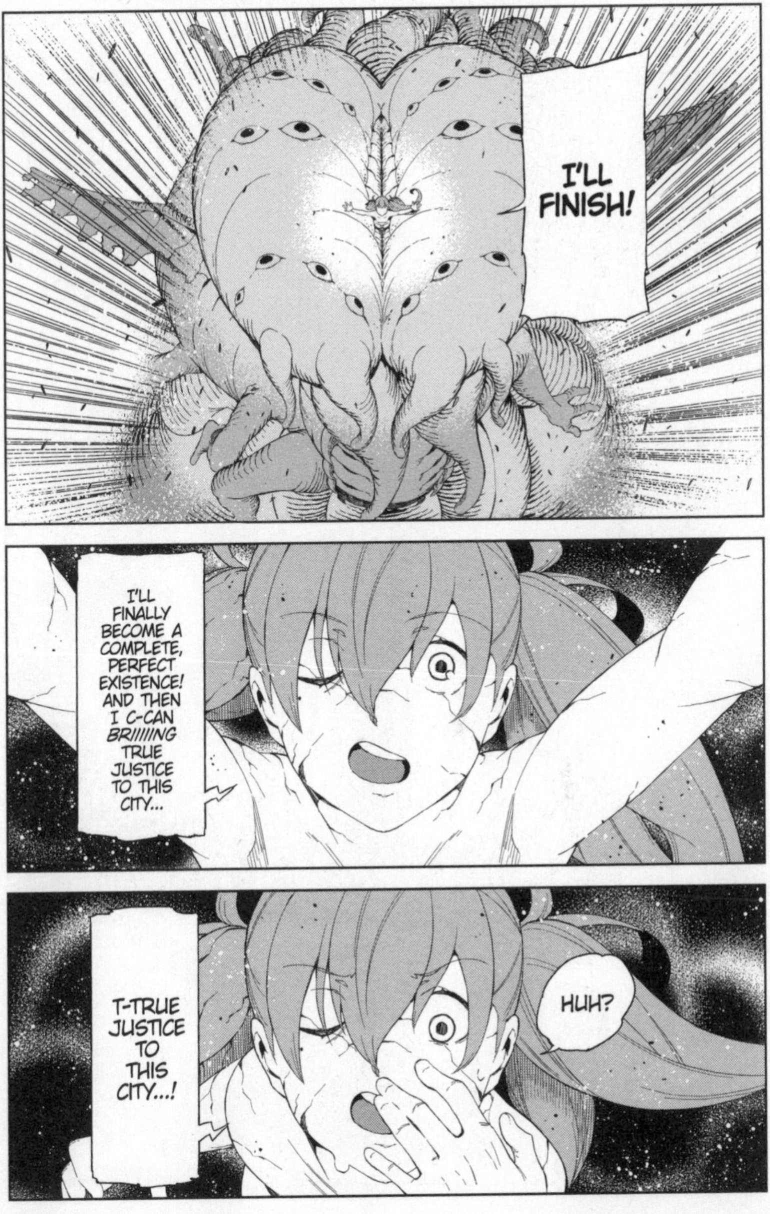
I'LL FINISH!
I'LL FINALLY BECOME A COMPLETE, PERFECT EXISTENCE! AND THEN I C-CAN BRIIIIING TRUE JUSTICE TO THIS CITY...
HUH?
T-TRUE JUSTICE TO THIS CITY...!

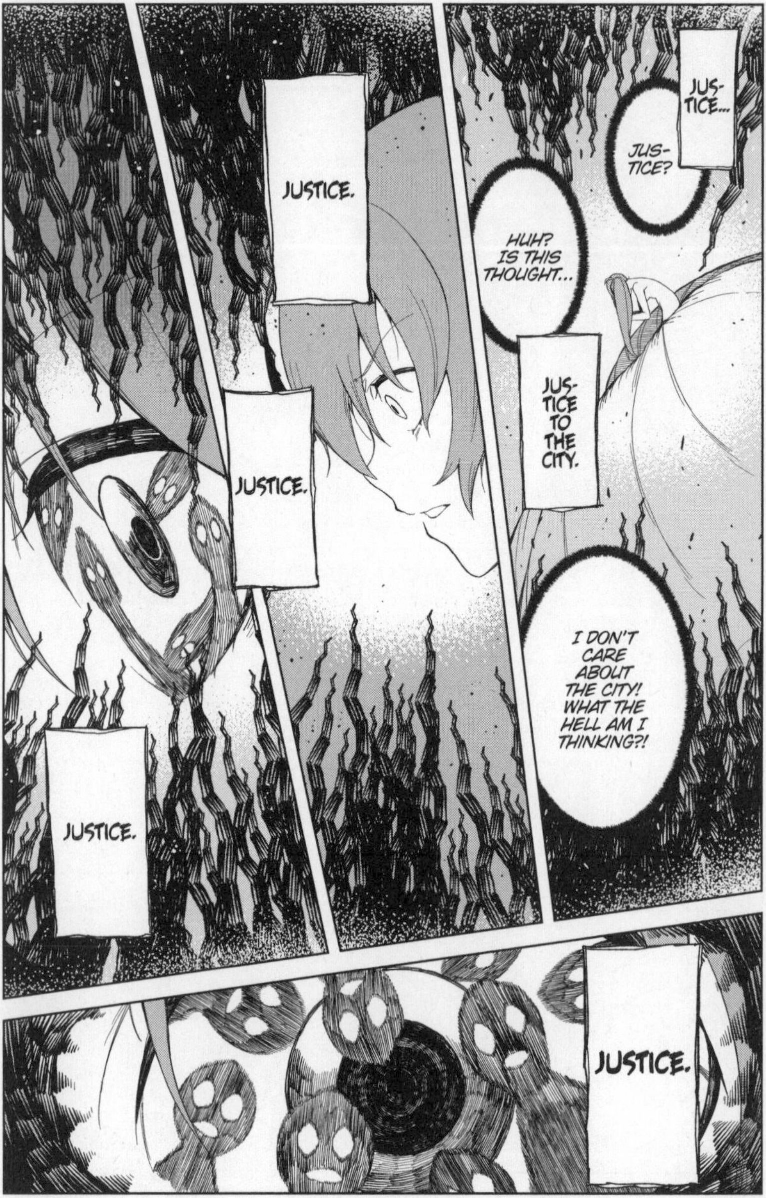
JUSTICE...
JUSTICE?
HUH? IS THIS THOUGHT...
JUSTICE TO THE CITY.
I DON'T CARE ABOUT THE CITY! WHAT THE HELL AM I THINKING?!
JUSTICE.
JUSTICE.
JUSTICE.
JUSTICE.

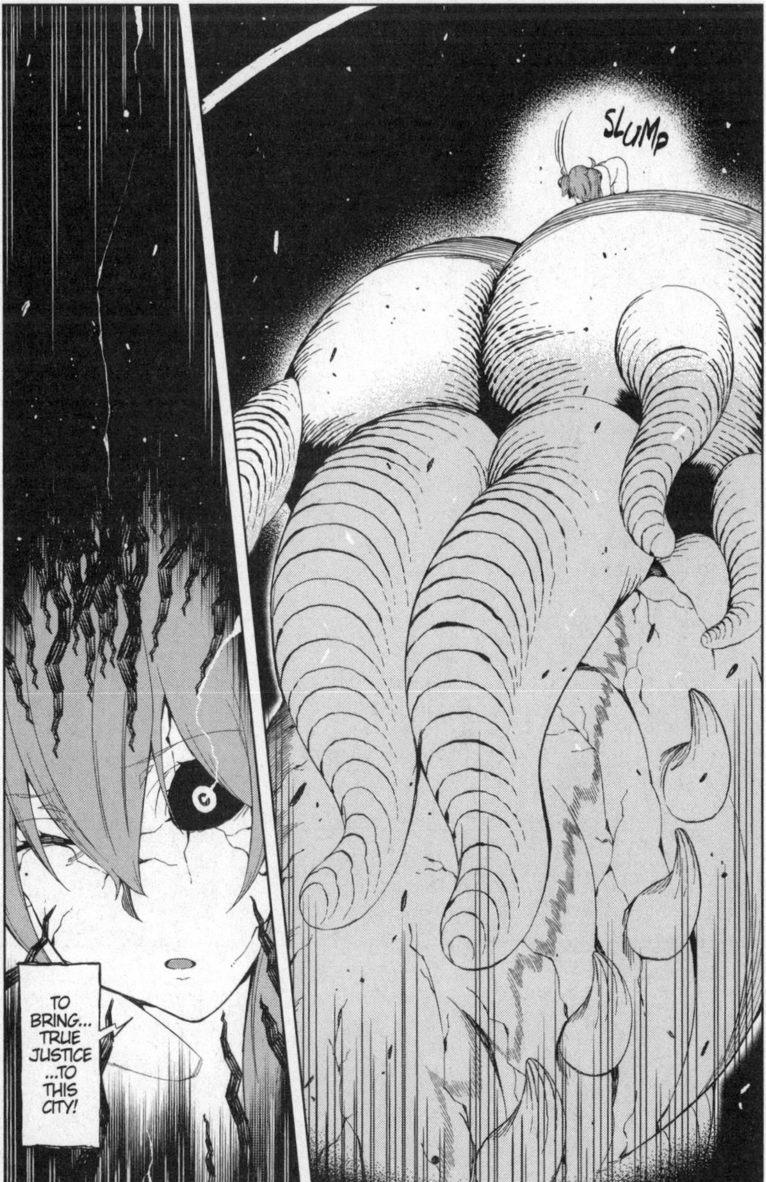
SLUMP
TO BRING... TRUE JUSTICE ...TO THIS CITY!

a certain
SCIENTIFIC
ACCELERATOR

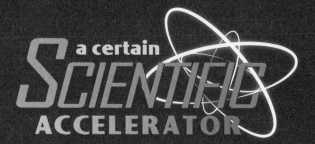

とある科学の一方通行

アクセラレータ

とある魔術の禁書目録外伝

CHAPTER 33

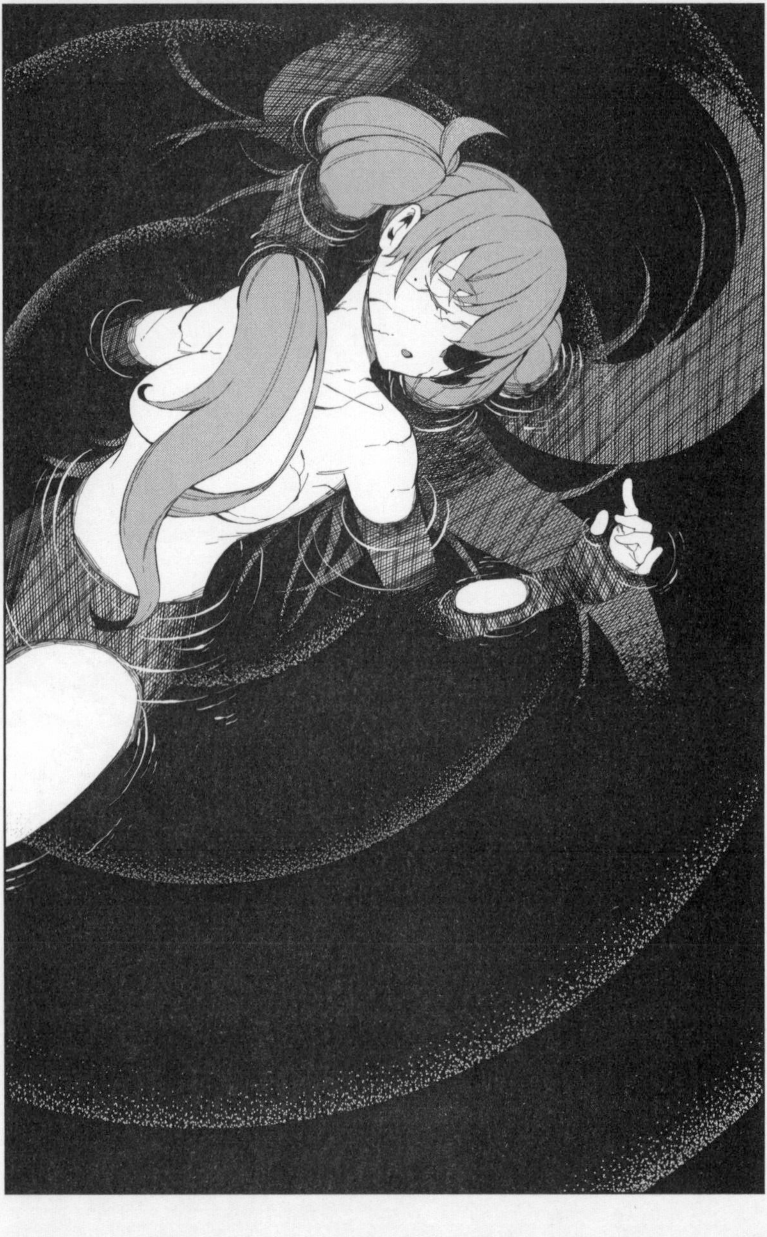

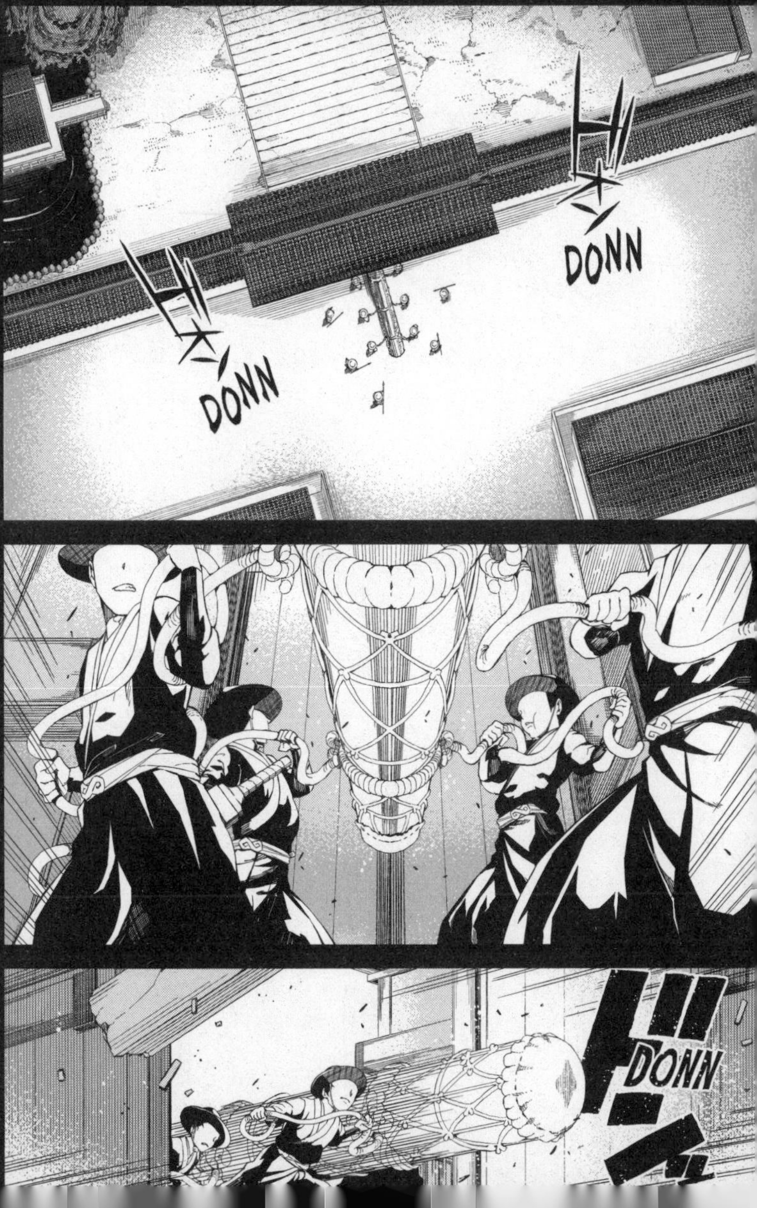
DONN
DONN
DONN

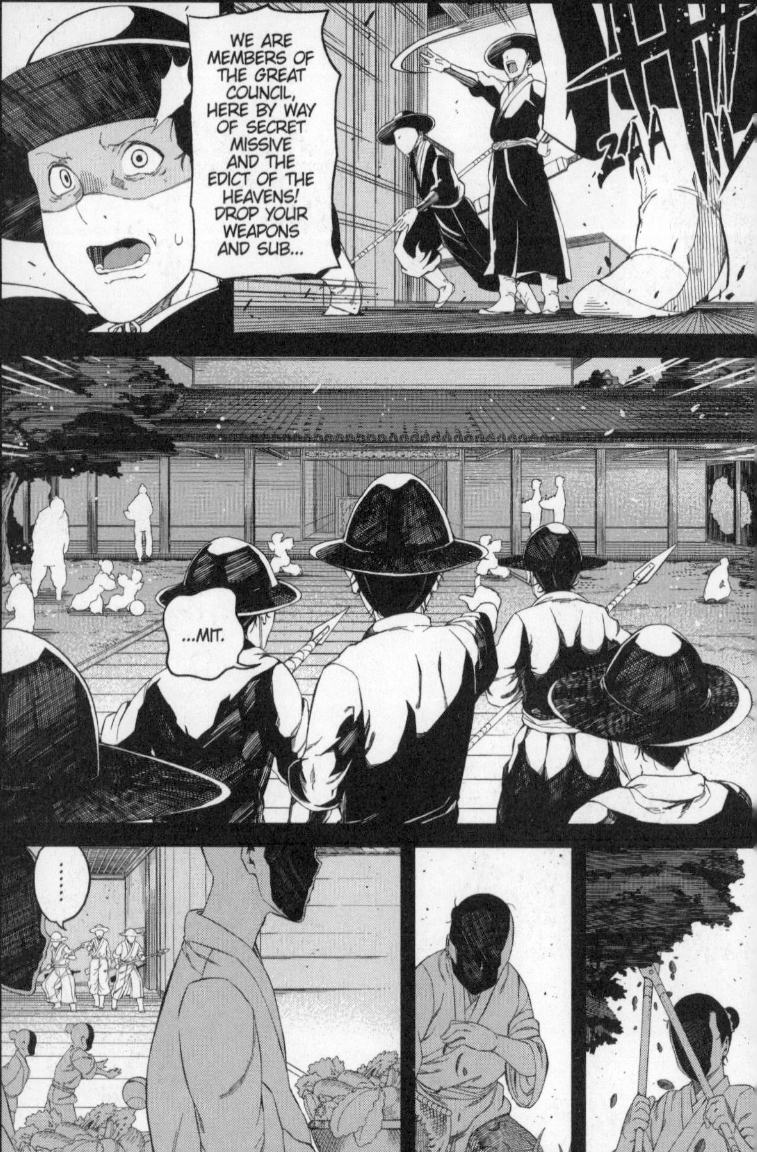
ZAA
WE ARE MEMBERS OF THE GREAT COUNCIL, HERE BY WAY OF SECRET MISSIVE AND THE EDICT OF THE HEAVENS! DROP YOUR WEAPONS AND SUB...
...MIT.
......

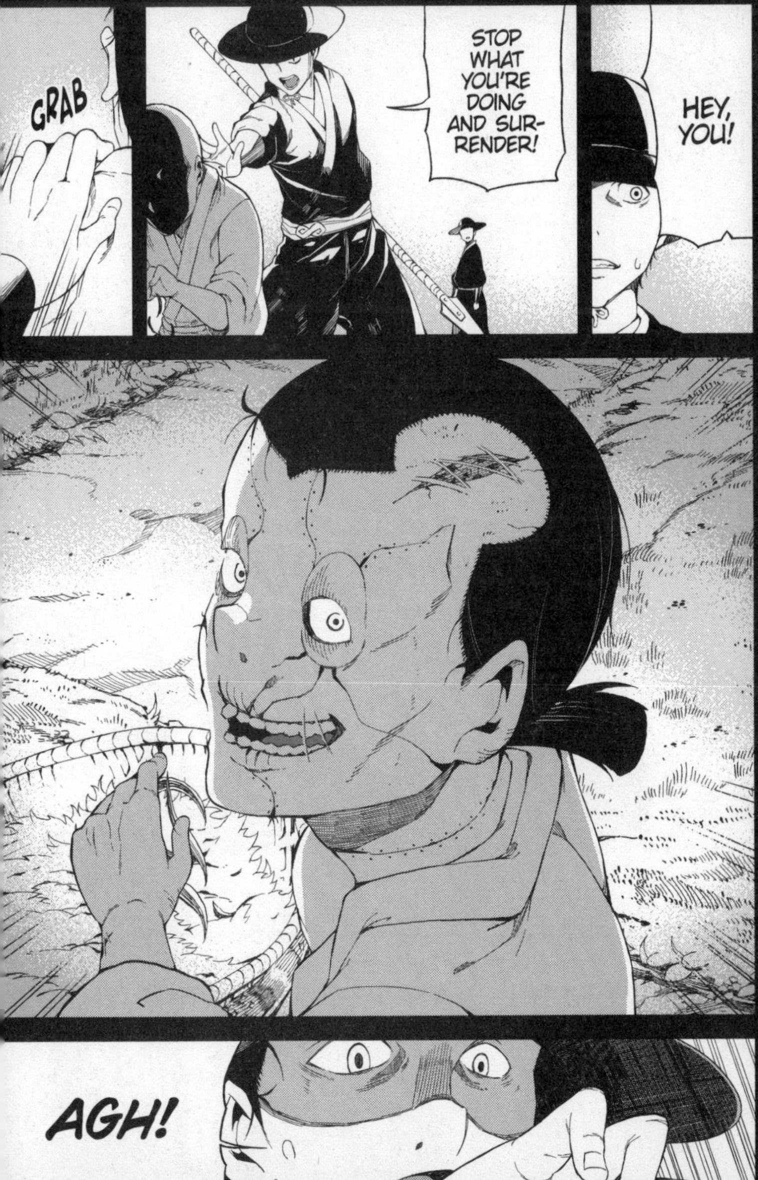
HEY, YOU!
STOP WHAT YOU'RE DOING AND SUR-RENDER!
GRAB
AGH!

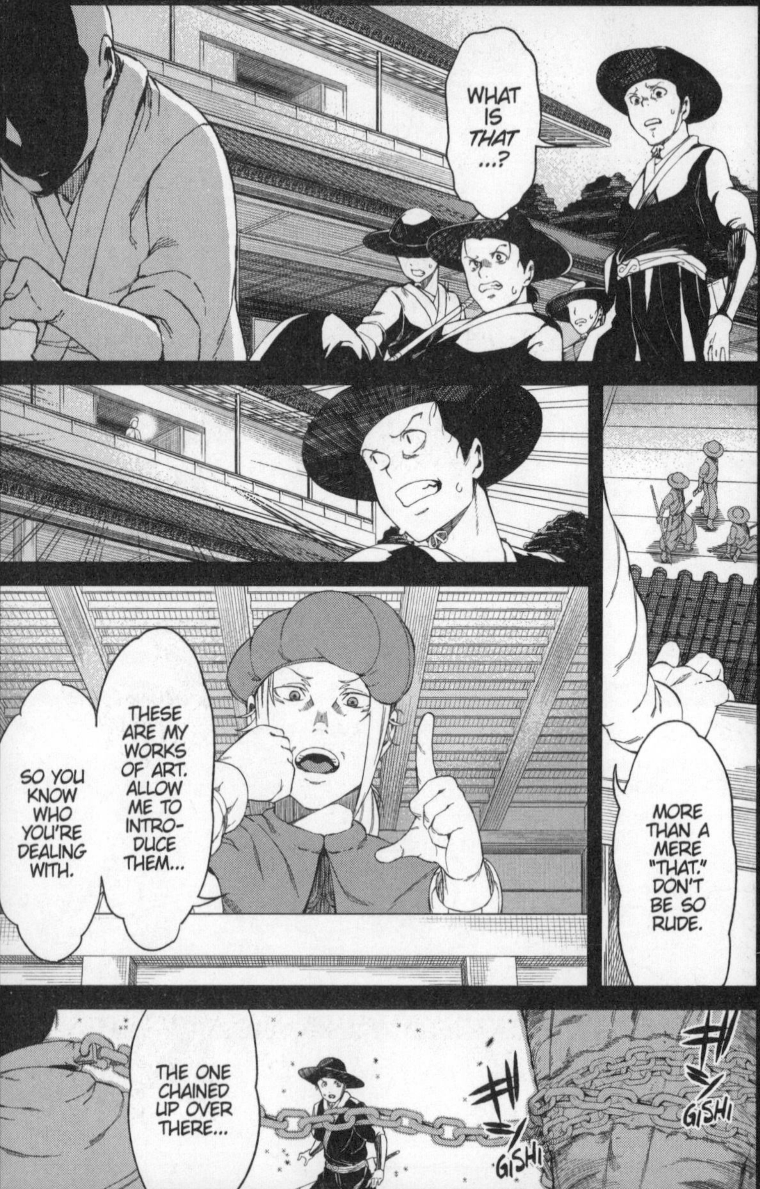
WHAT IS *THAT* ...?
MORE THAN A MERE "THAT." DON'T BE SO RUDE.
THESE ARE MY WORKS OF ART. ALLOW ME TO INTRO-DUCE THEM...
SO YOU KNOW WHO YOU'RE DEALING WITH.
THE ONE CHAINED UP OVER THERE...
GISHI
GISHI

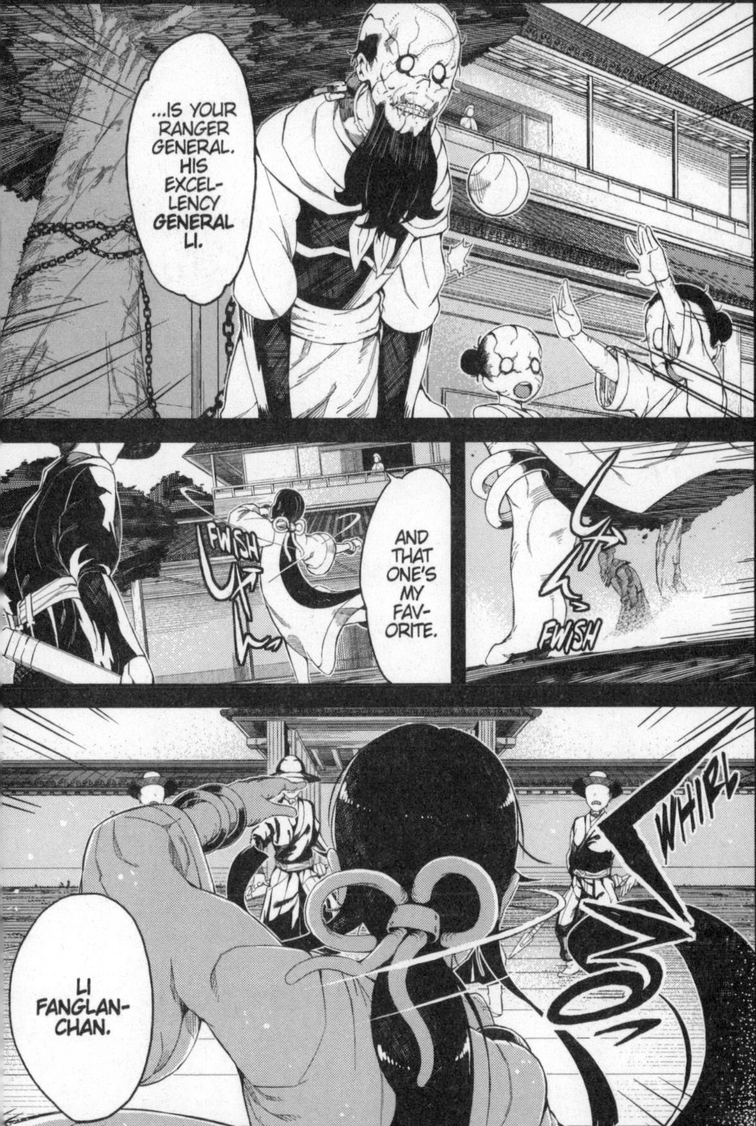
...IS YOUR RANGER GENERAL. HIS EXCEL-LENCY GENERAL LI.
FWISH
AND THAT ONE'S MY FAV-ORITE.
FWISH
WHIRL
LI FANGLAN-CHAN.

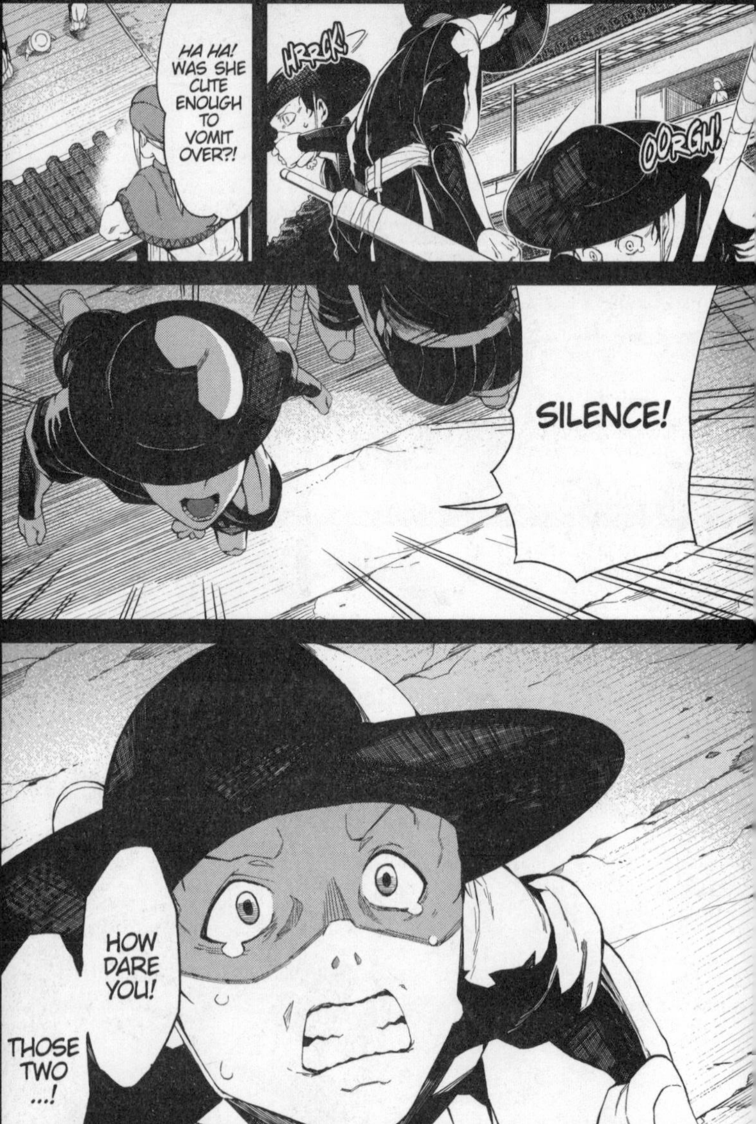
HRRCK!
OORGH!
HA HA! WAS SHE CUTE ENOUGH TO VOMIT OVER?!
SILENCE!
HOW DARE YOU!
THOSE TWO ...!

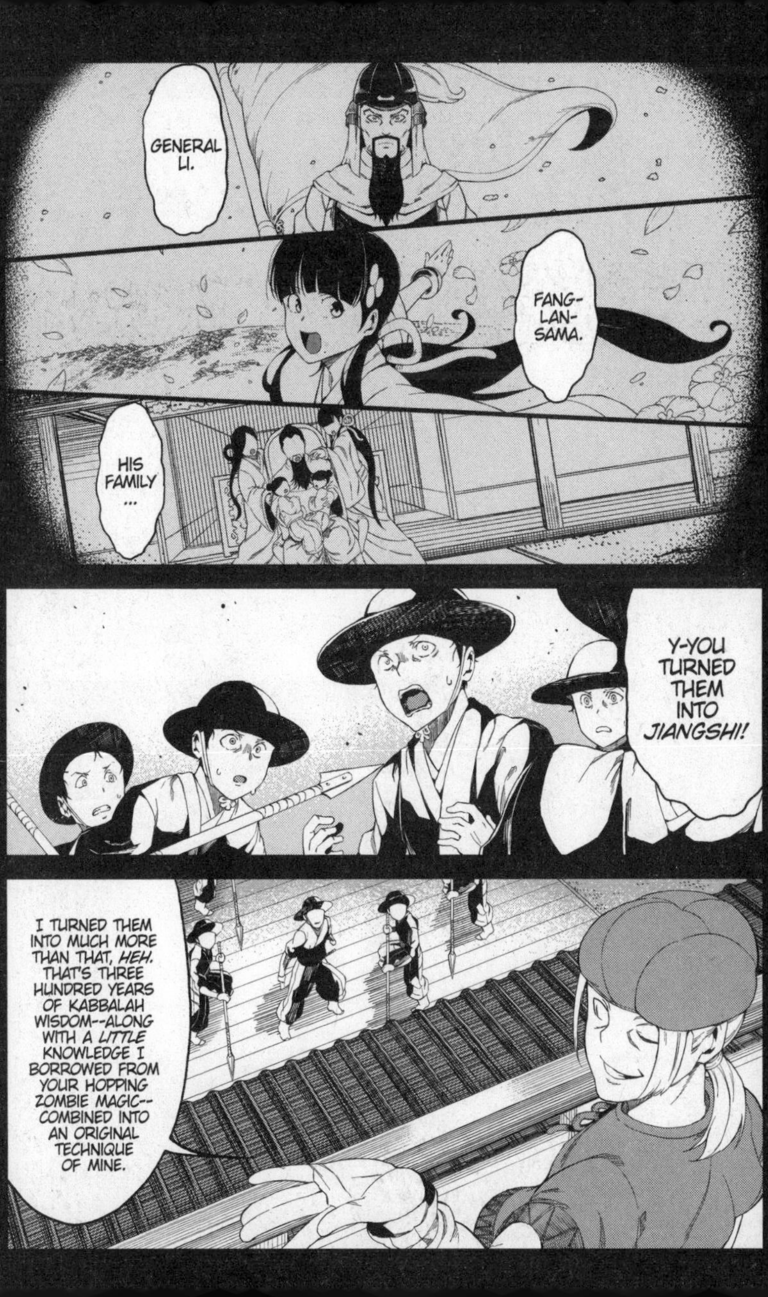
GENERAL LI.
FANG-LAN-SAMA.
HIS FAMILY ...
Y-YOU TURNED THEM INTO JIANGSHI!
I TURNED THEM INTO MUCH MORE THAN THAT, *HEH.* THAT'S THREE HUNDRED YEARS OF KABBALAH WISDOM--ALONG WITH A *LITTLE* KNOWLEDGE I BORROWED FROM YOUR HOPPING ZOMBIE MAGIC--COMBINED INTO AN ORIGINAL TECHNIQUE OF MINE.

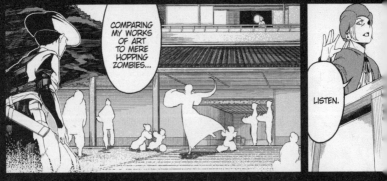

COMPARING MY WORKS OF ART TO MERE HOPPING ZOMBIES...

LISTEN.

GLARE

IT'S INSULTING.

DEVOUR THEM!

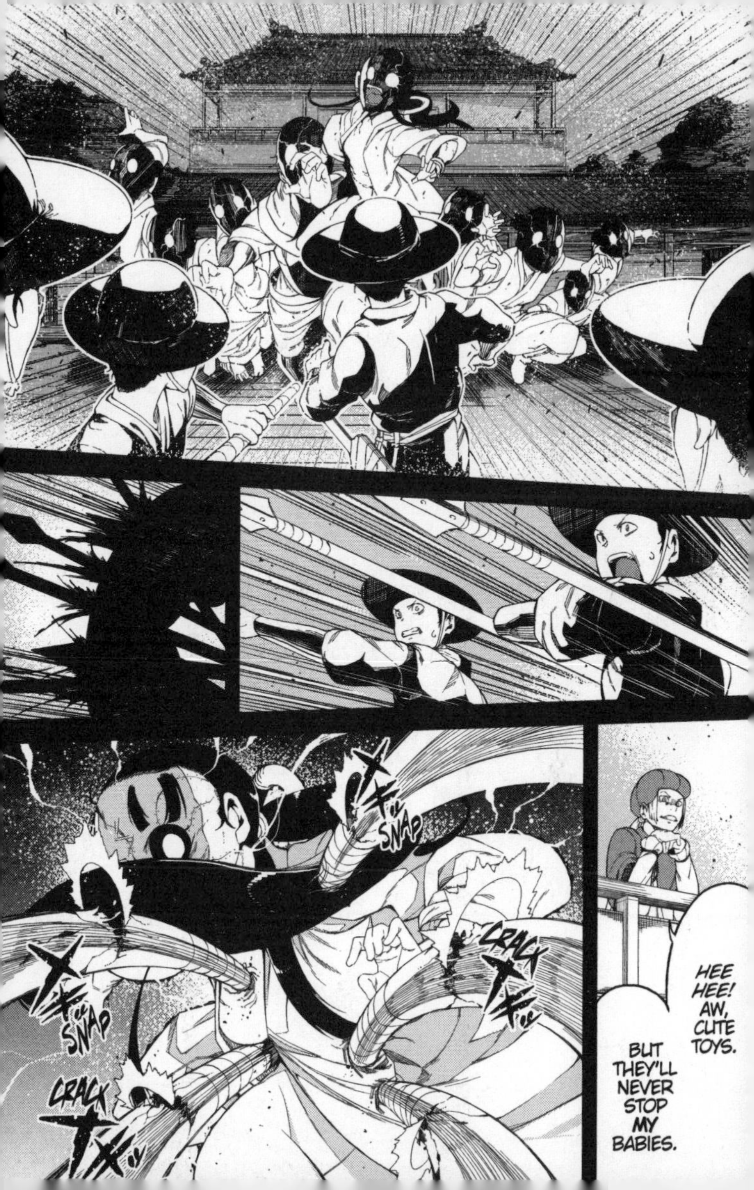
HEE HEE! AW, CUTE TOYS.
BUT THEY'LL NEVER STOP MY BABIES.
SNAP
CRACK
SNAP
CRACK

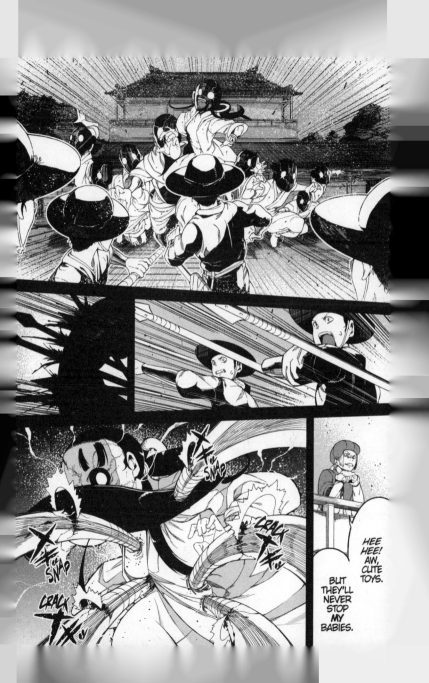

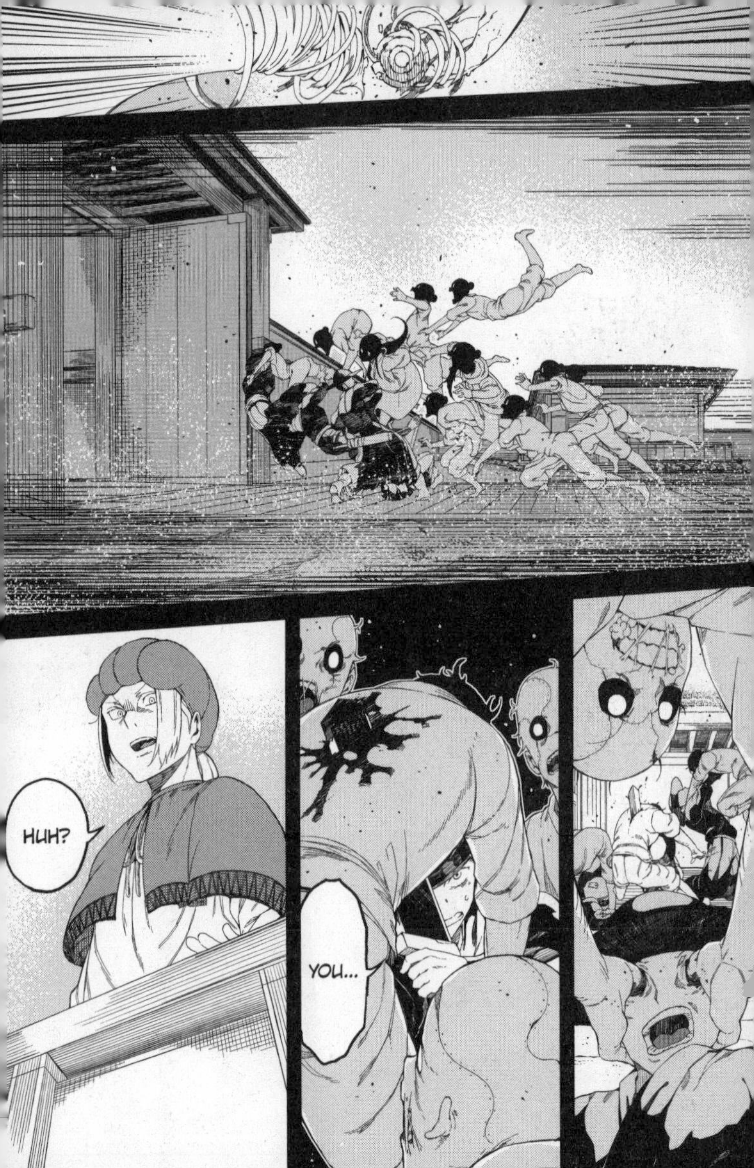
YOU...
HUH?

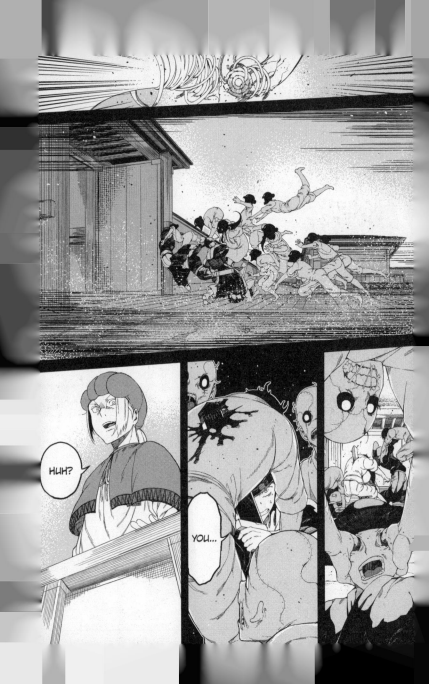

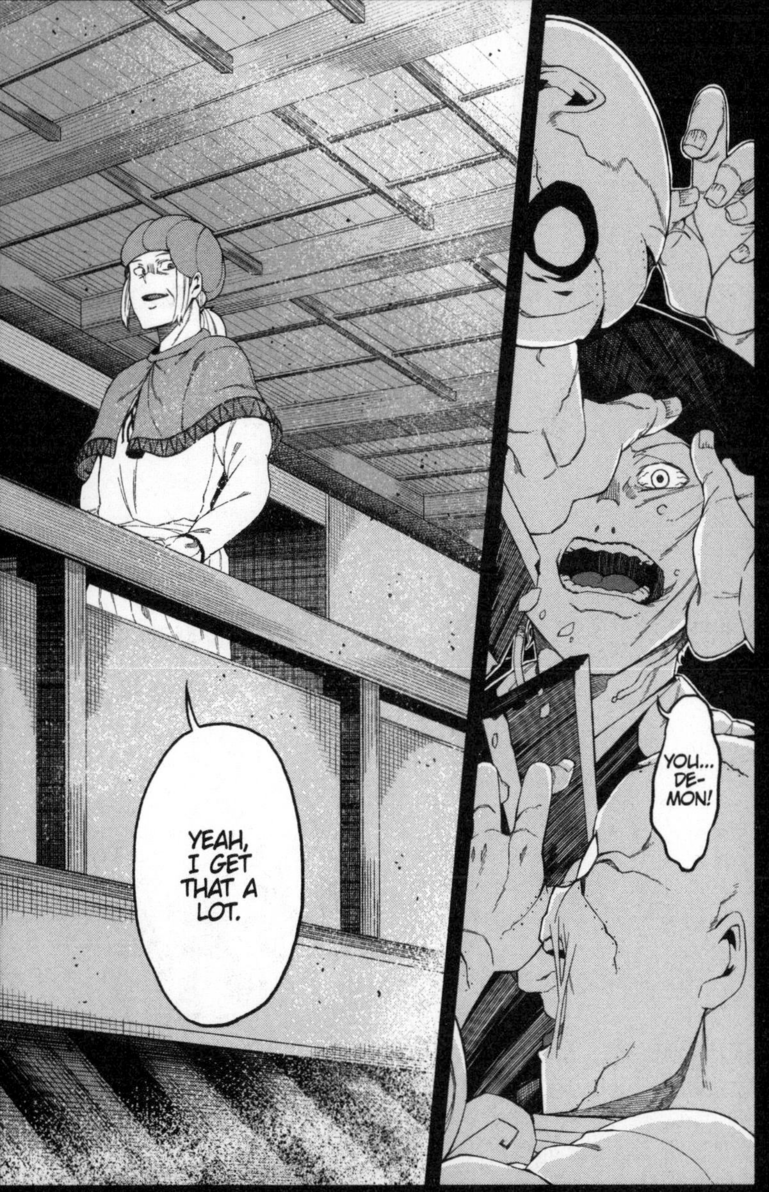
YOU... DE-MON!
YEAH, I GET THAT A LOT.

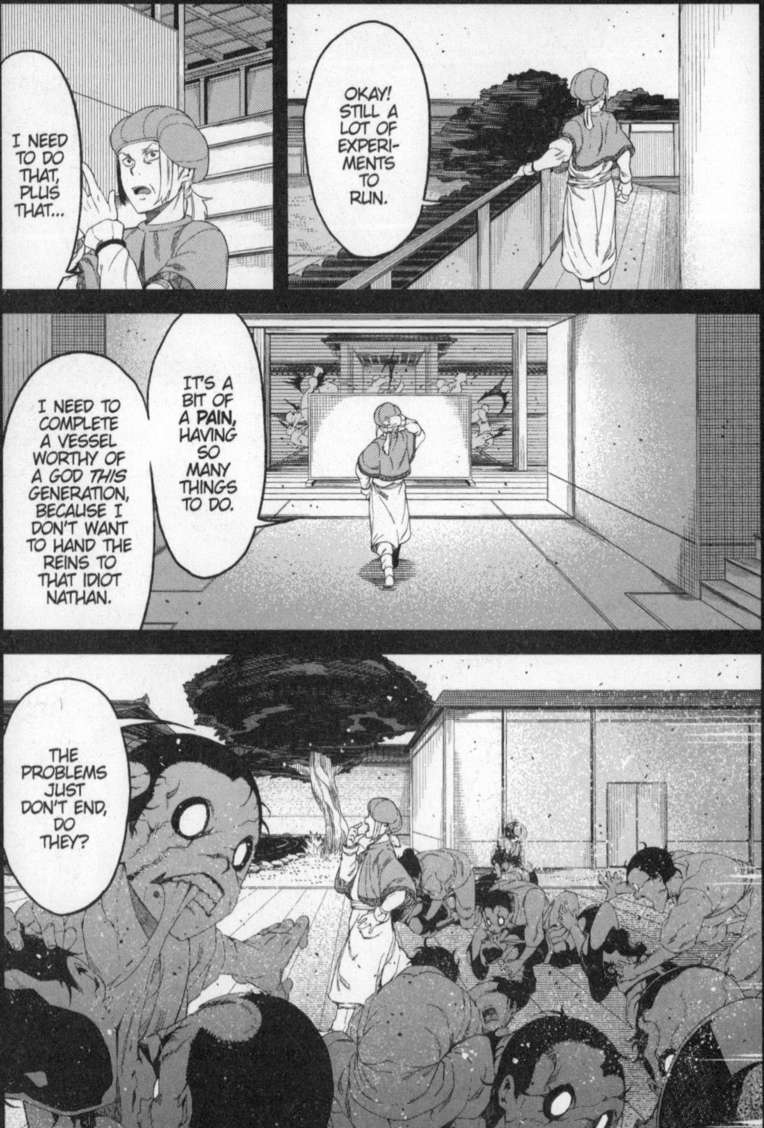
OKAY! STILL A LOT OF EXPERI-MENTS TO RUN.
I NEED TO DO THAT, PLUS THAT...
IT'S A BIT OF A **PAIN**, HAVING SO MANY THINGS TO DO.
I NEED TO COMPLETE A VESSEL WORTHY OF A GOD *THIS* GENERATION, BECAUSE I DON'T WANT TO HAND THE REINS TO THAT IDIOT NATHAN.
THE PROBLEMS JUST DON'T END, DO THEY?

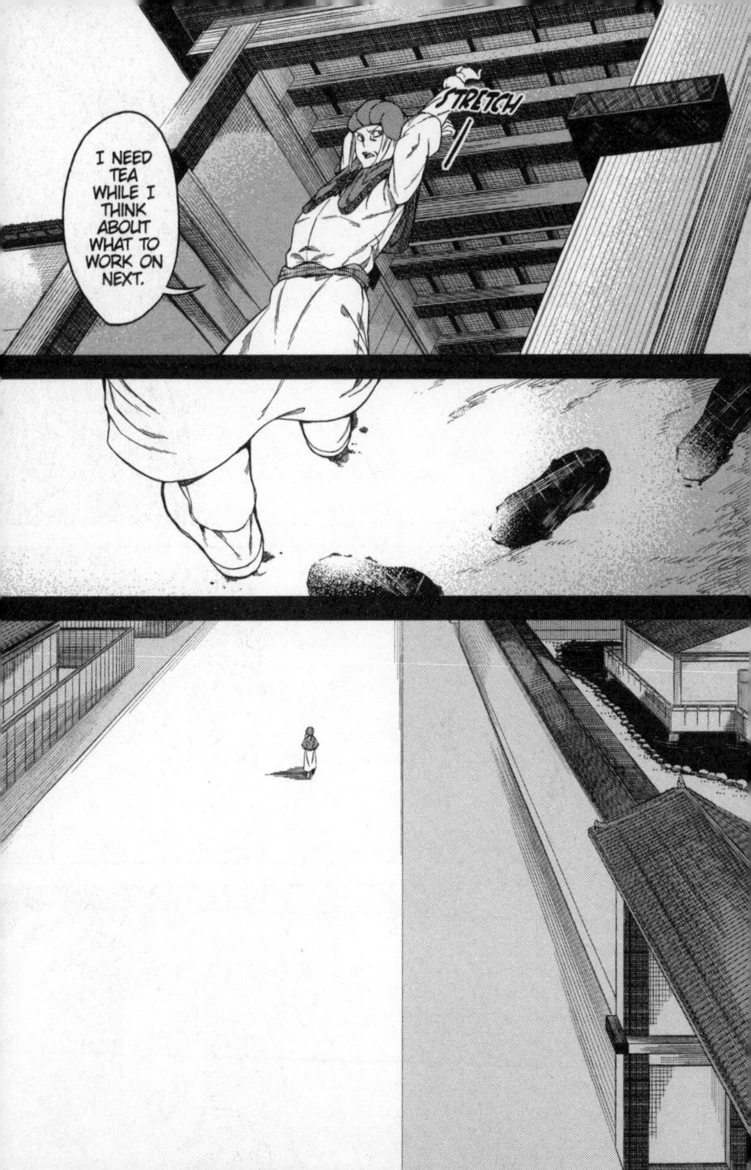
STRETCH
I NEED TEA WHILE I THINK ABOUT WHAT TO WORK ON NEXT.

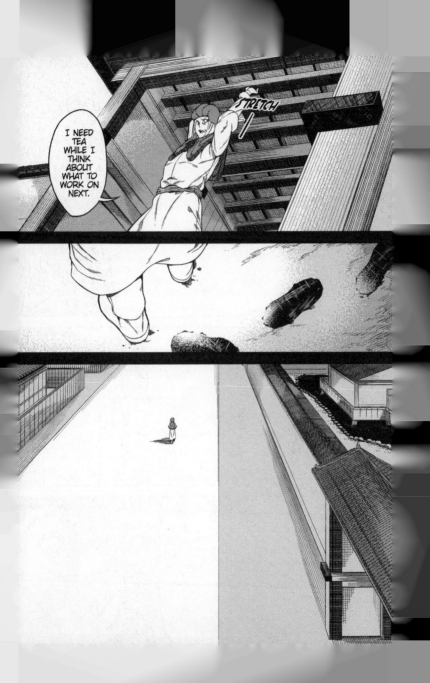

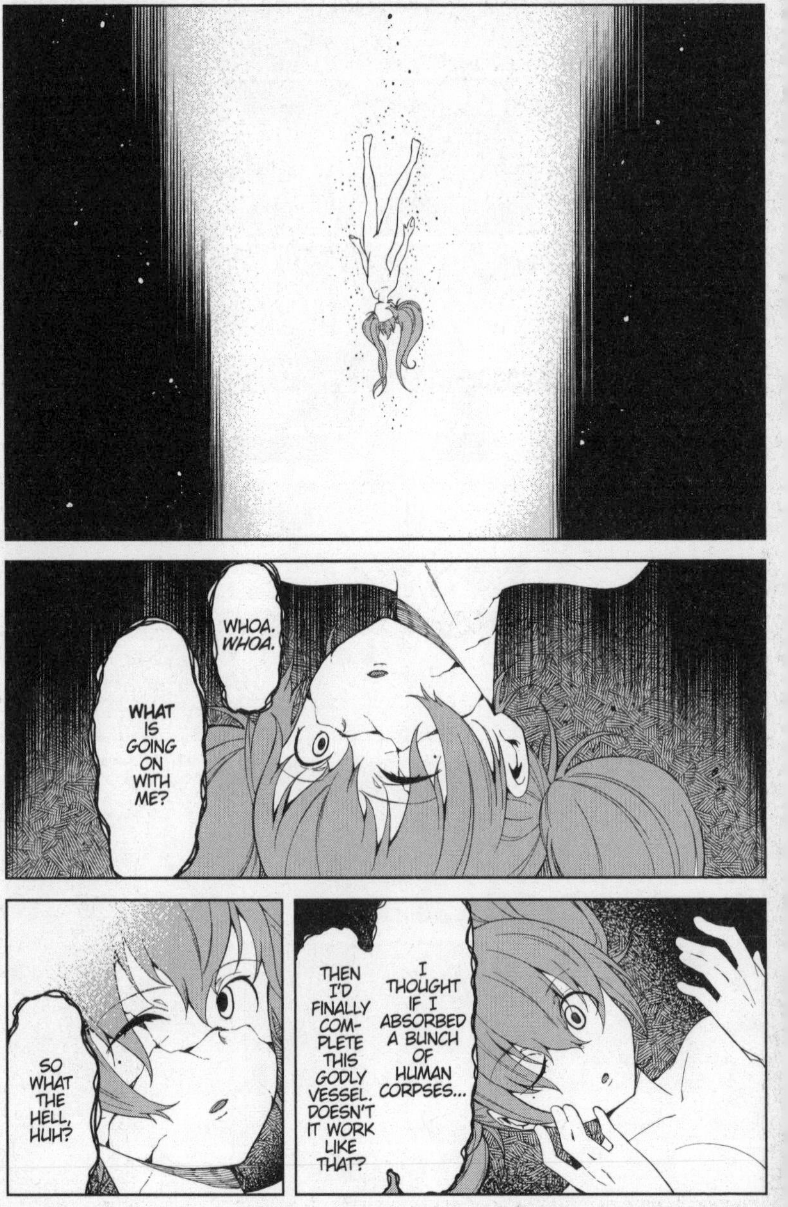
WHOA. WHOA.
WHAT IS GOING ON WITH ME?
I THOUGHT IF I ABSORBED A BUNCH OF HUMAN CORPSES...
THEN I'D FINALLY COMPLETE THIS GODLY VESSEL. DOESN'T IT WORK LIKE THAT?
SO WHAT THE HELL, HUH?

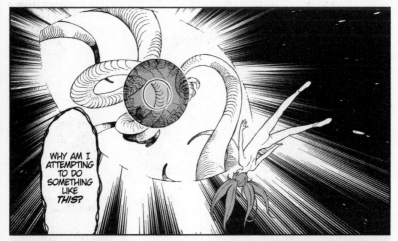

WHY AM I ATTEMPTING TO DO SOMETHING LIKE *THIS?*

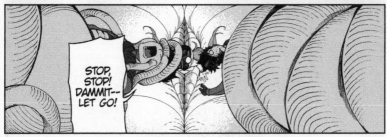

STOP, STOP! DAMMIT-- LET GO!

DIS-PENSING JUSTICE.

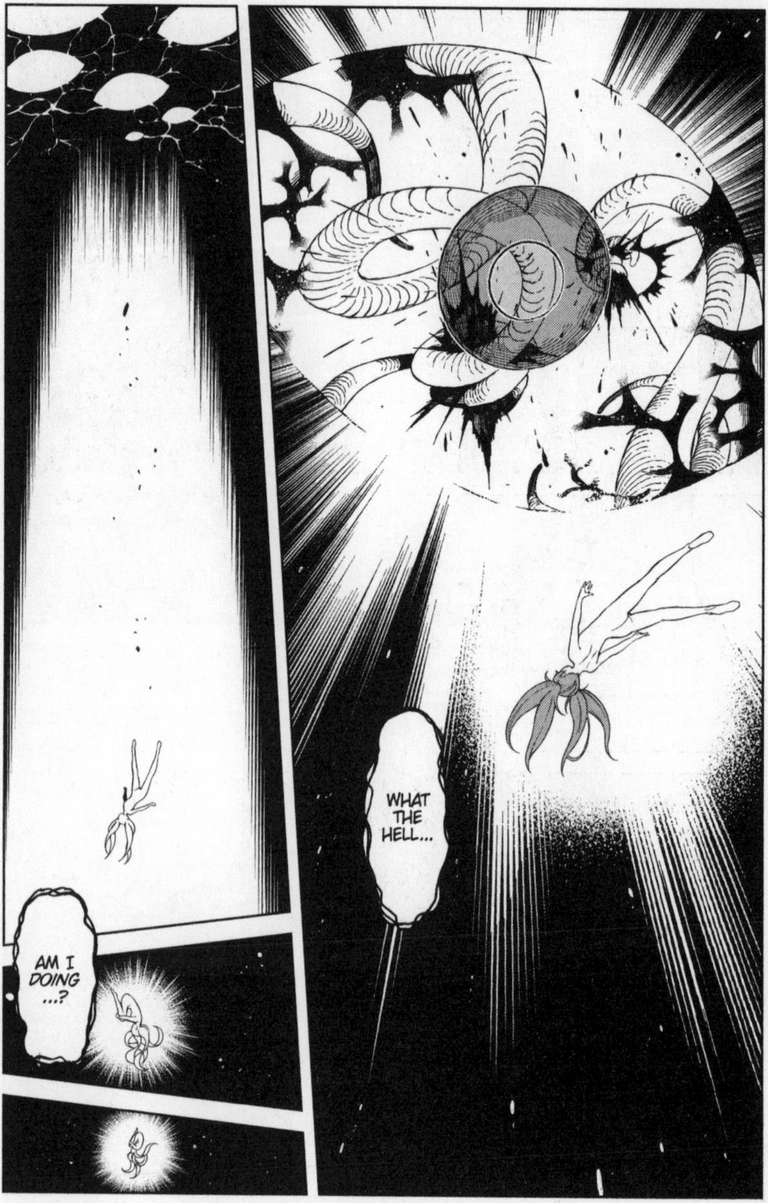
WHAT THE HELL...
AM I DOING ...?

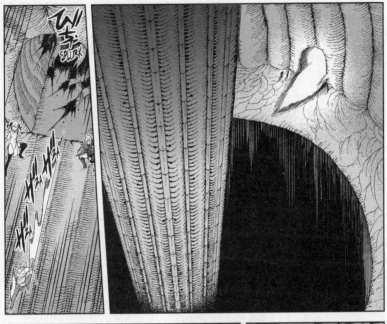

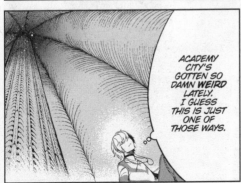

SPLURK
ZA
ZA
ZA
ZA
ANOTHER INJURY OUT OF NOWHERE.
ACADEMY CITY'S GOTTEN SO DAMN WEIRD LATELY. I GUESS THIS IS JUST ONE OF THOSE WAYS.

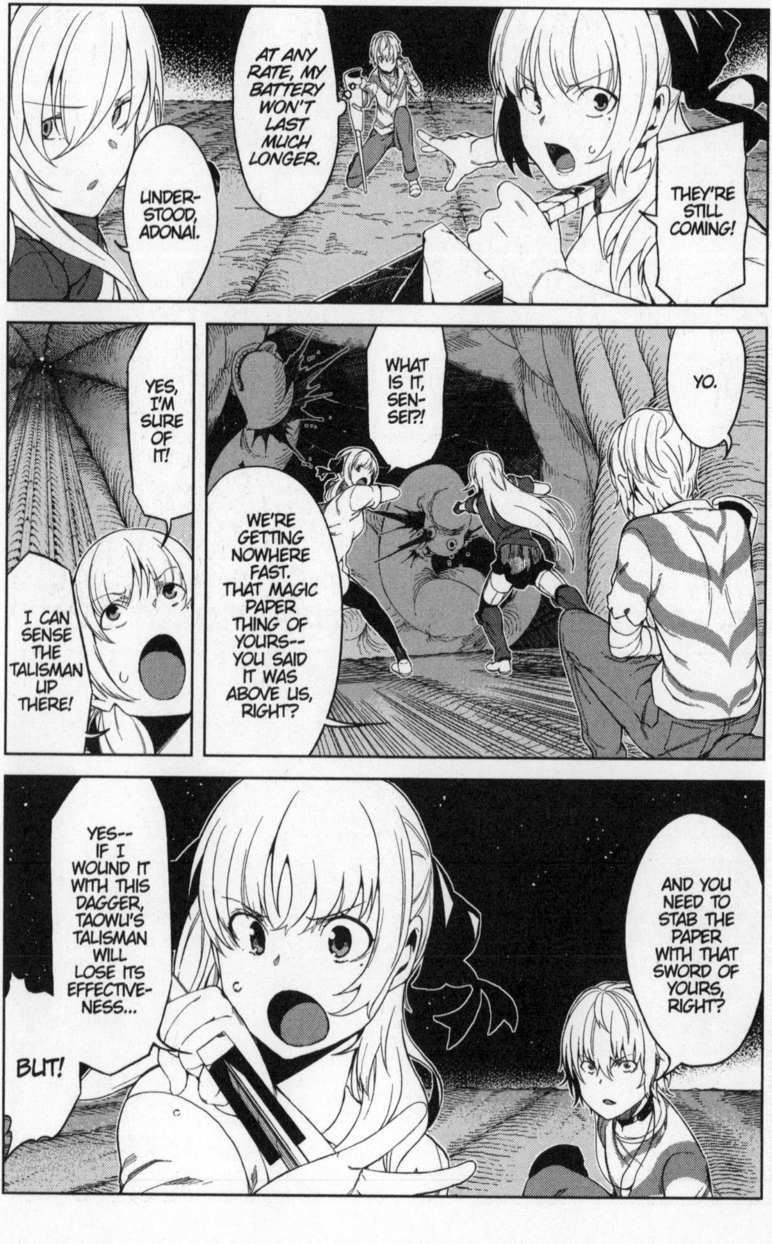
THEY'RE STILL COMING!
AT ANY RATE, MY BATTERY WON'T LAST MUCH LONGER.
UNDERSTOOD, ADONAI.
YO.
WHAT IS IT, SENSEI?!
WE'RE GETTING NOWHERE FAST. THAT MAGIC PAPER THING OF YOURS-- YOU SAID IT WAS ABOVE US, RIGHT?
YES, I'M SURE OF IT!
I CAN SENSE THE TALISMAN UP THERE!
AND YOU NEED TO STAB THE PAPER WITH THAT SWORD OF YOURS, RIGHT?
YES-- IF I WOUND IT WITH THIS DAGGER, TAOWU'S TALISMAN WILL LOSE ITS EFFECTIVENESS...
BUT!

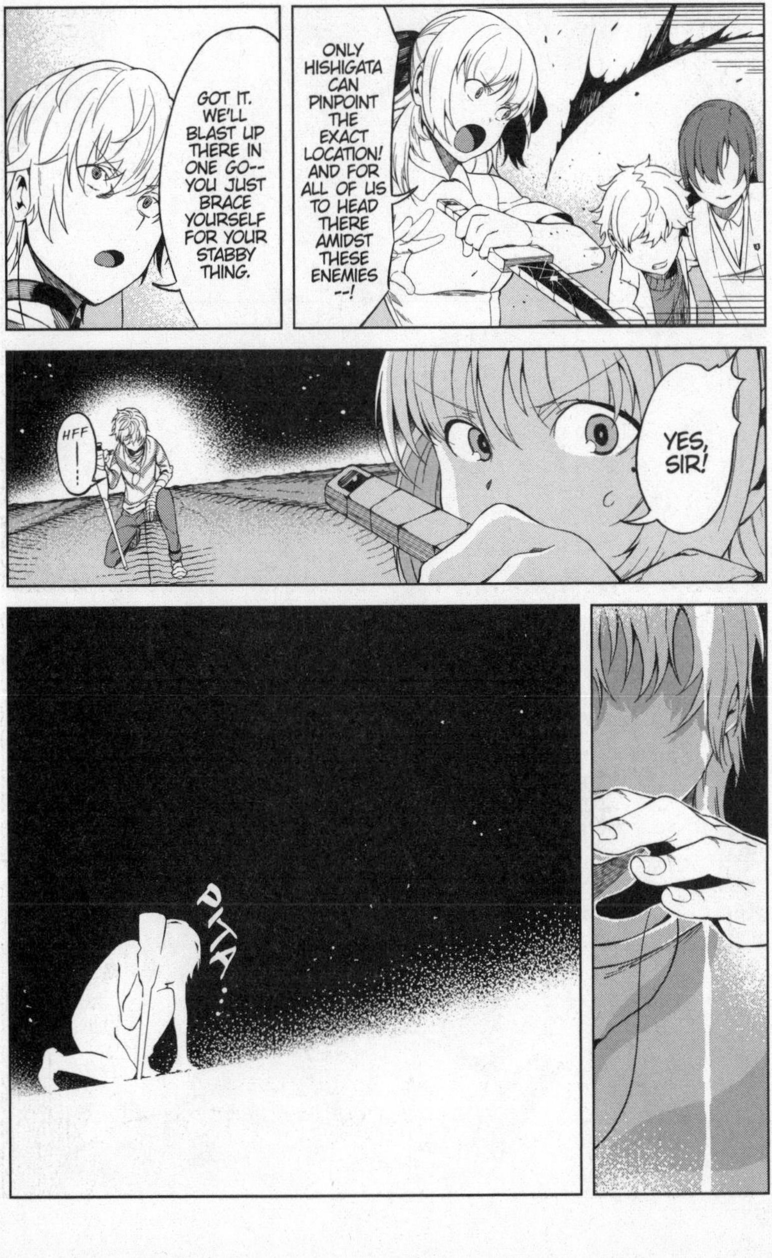
ONLY HISHIGATA CAN PINPOINT THE EXACT LOCATION! AND FOR ALL OF US TO HEAD THERE AMIDST THESE ENEMIES --!
GOT IT. WE'LL BLAST UP THERE IN ONE GO-- YOU JUST BRACE YOURSELF FOR YOUR STABBY THING.
YES, SIR!
HFF ...!
PITA...

THERE'S NO WIND HERE.

BUT BY CONTROLLING THE FORCE OF THE EARTH'S ROTATION WHERE WE'RE STANDING...

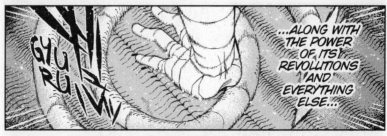

GYU RU

...ALONG WITH THE POWER OF ITS REVOLUTIONS AND EVERYTHING ELSE...

...AND TRANSFORMING THAT INTO WHAT I WANT...!

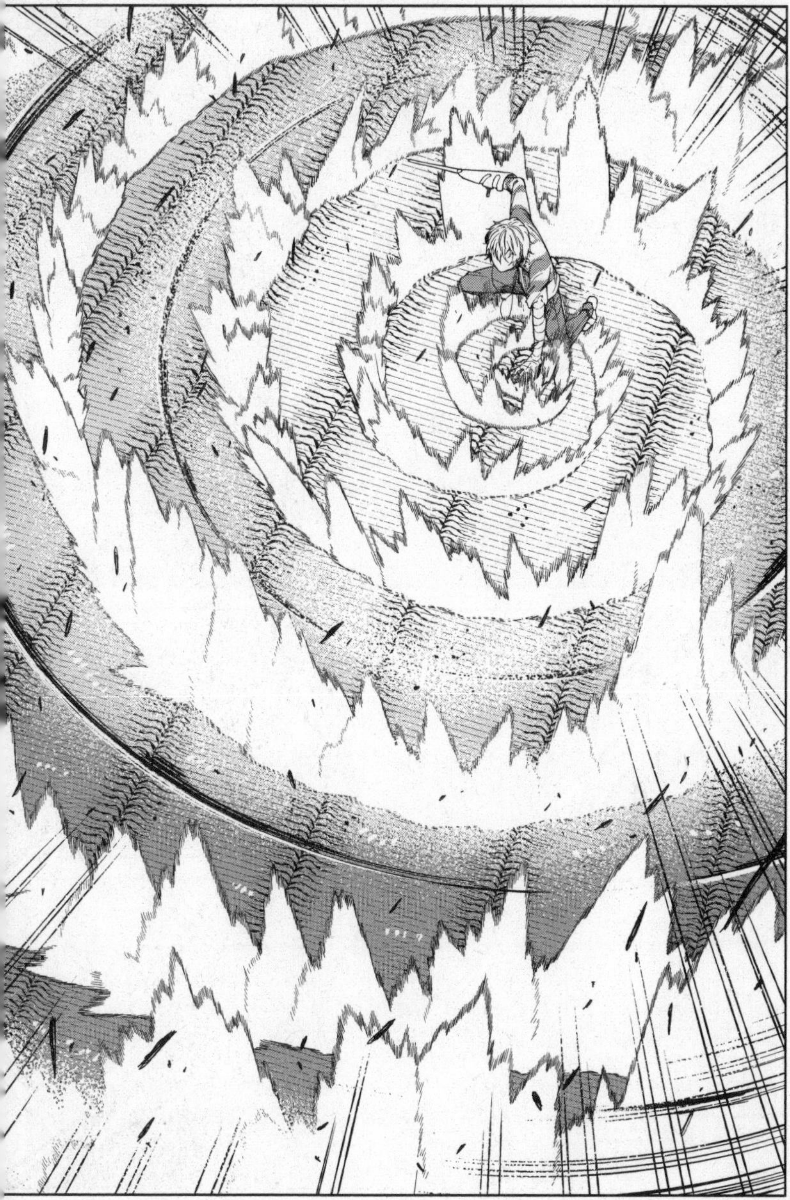

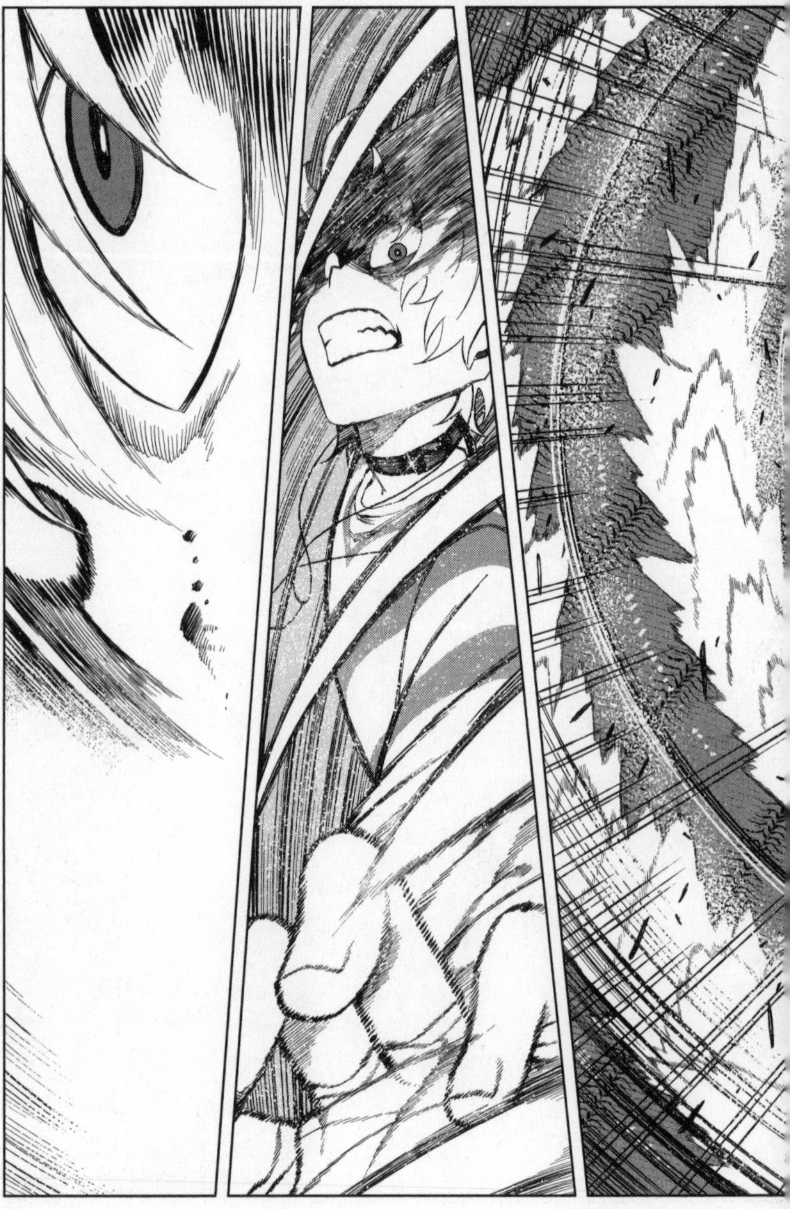

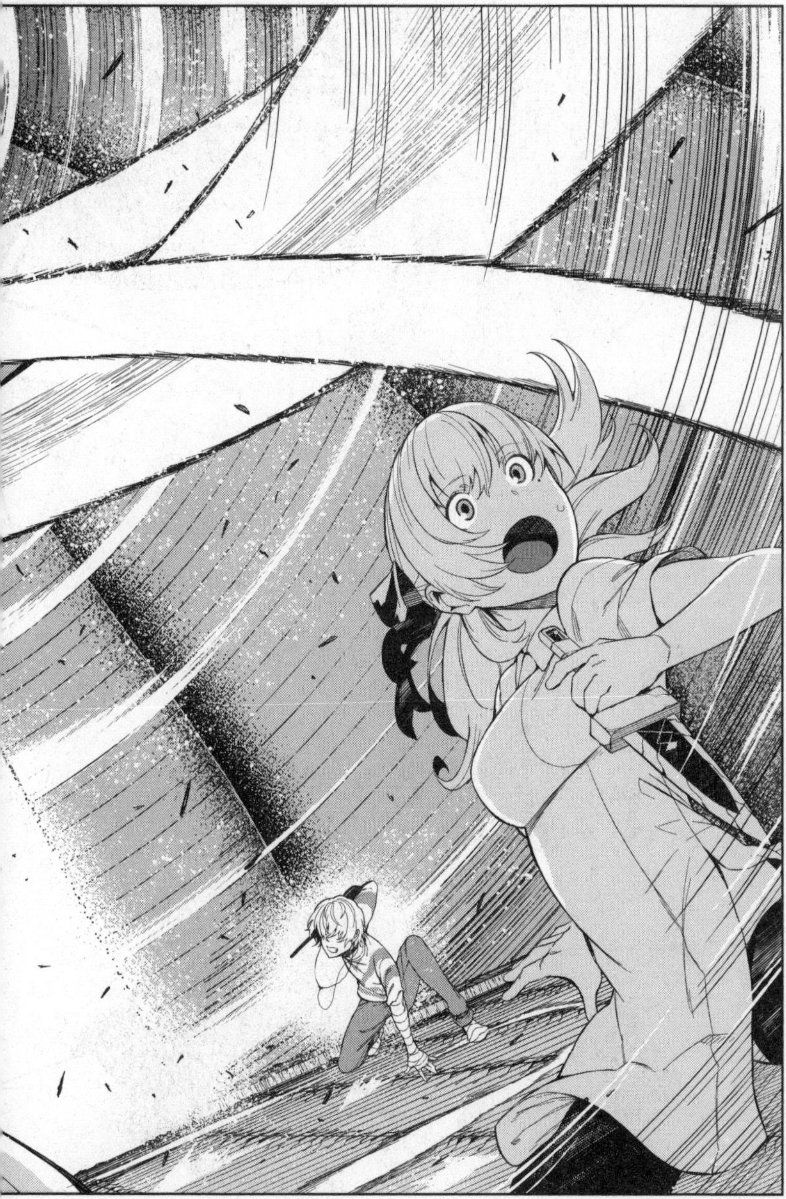

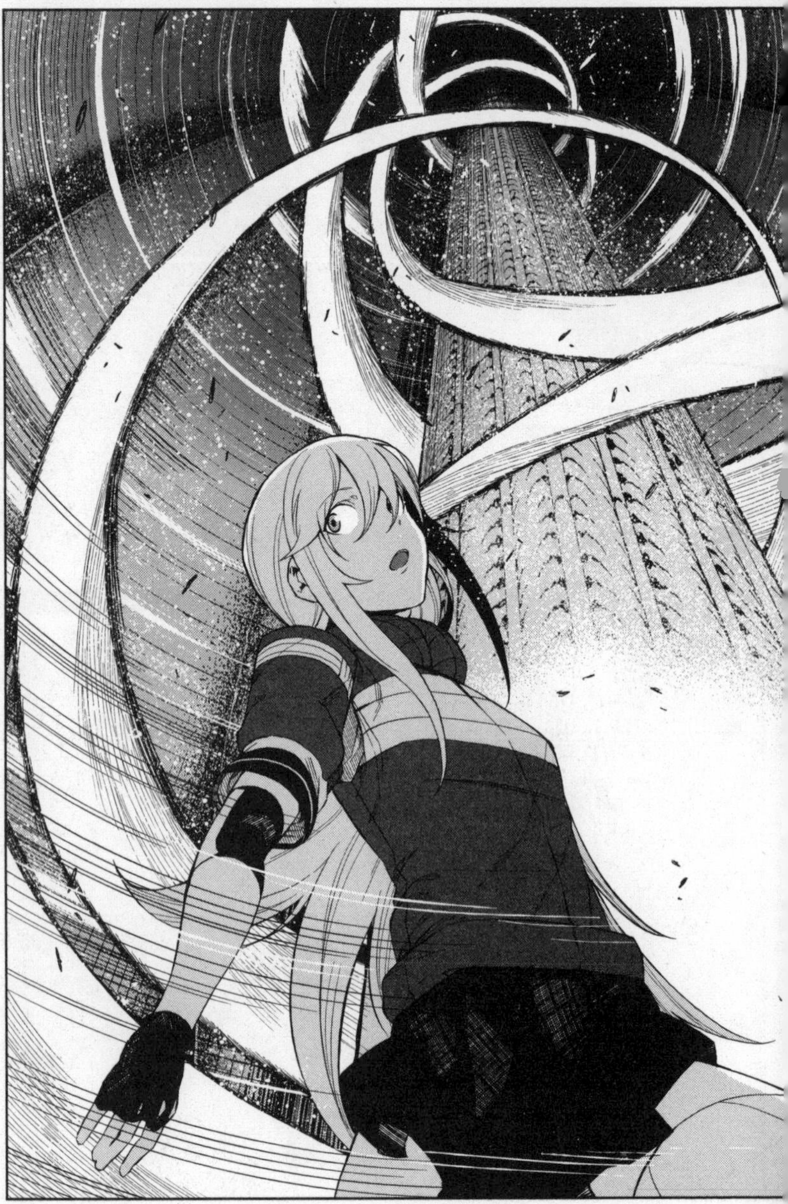

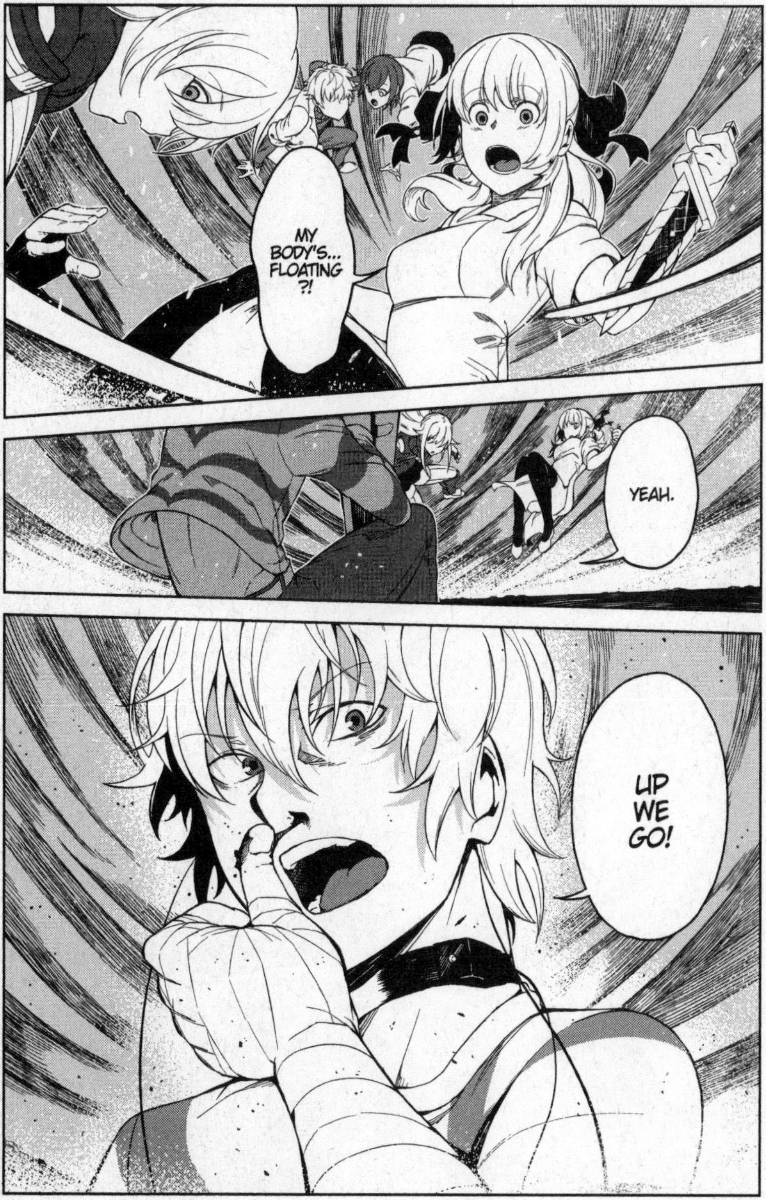
MY BODY'S... FLOATING ?!
YEAH.
UP WE GO!

a certain
SCIENTIFIC
ACCELERATOR

とある科学の一方通行

アクセラレータ

とある魔術の禁書目録外伝

CHAPTER 34

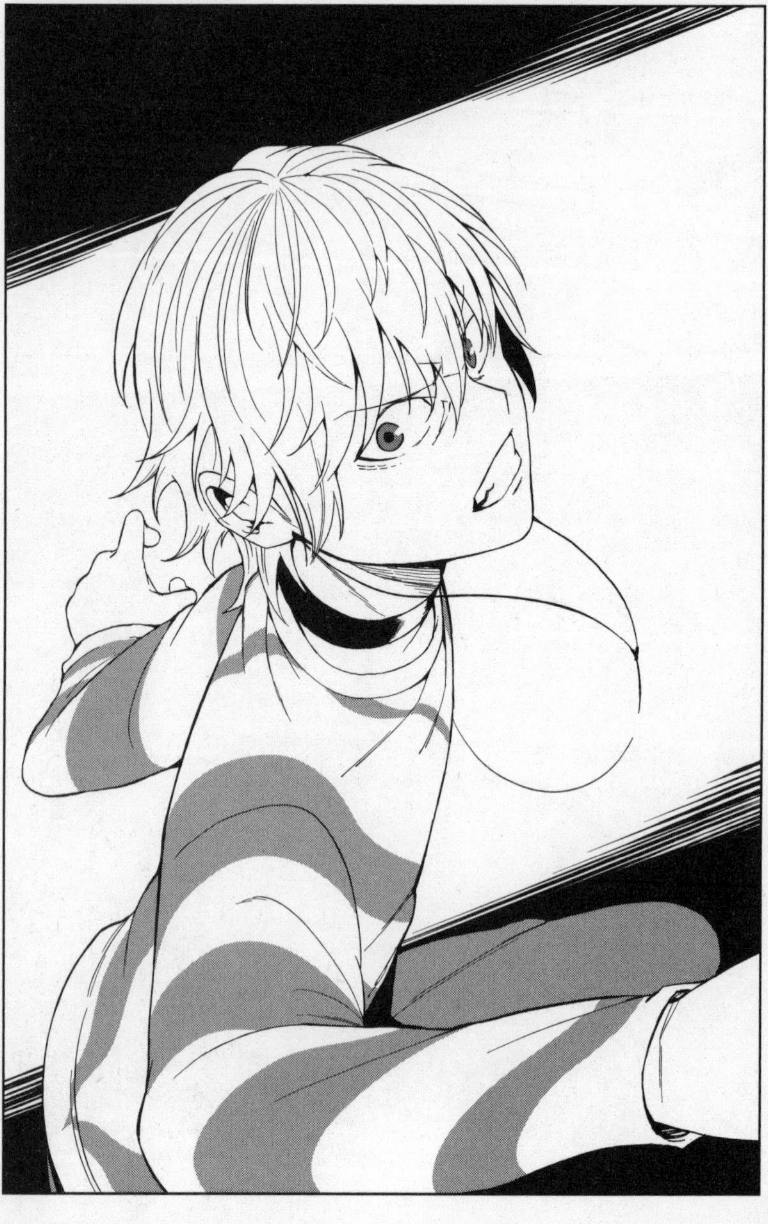

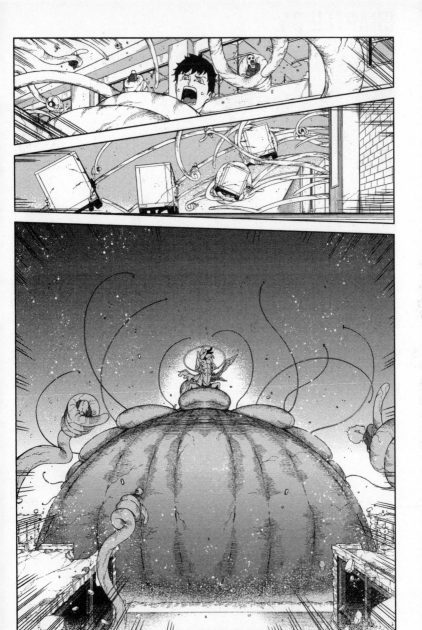

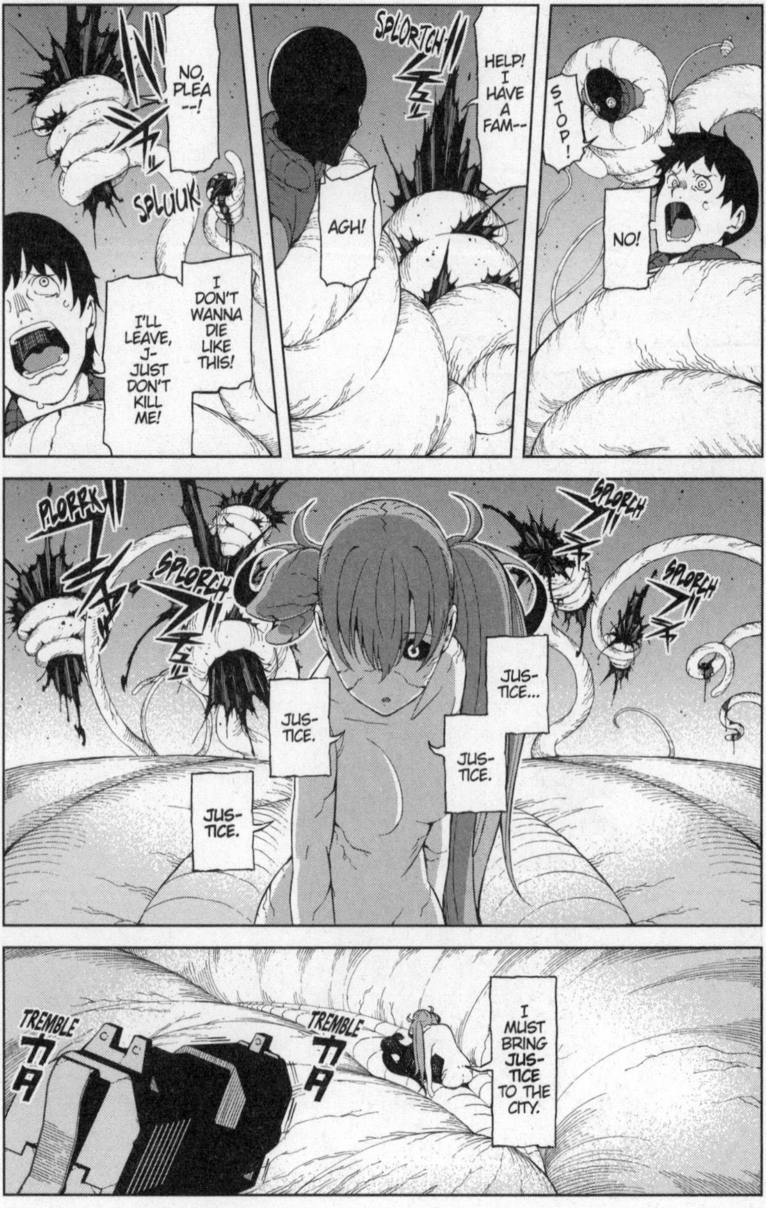
STOP!
NO!
SPLORTCH
HELP! I HAVE A FAM--
AGH!
NO, PLEA--!
SPLUUK
I DON'T WANNA DIE LIKE THIS!
I'LL LEAVE, J-JUST DON'T KILL ME!
SPLORCH
SPLORCH
SPLORCH
PLORRK
JUS-TICE...
JUS-TICE.
JUS-TICE.
JUS-TICE.
I MUST BRING JUS-TICE TO THE CITY.
TREMBLE
カタ
TREMBLE
カタ

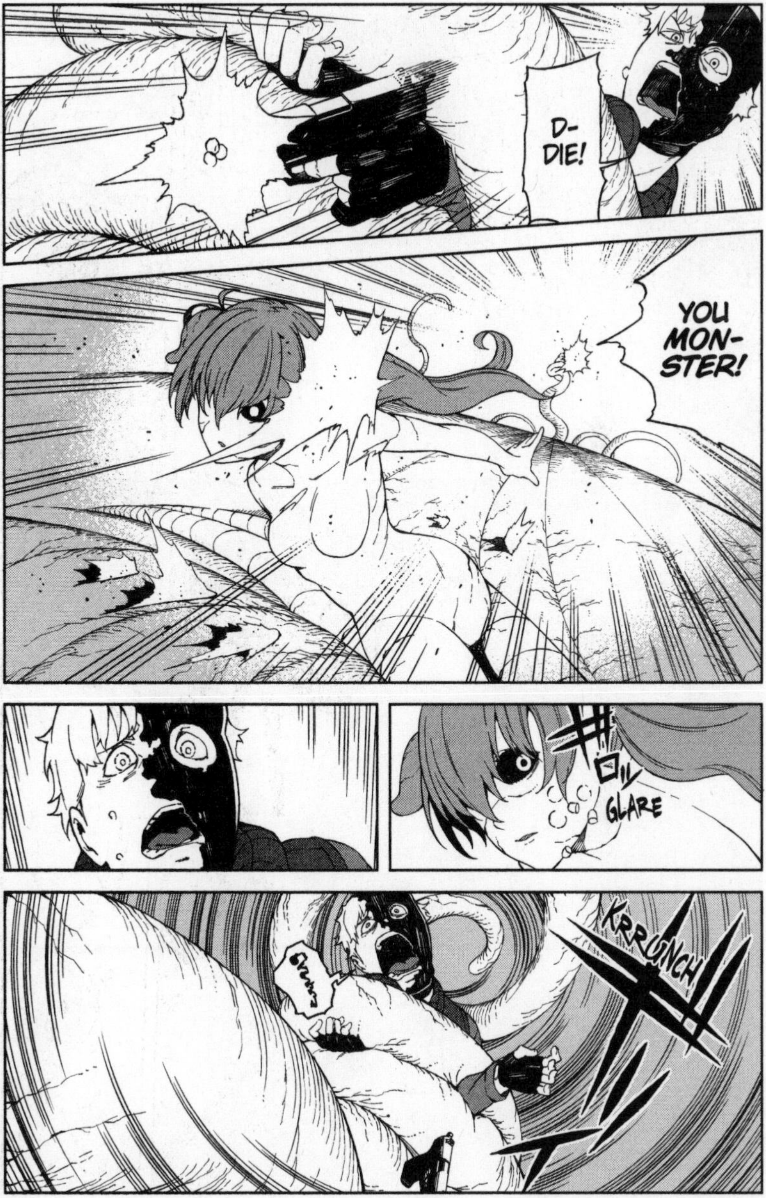
D-
DIE!
YOU MONSTER!
GLARE
KRRUNCH

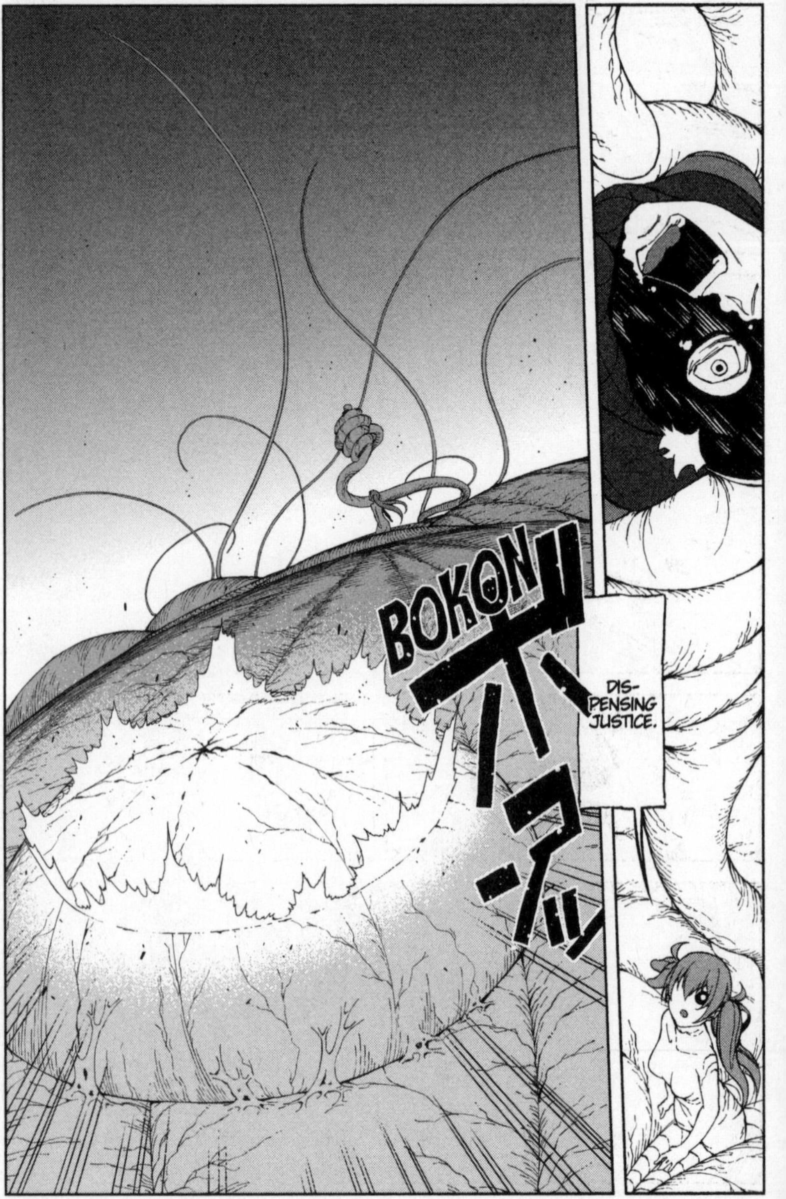
DIS-
PENSING
JUSTICE.
BOKON

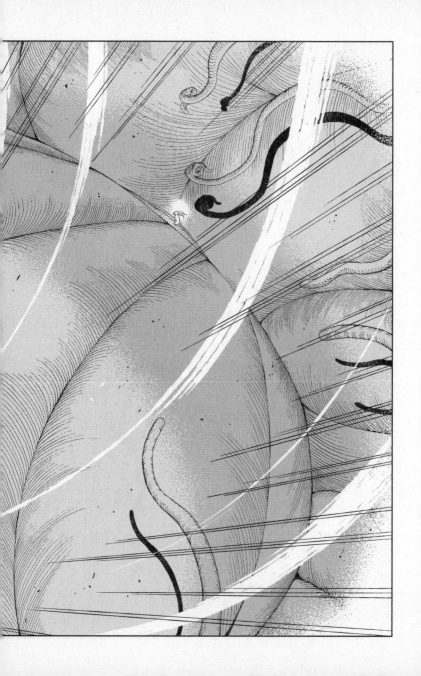

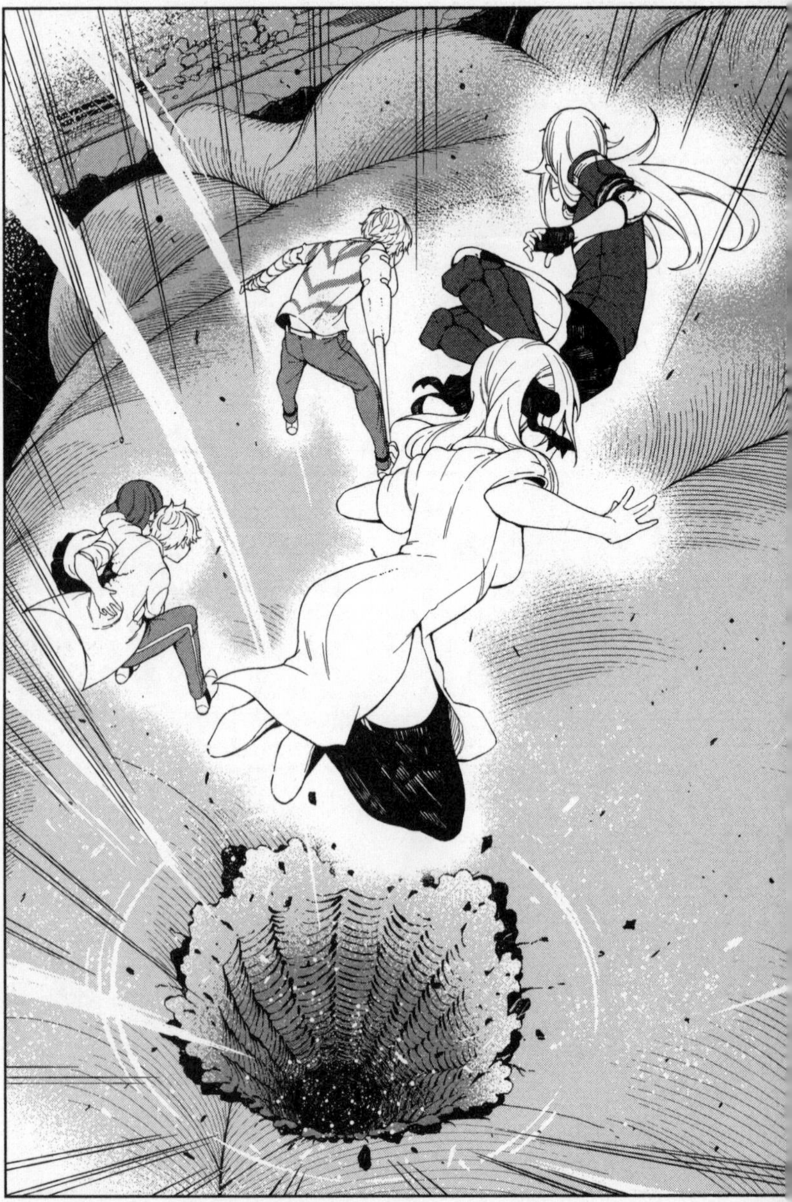

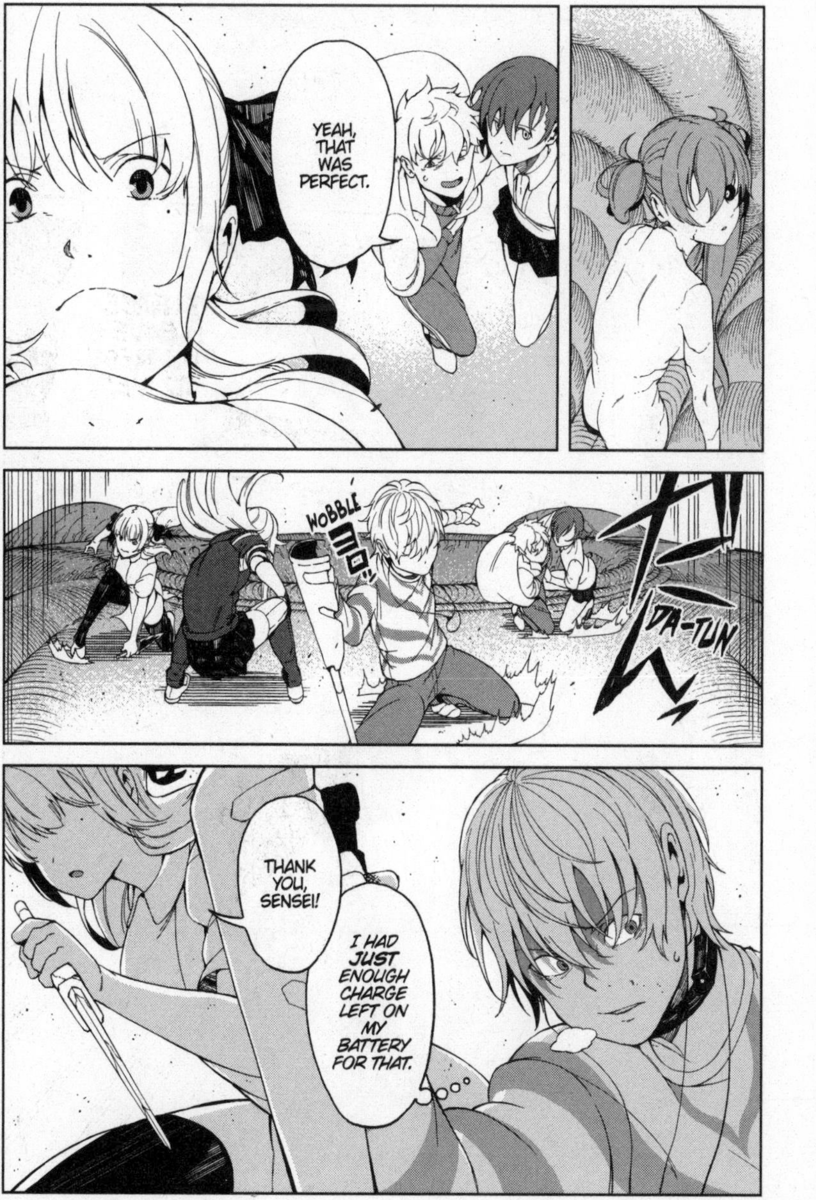
YEAH, THAT WAS PERFECT.
DA-TUN
WOBBLE
THANK YOU, SENSEI!
I HAD JUST ENOUGH CHARGE LEFT ON MY BATTERY FOR THAT.

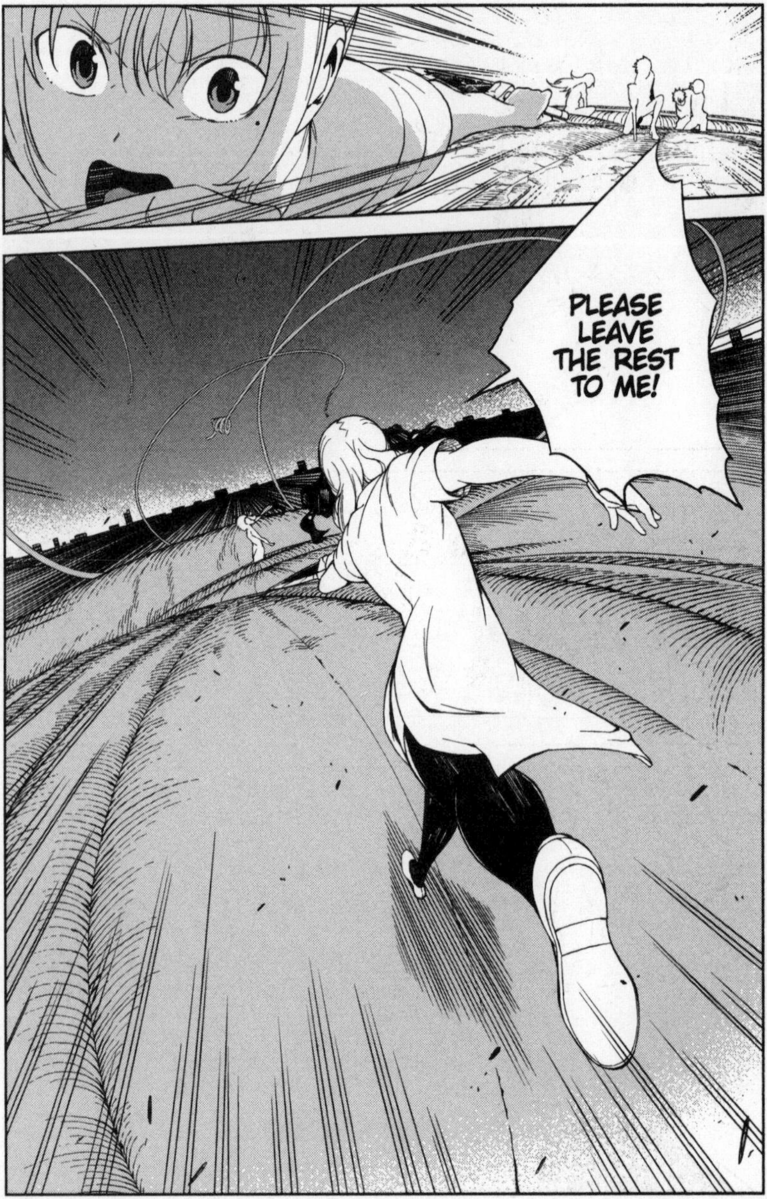
PLEASE LEAVE THE REST TO ME!

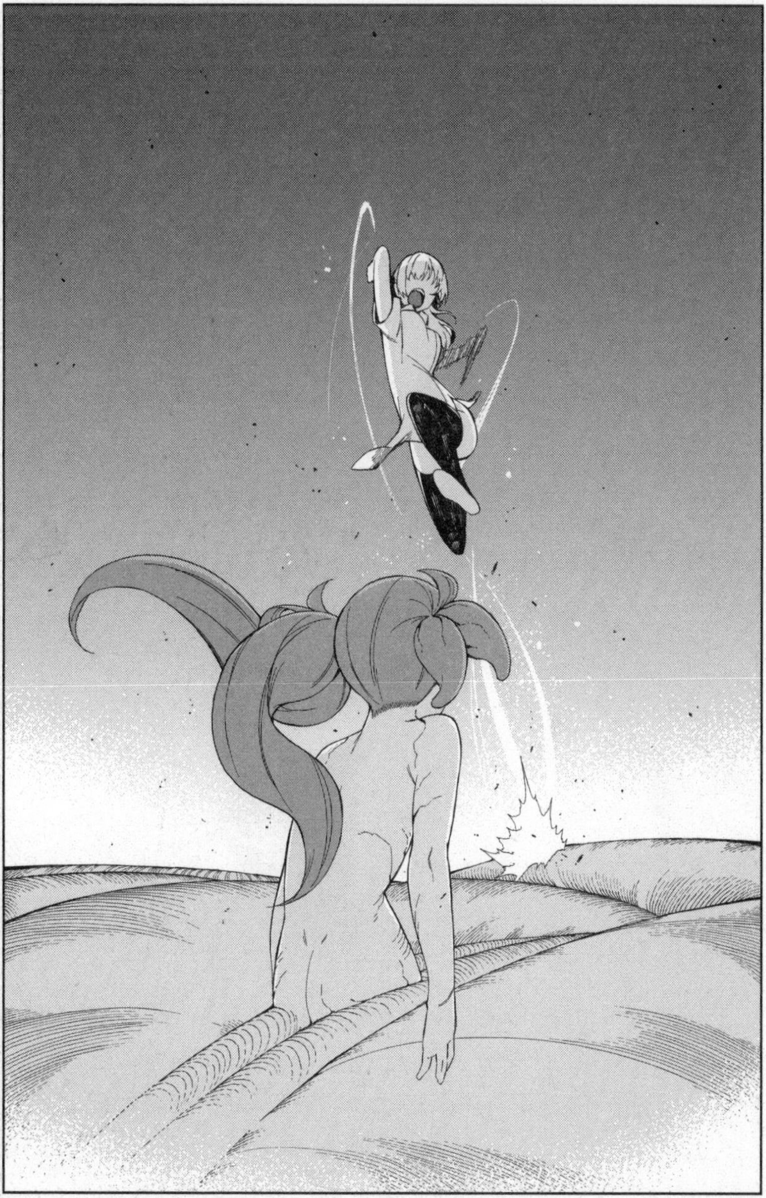

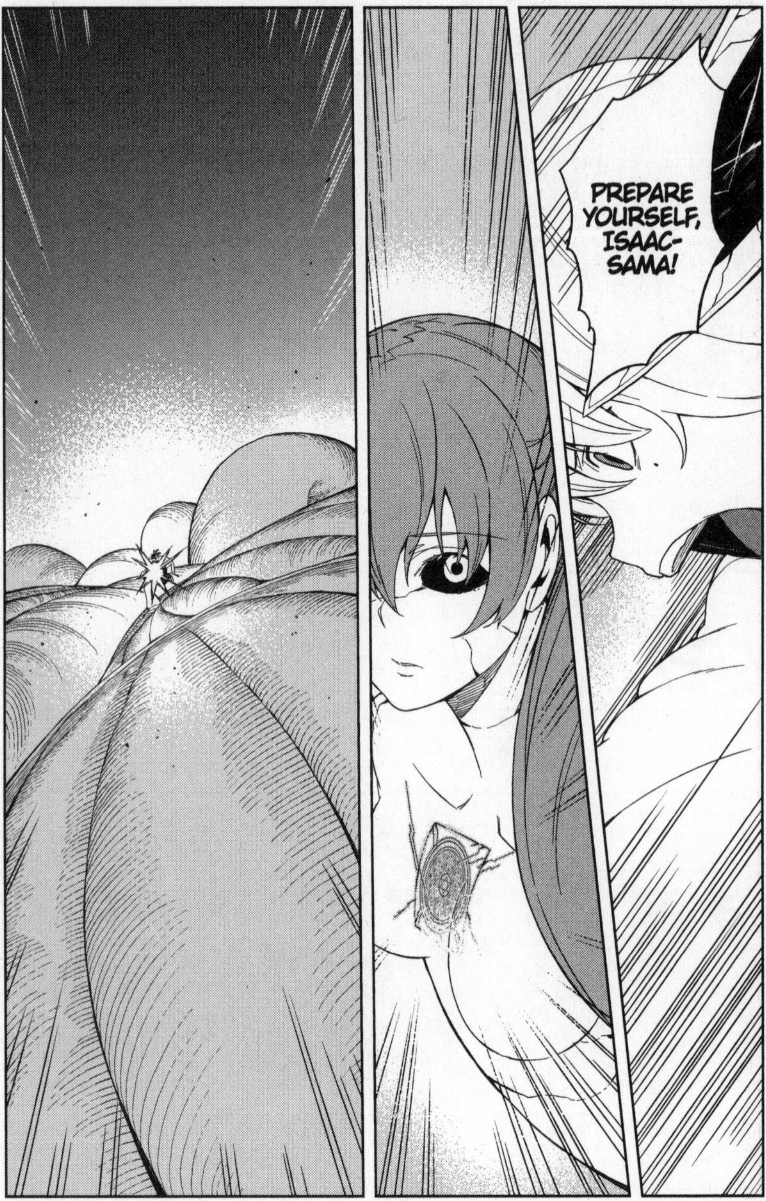
PREPARE YOURSELF, ISAAC-SAMA!

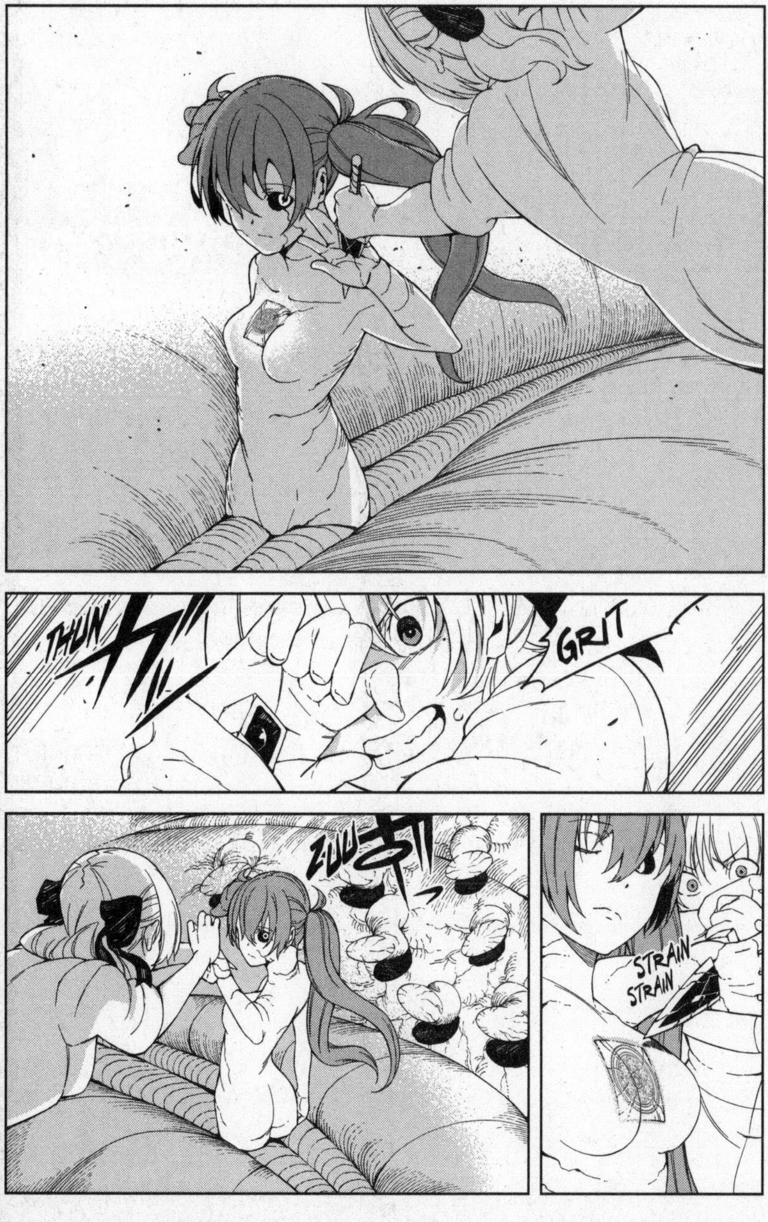
GRIT
THUN
STRAIN
STRAIN
Z-UU

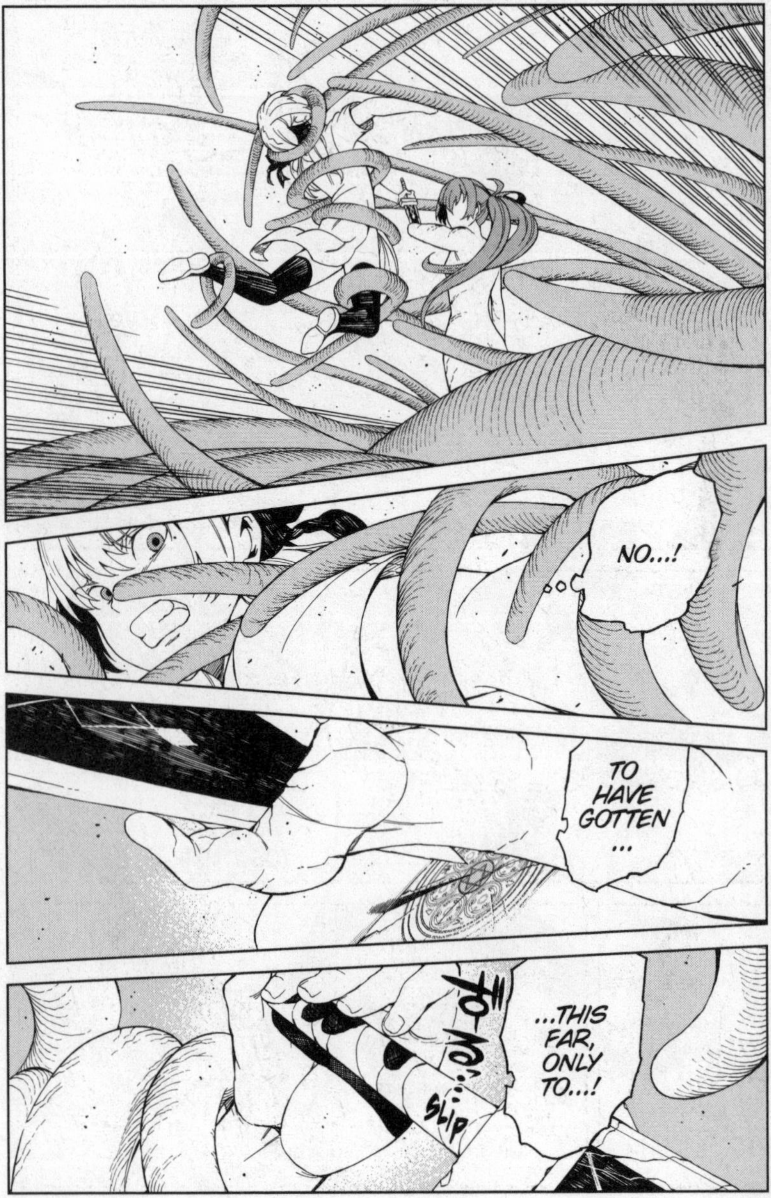
NO...!
TO HAVE GOTTEN ...
...THIS FAR, ONLY TO...!
SLIP

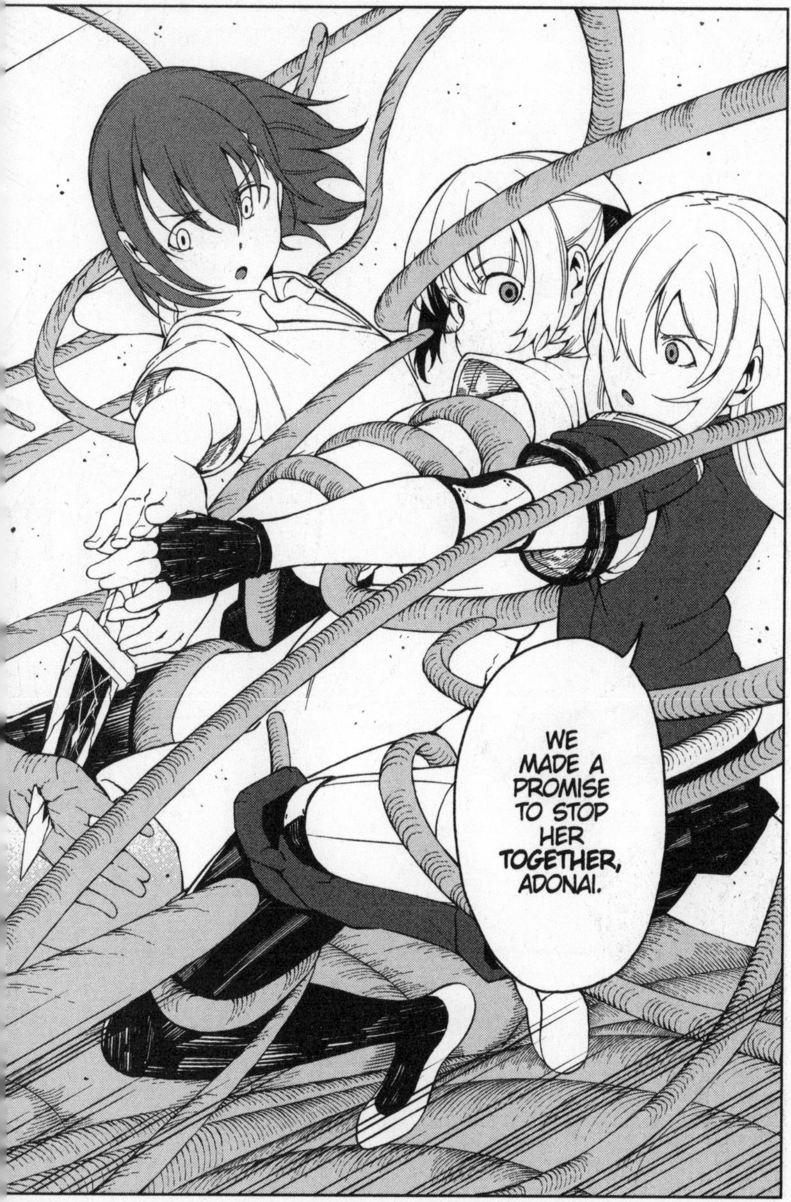
WE MADE A PROMISE TO STOP HER TOGETHER, ADONAI.

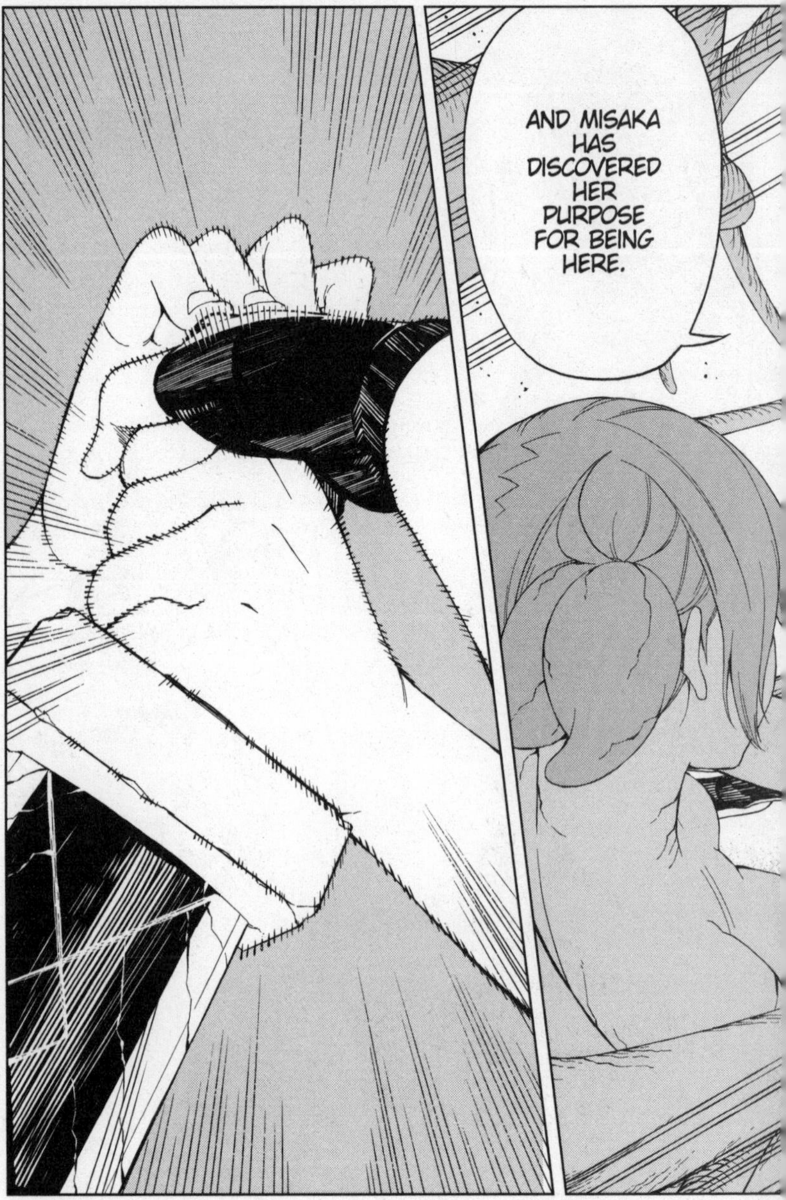
AND MISAKA HAS DISCOVERED HER PURPOSE FOR BEING HERE.

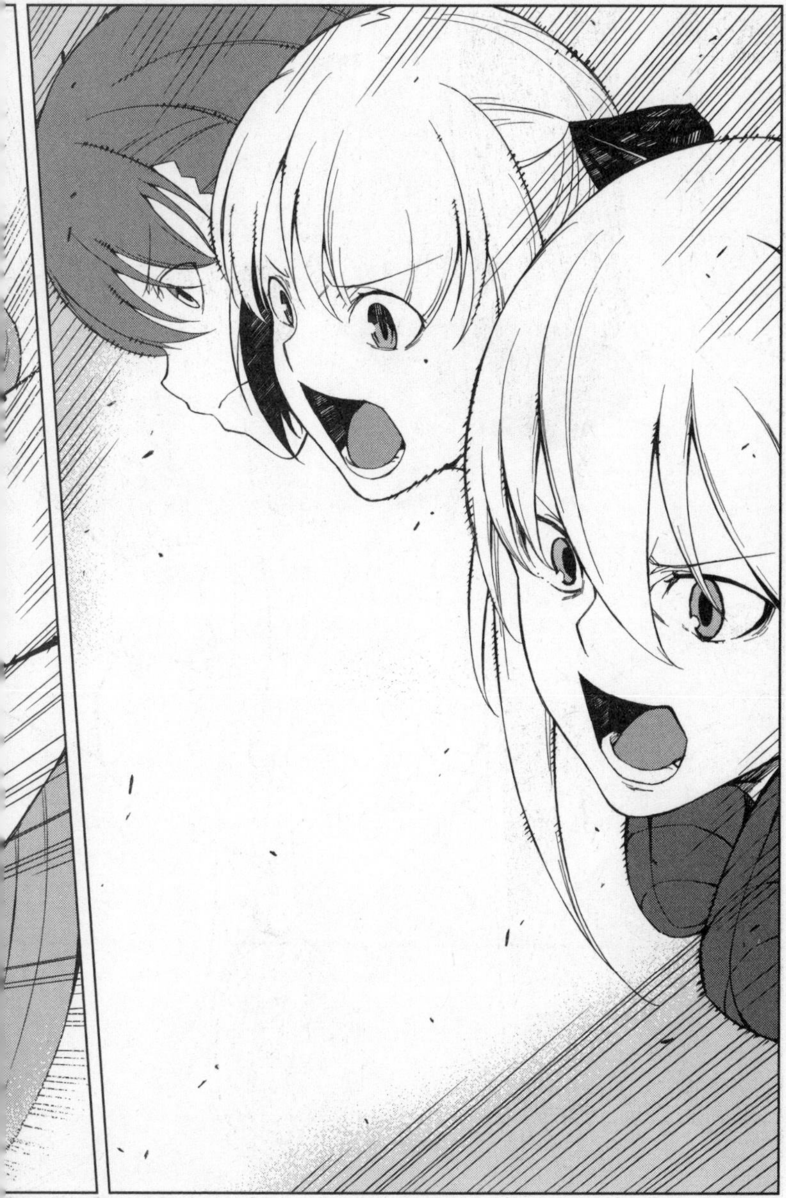

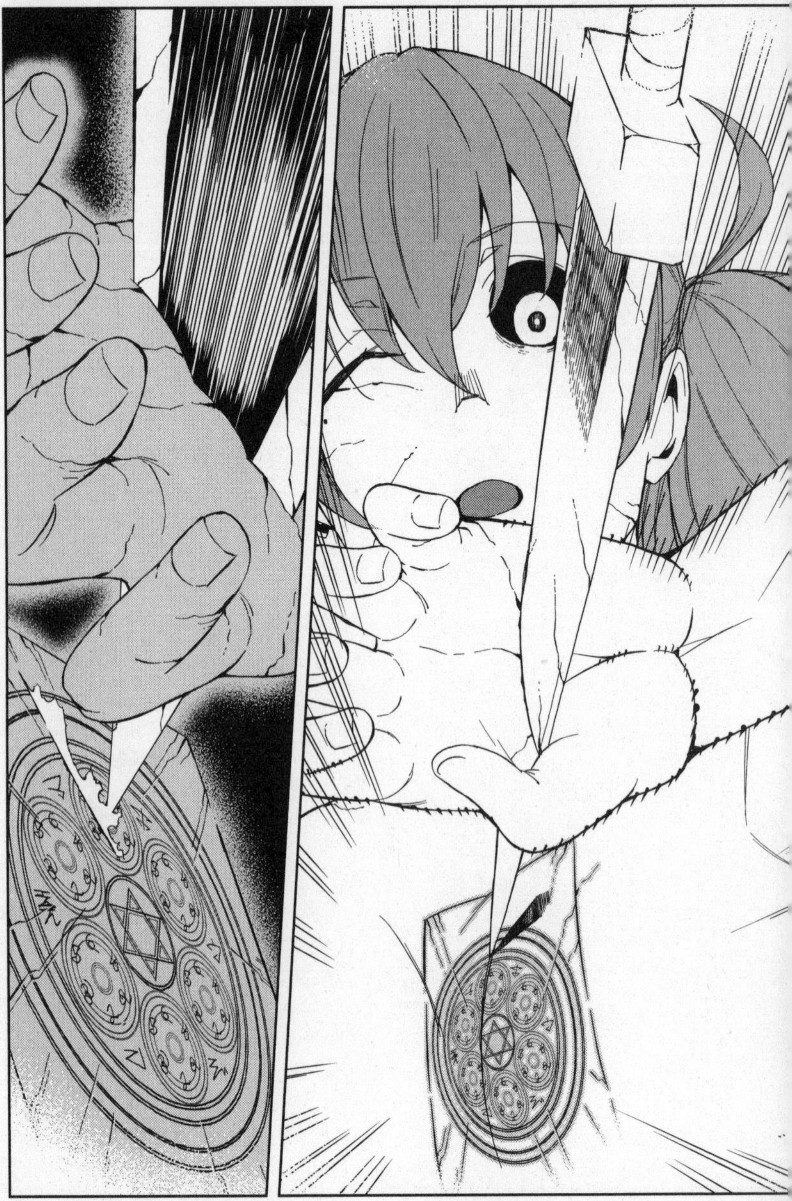

とある科学の一方通行

アクセラレータ

とある魔術の禁書目録外伝

CHAPTER 35

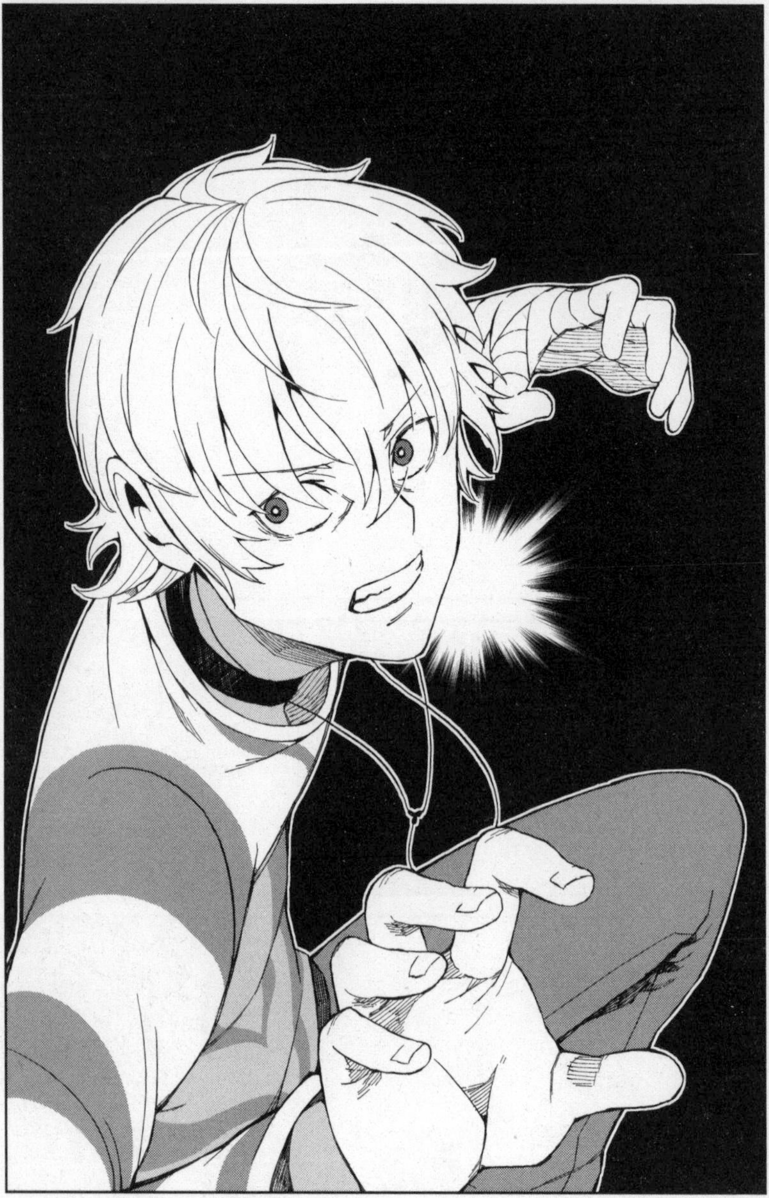

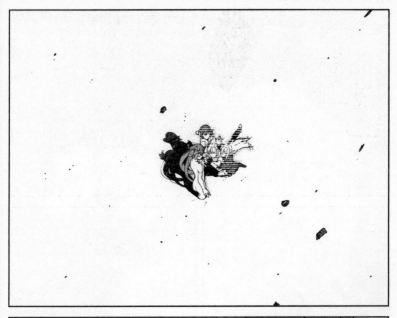

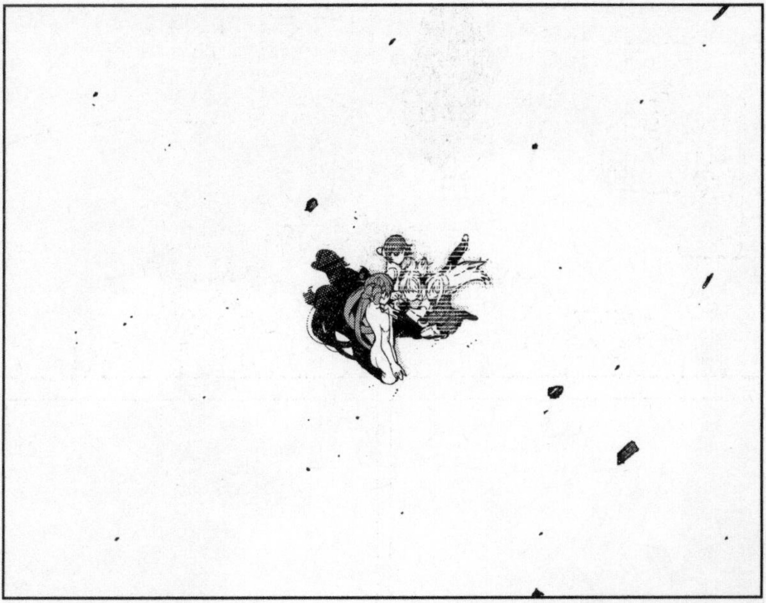
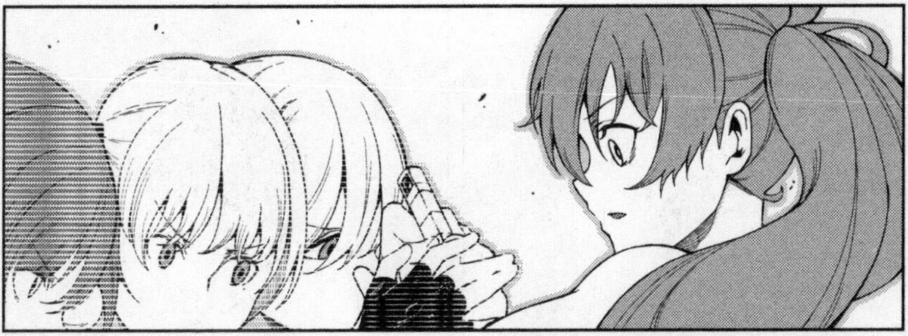
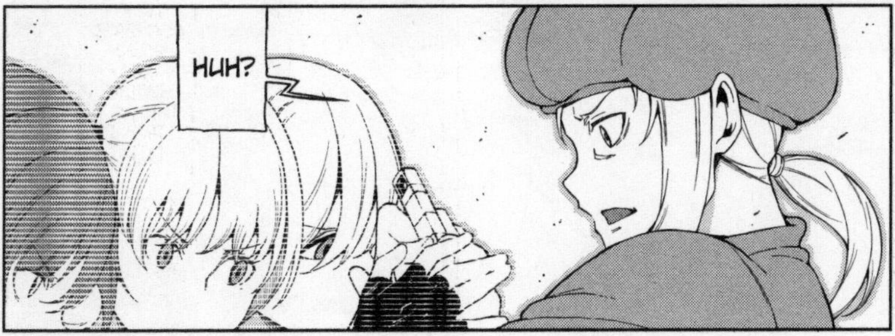
HUH?

OH. I GET IT.

I FAILED AGAIN, DIDN'T I?

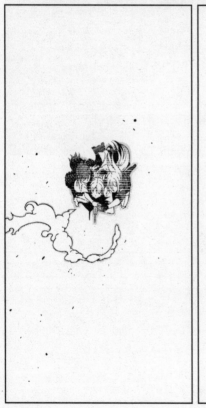

I THINK I MUTTERED SOMETHING SIMILAR THE LAST TIME I DIED...

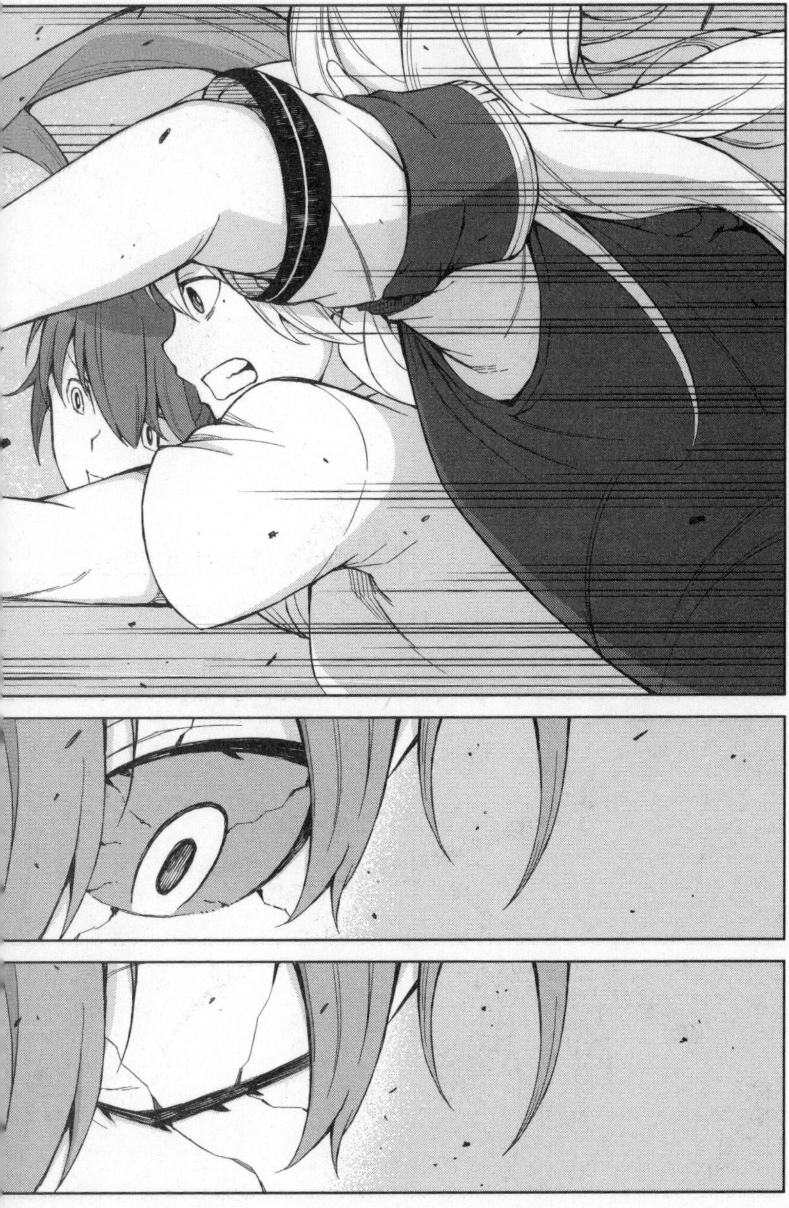

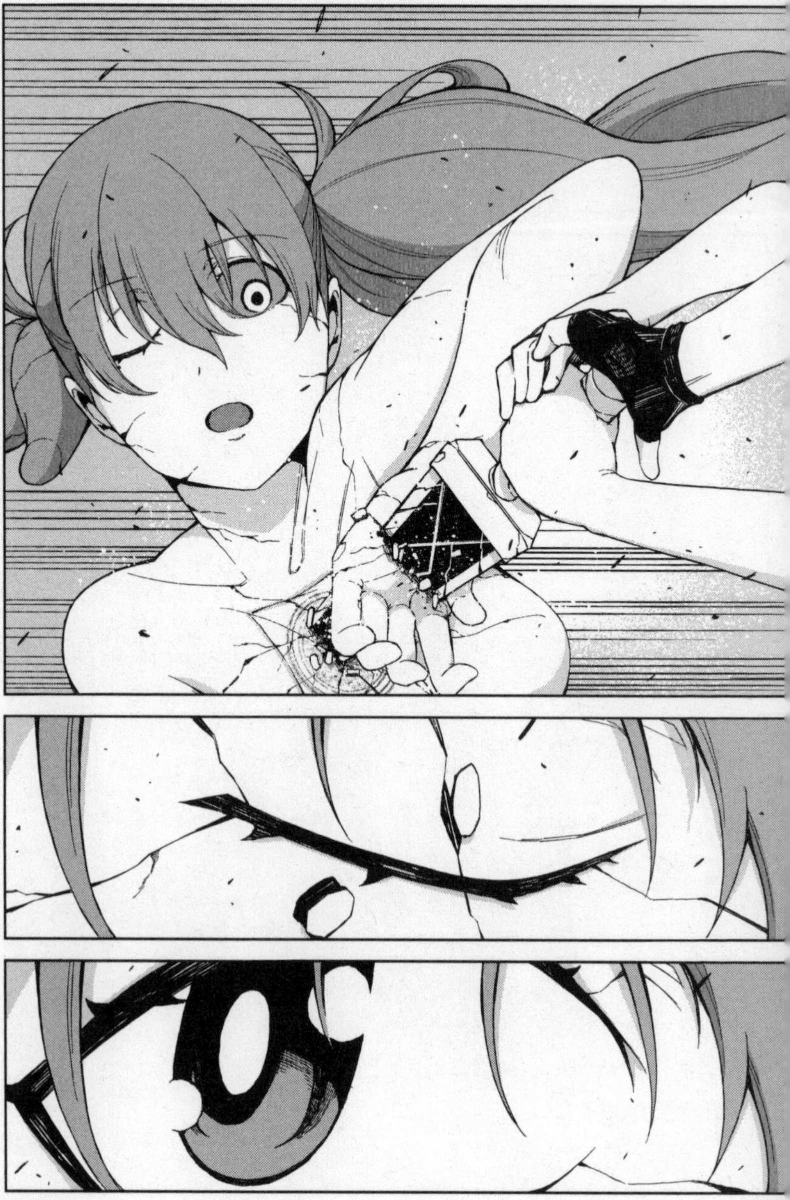

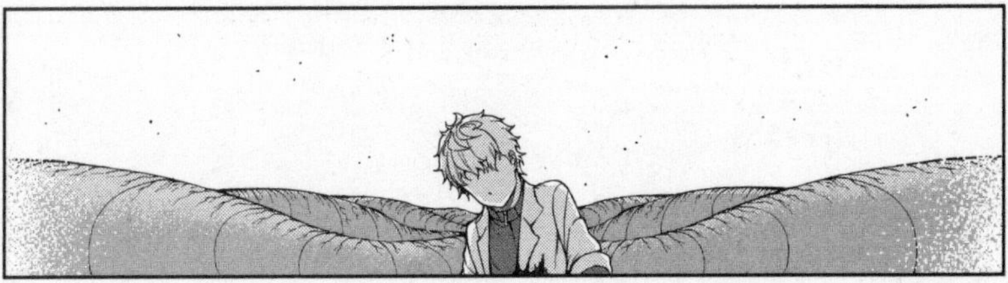
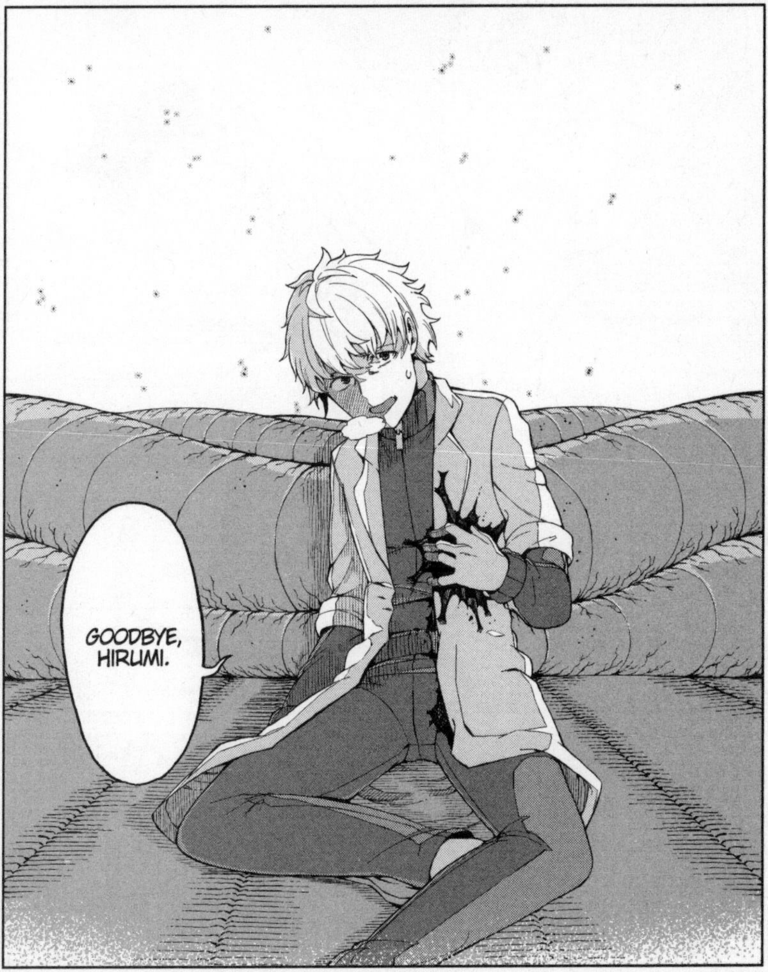
GOODBYE,
HIRUMI.

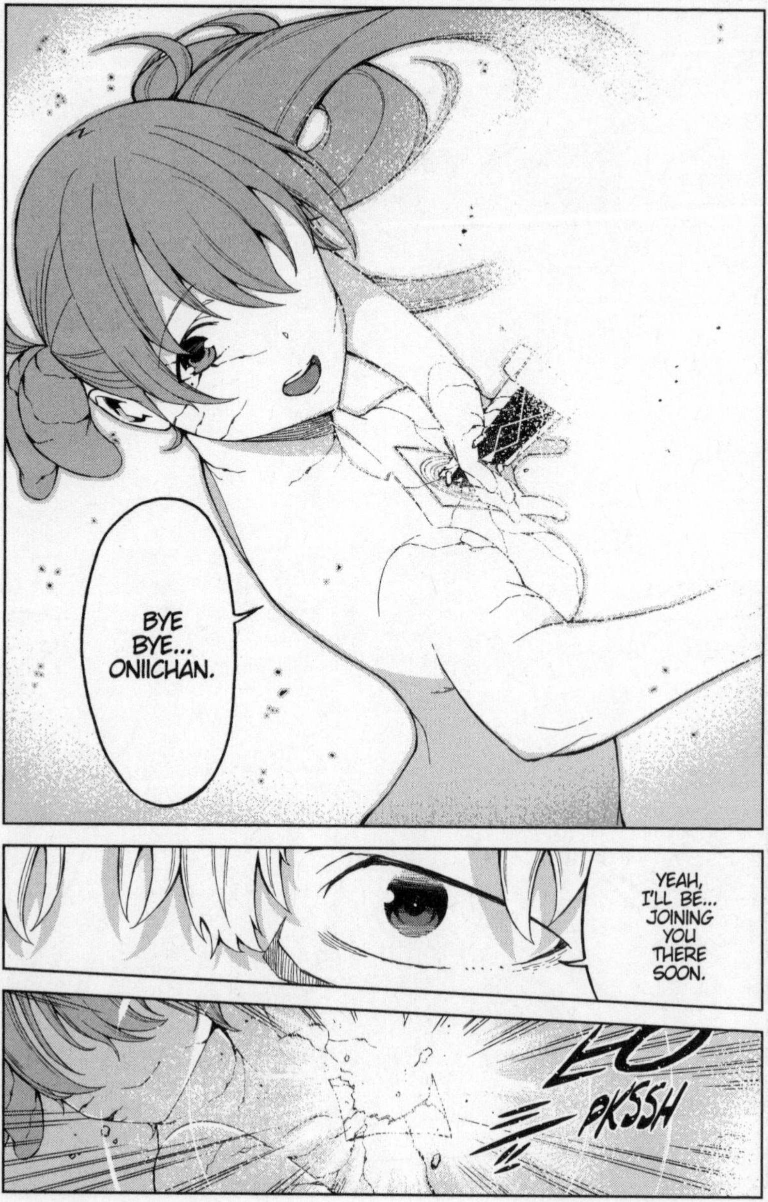
BYE BYE... ONIICHAN.
YEAH, I'LL BE... JOINING YOU THERE SOON.
...
PKSSH

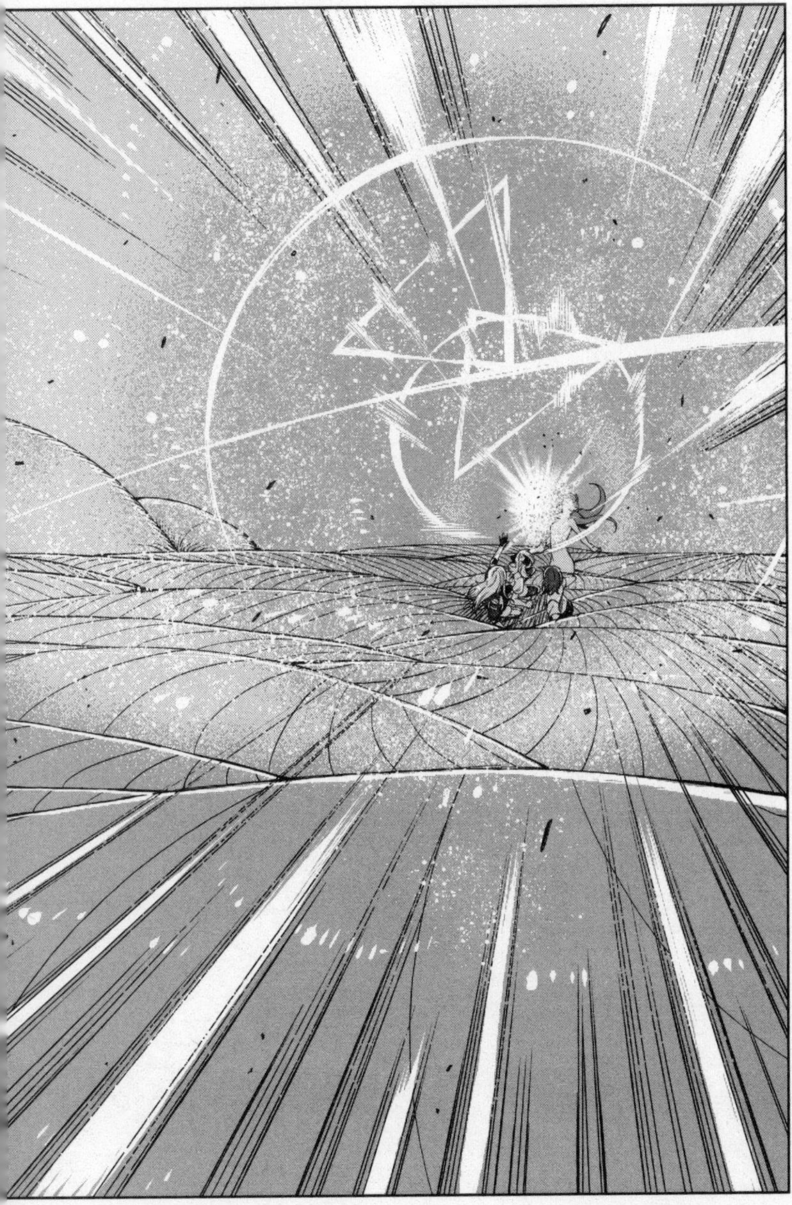

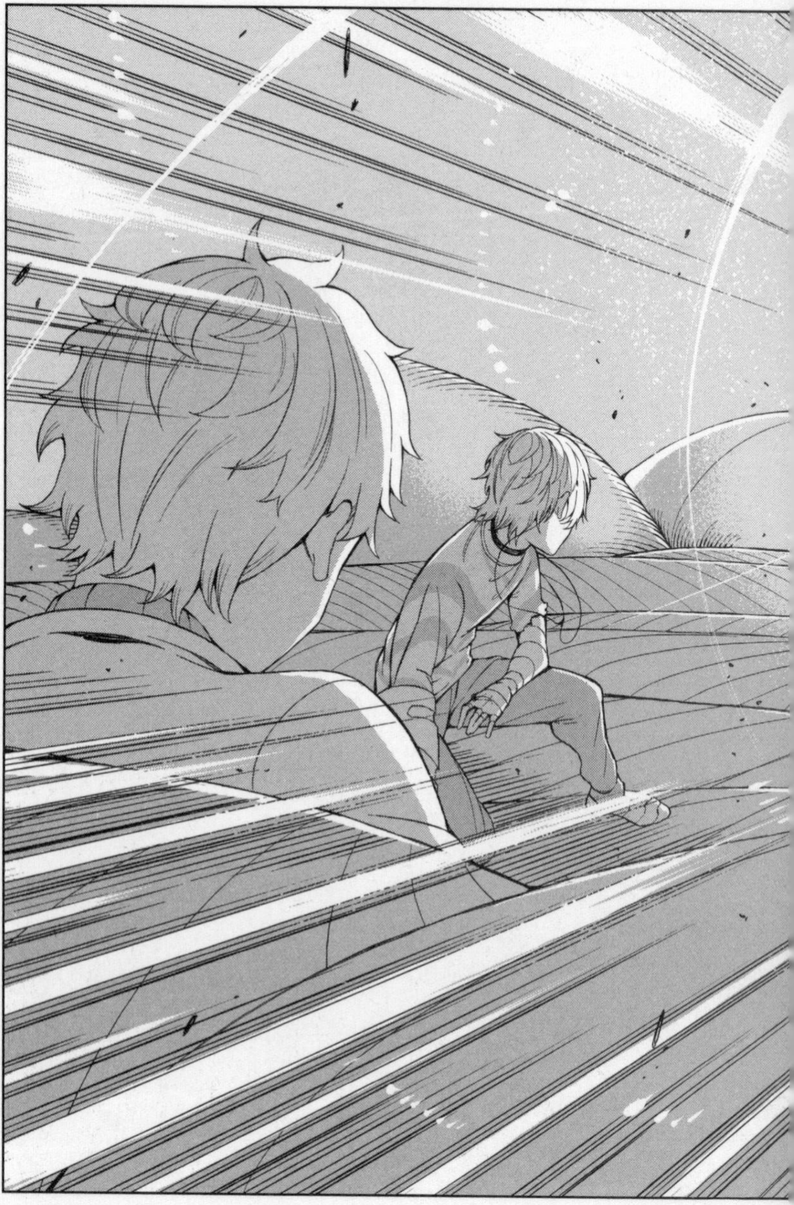

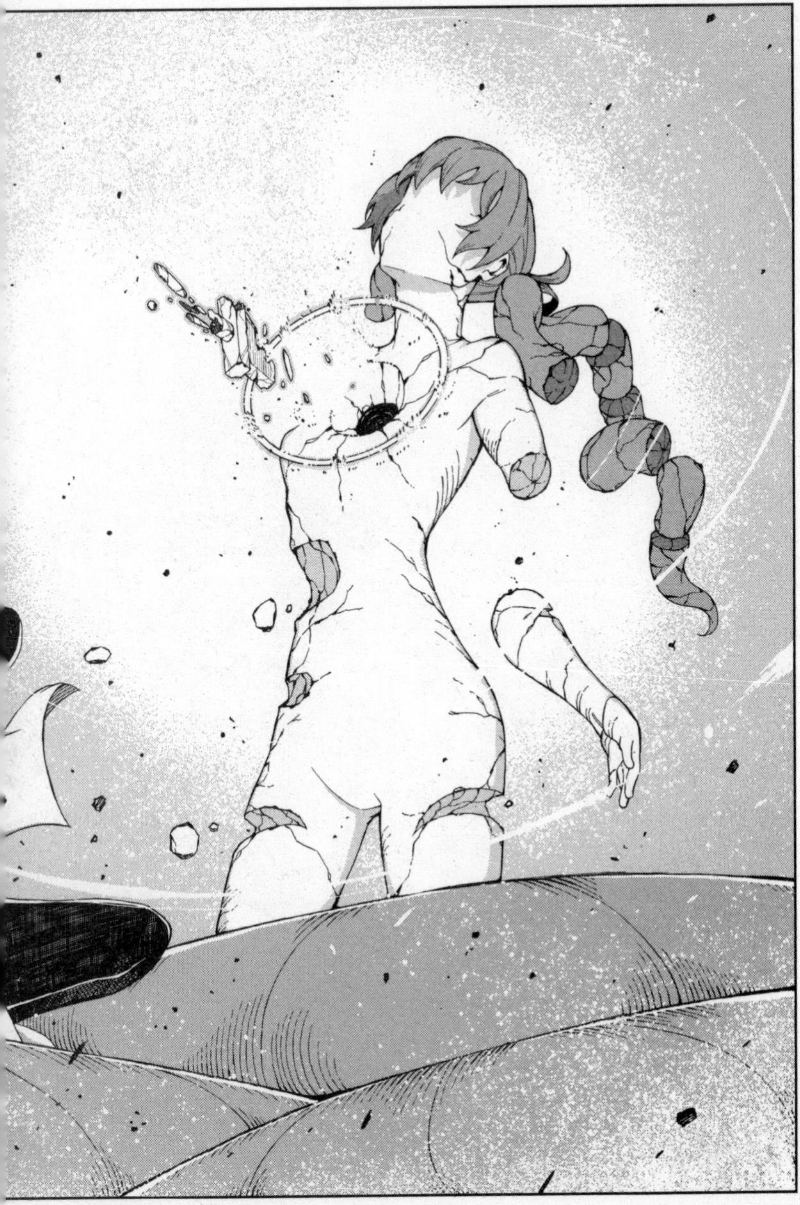

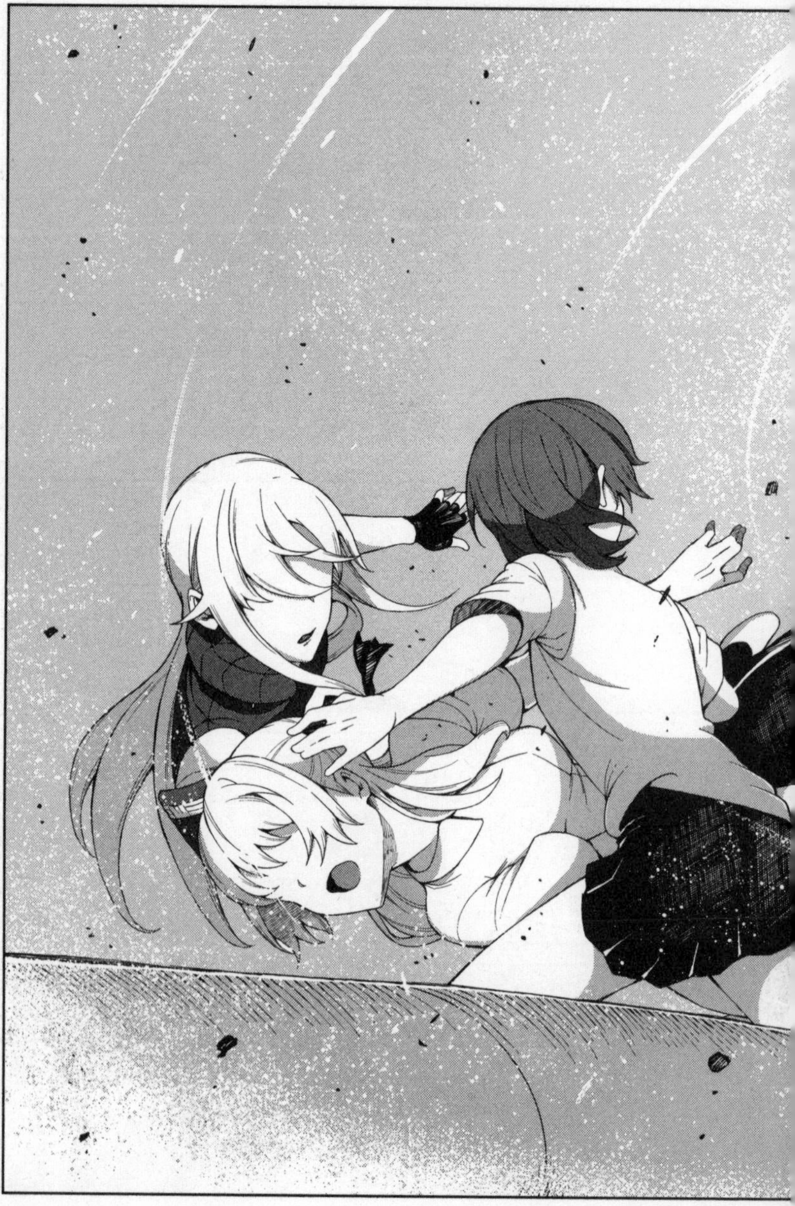

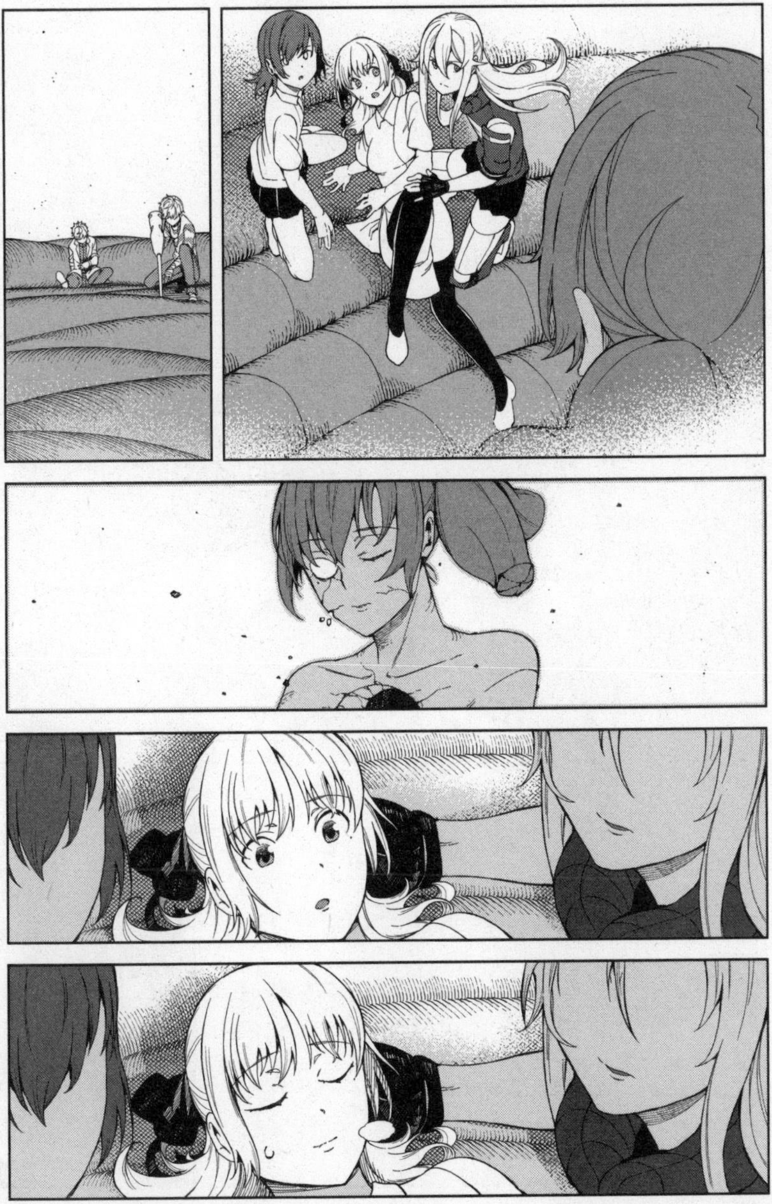

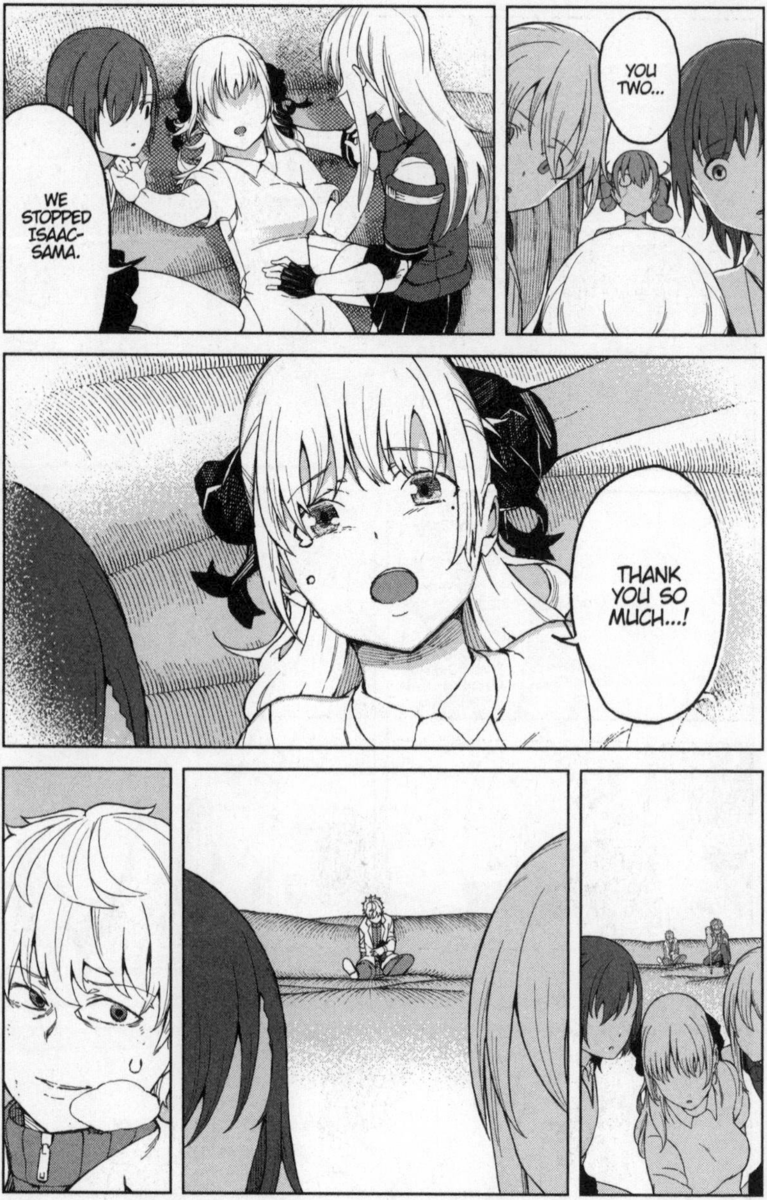
YOU TWO...
WE STOPPED ISAAC-SAMA.
THANK YOU SO MUCH...!

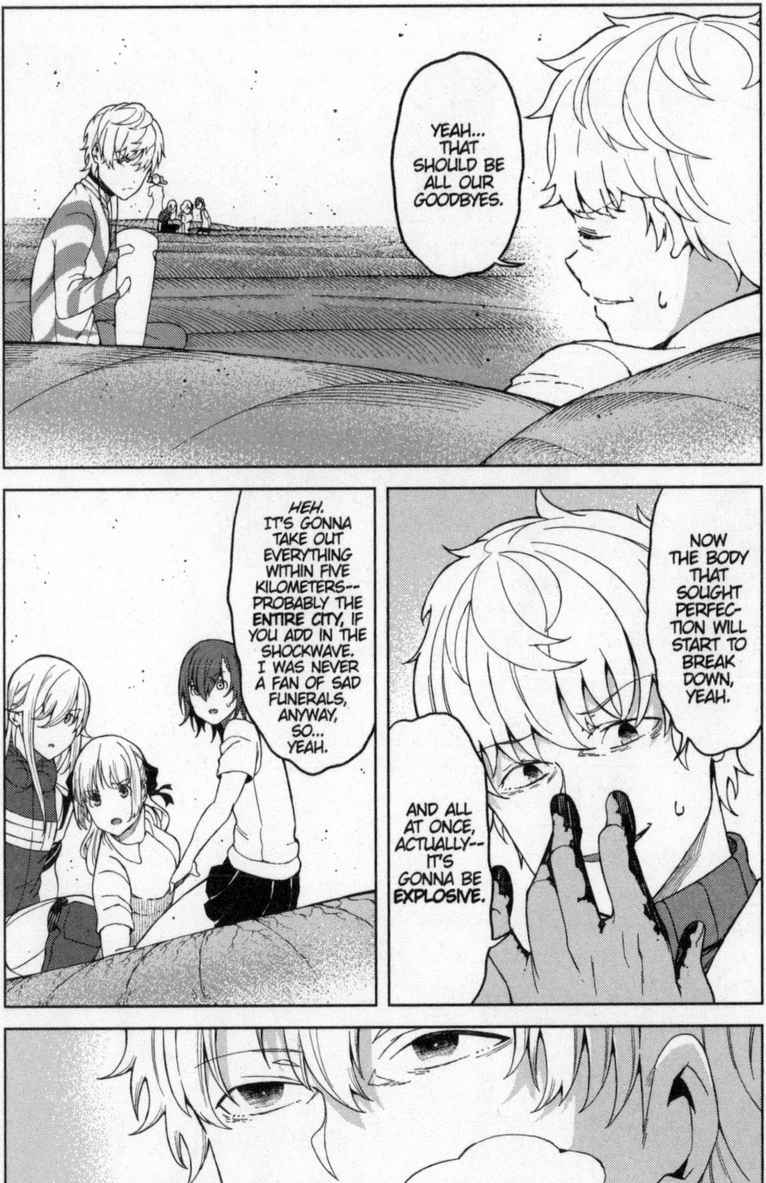
YEAH... THAT SHOULD BE ALL OUR GOODBYES.
NOW THE BODY THAT SOUGHT PERFECTION WILL START TO BREAK DOWN, YEAH.
AND ALL AT ONCE, ACTUALLY-- IT'S GONNA BE **EXPLOSIVE.**
HEH. IT'S GONNA TAKE OUT EVERYTHING WITHIN FIVE KILOMETERS-- PROBABLY THE **ENTIRE CITY,** IF YOU ADD IN THE SHOCKWAVE. I WAS NEVER A FAN OF SAD FUNERALS, ANYWAY, SO... YEAH.

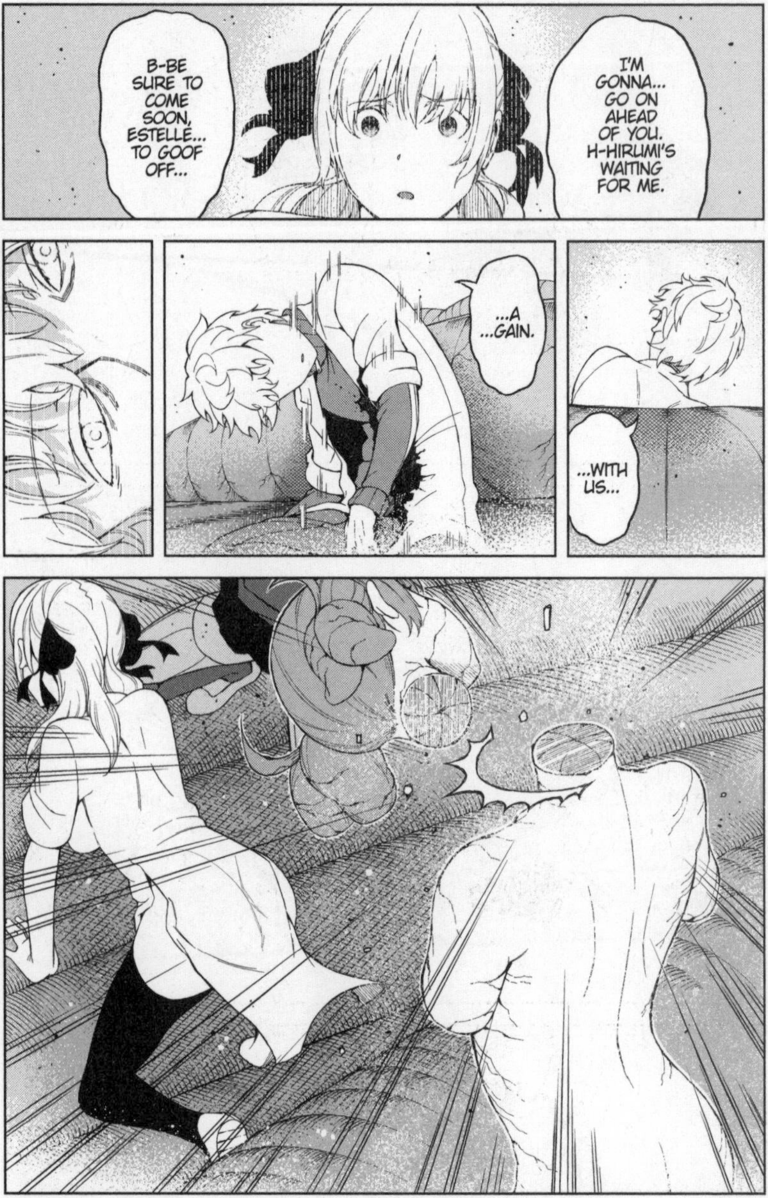
I'M GONNA... GO ON AHEAD OF YOU. H-HIRUMI'S WAITING FOR ME.
B-BE SURE TO COME SOON, ESTELLE... TO GOOF OFF...
...WITH US...
...A ...GAIN.

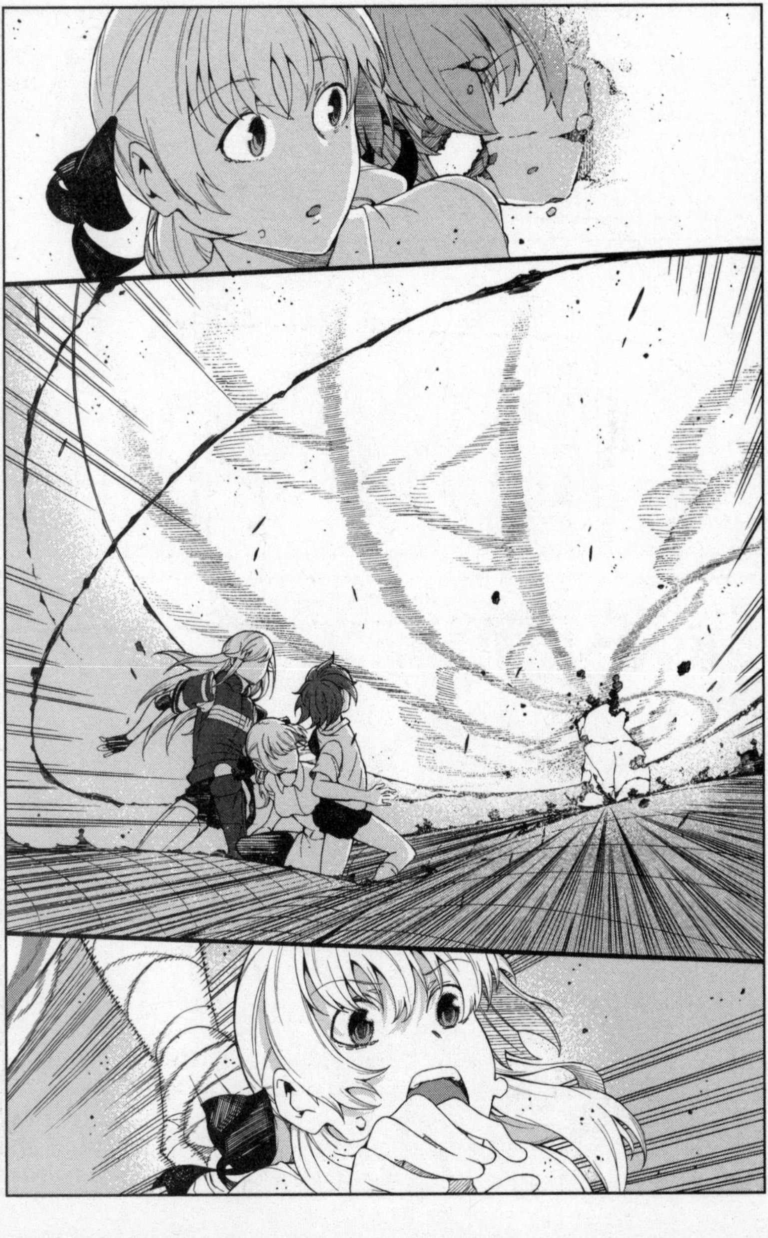

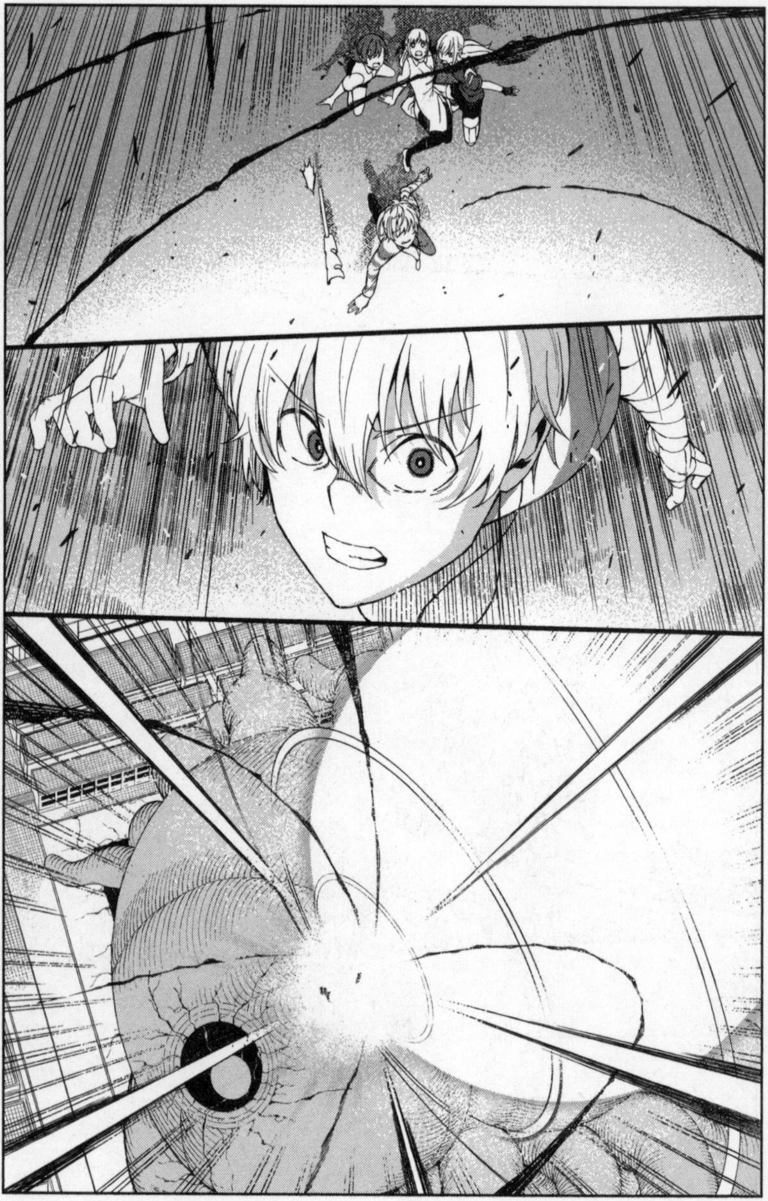

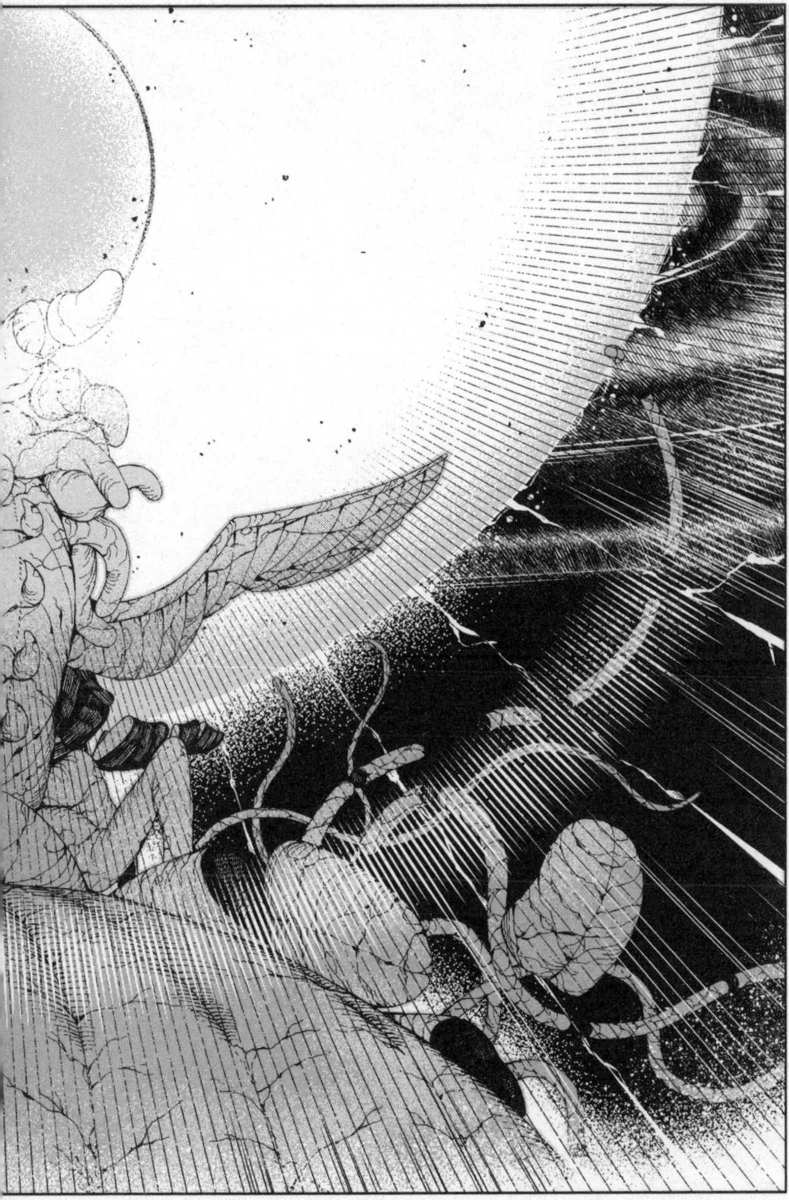

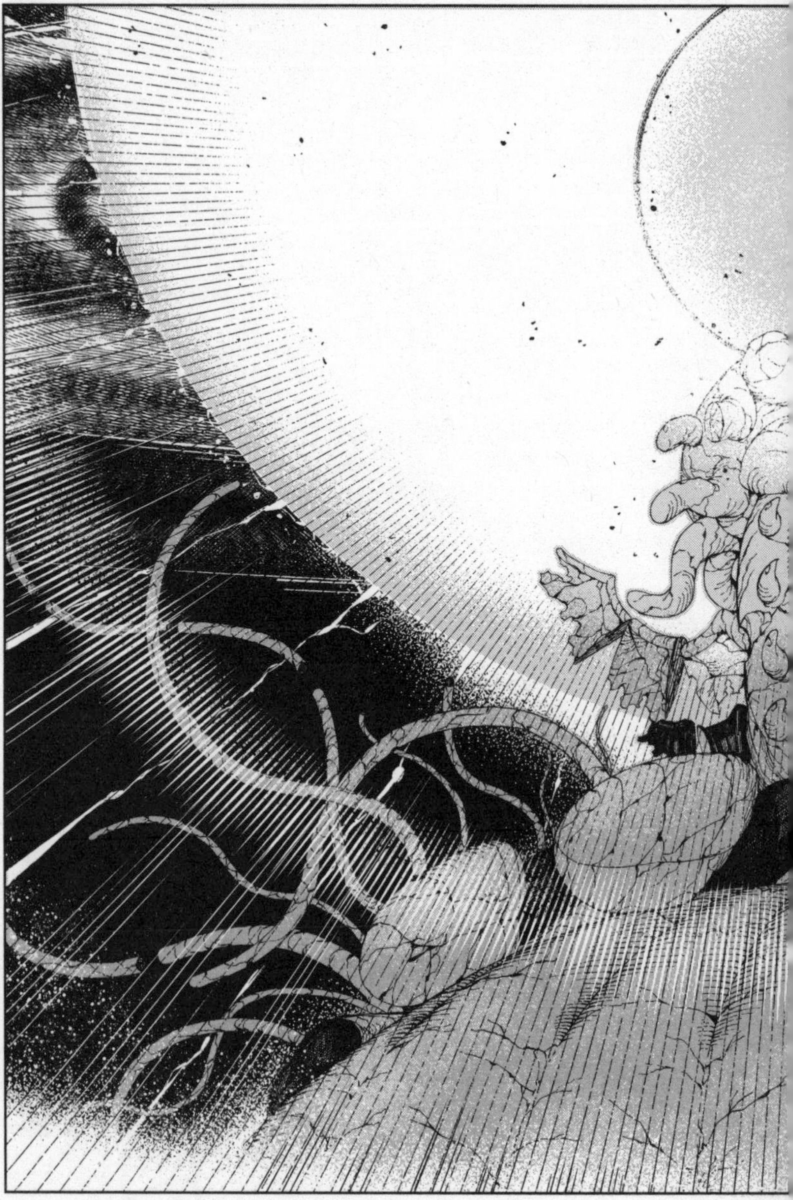

とある科学の一方通行

アクセラレータ

とある魔術の禁書目録外伝

CHAPTER 36

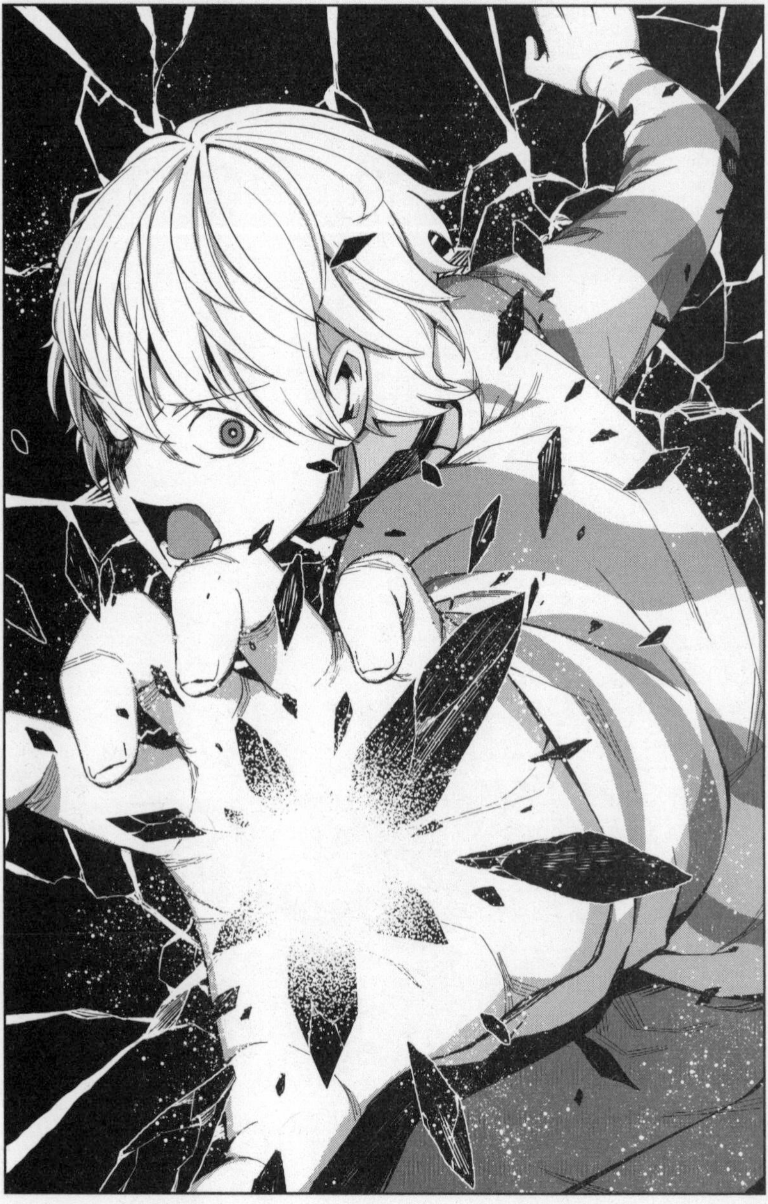

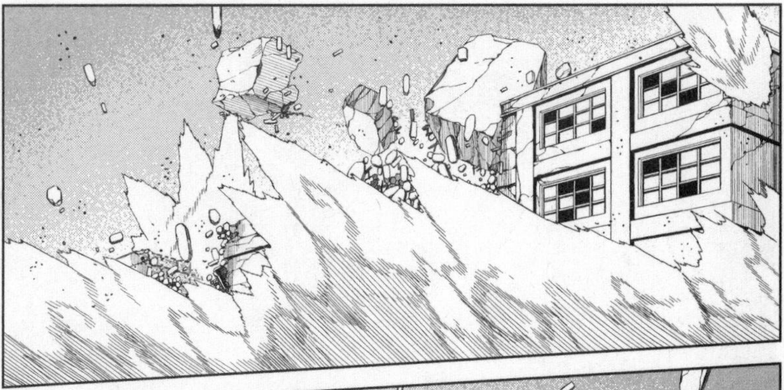
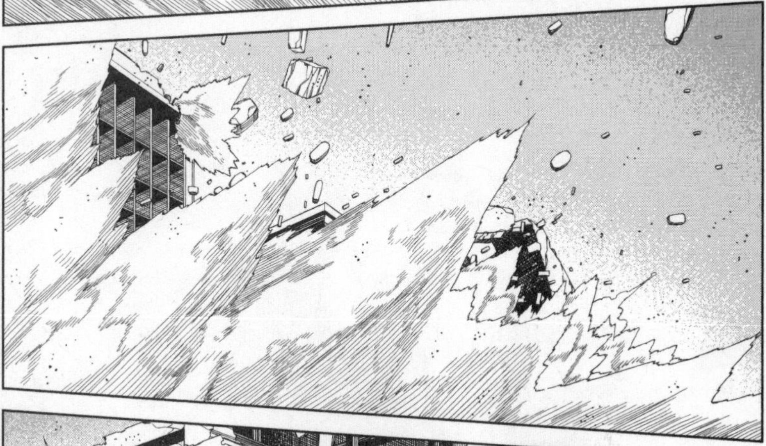
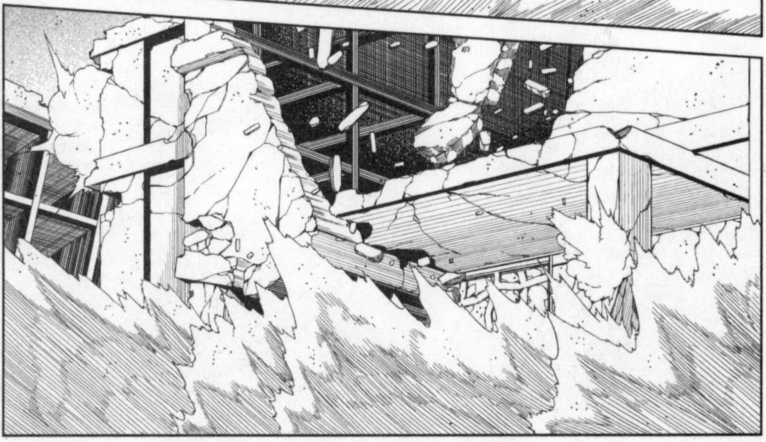

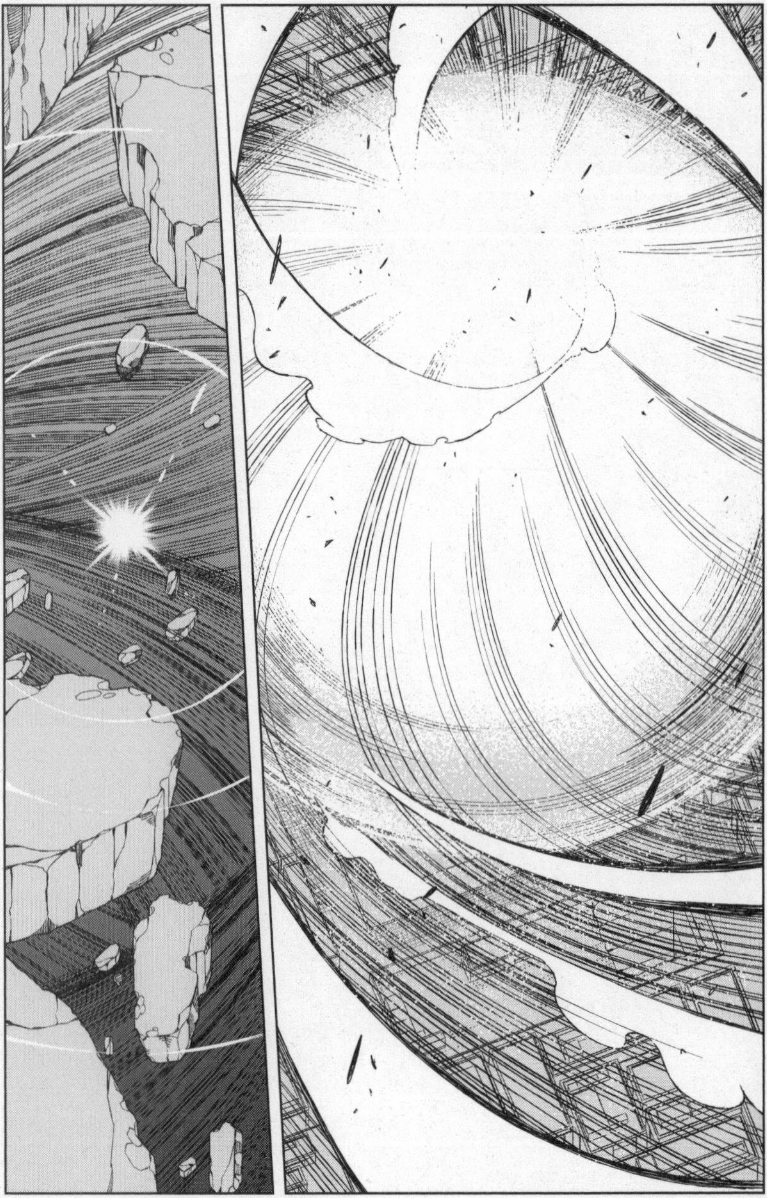

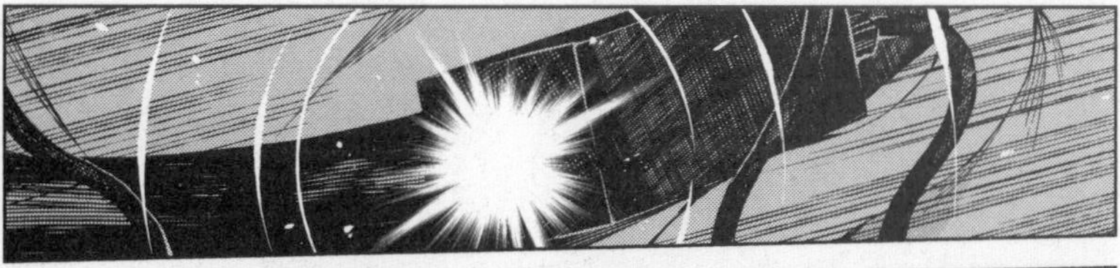
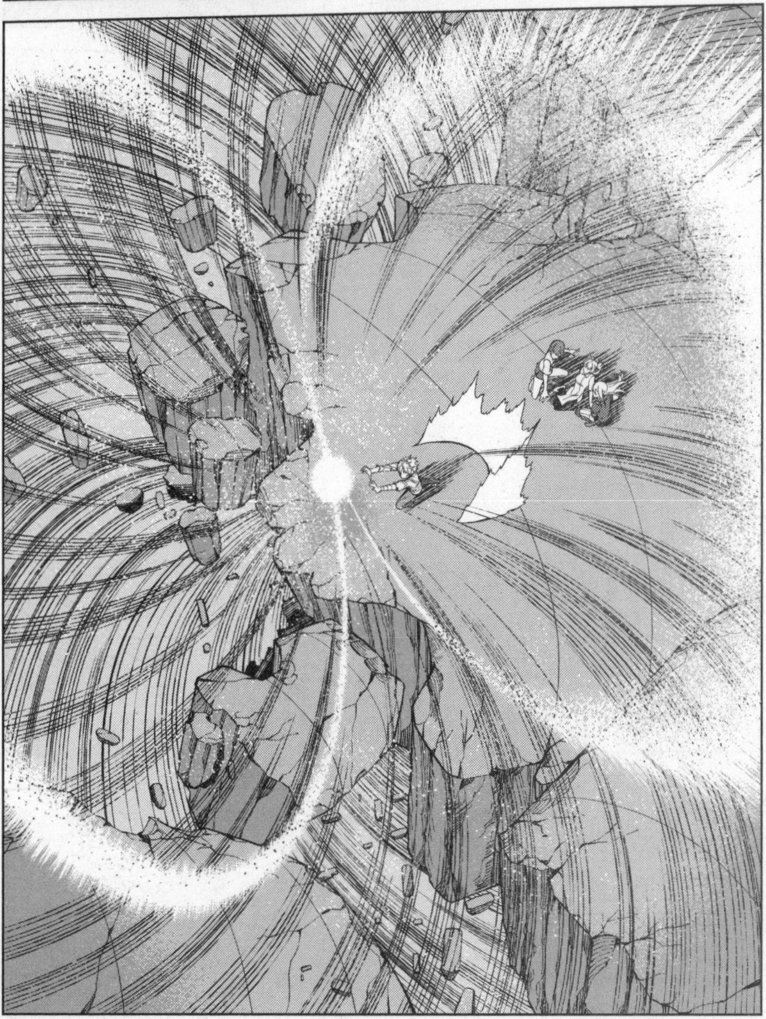

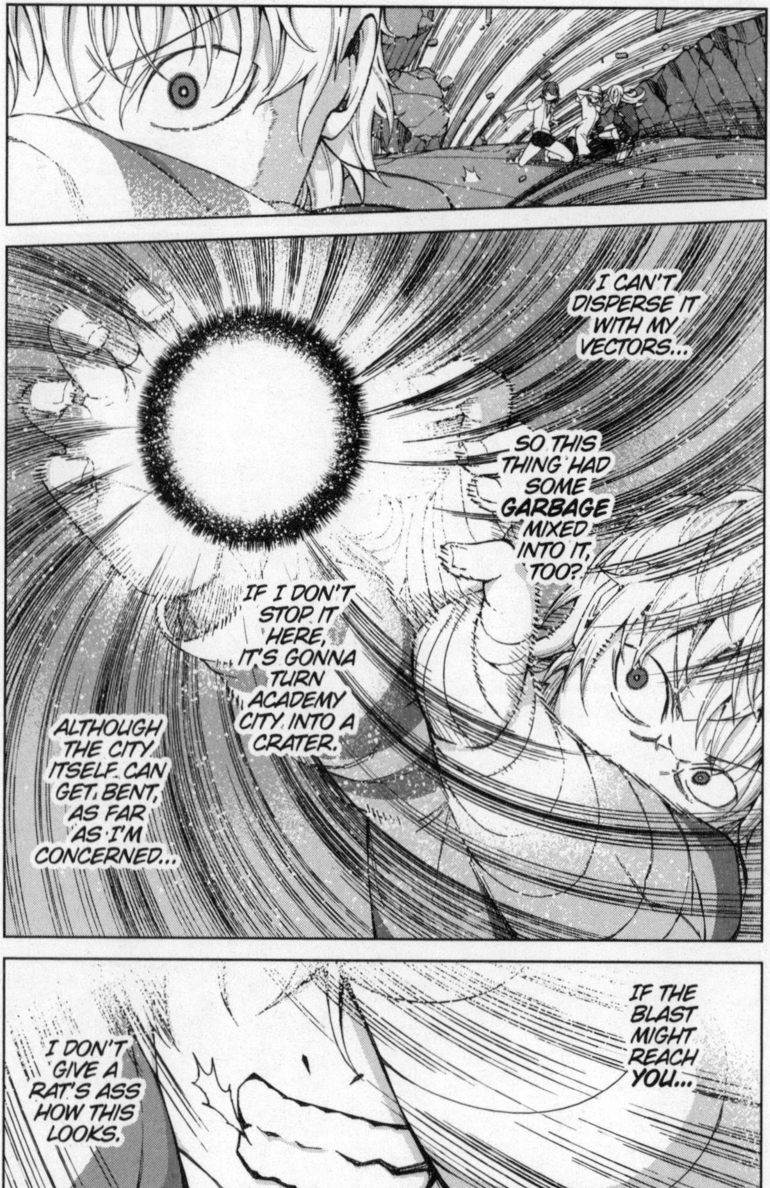

I CAN'T DISPERSE IT WITH MY VECTORS...
SO THIS THING HAD SOME GARBAGE MIXED INTO IT, TOO?
IF I DON'T STOP IT HERE, IT'S GONNA TURN ACADEMY CITY INTO A CRATER.
ALTHOUGH THE CITY ITSELF CAN GET BENT, AS FAR AS I'M CONCERNED...
IF THE BLAST MIGHT REACH YOU...
I DON'T GIVE A RAT'S ASS HOW THIS LOOKS.

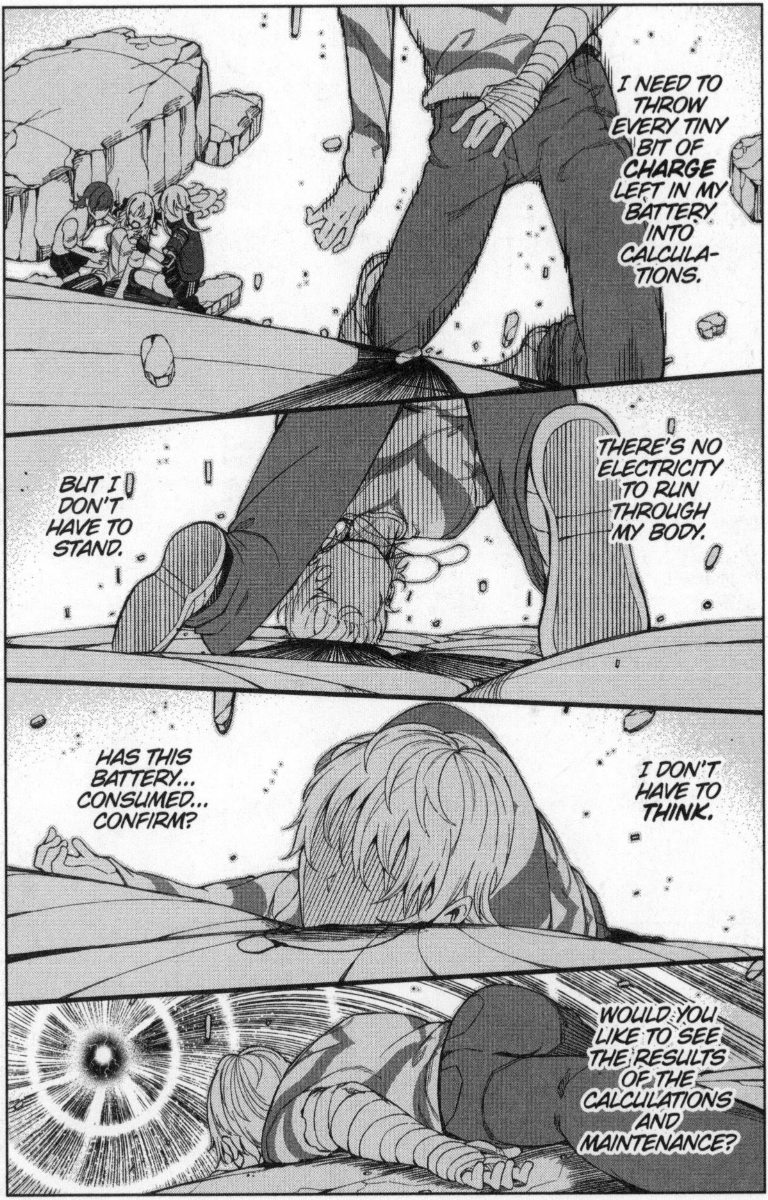
I NEED TO THROW EVERY TINY BIT OF CHARGE LEFT IN MY BATTERY INTO CALCULATIONS.
THERE'S NO ELECTRICITY TO RUN THROUGH MY BODY.
BUT I DON'T HAVE TO STAND.
I DON'T HAVE TO THINK.
HAS THIS BATTERY... CONSUMED... CONFIRM?
WOULD YOU LIKE TO SEE THE RESULTS OF THE CALCULATIONS AND MAINTENANCE?

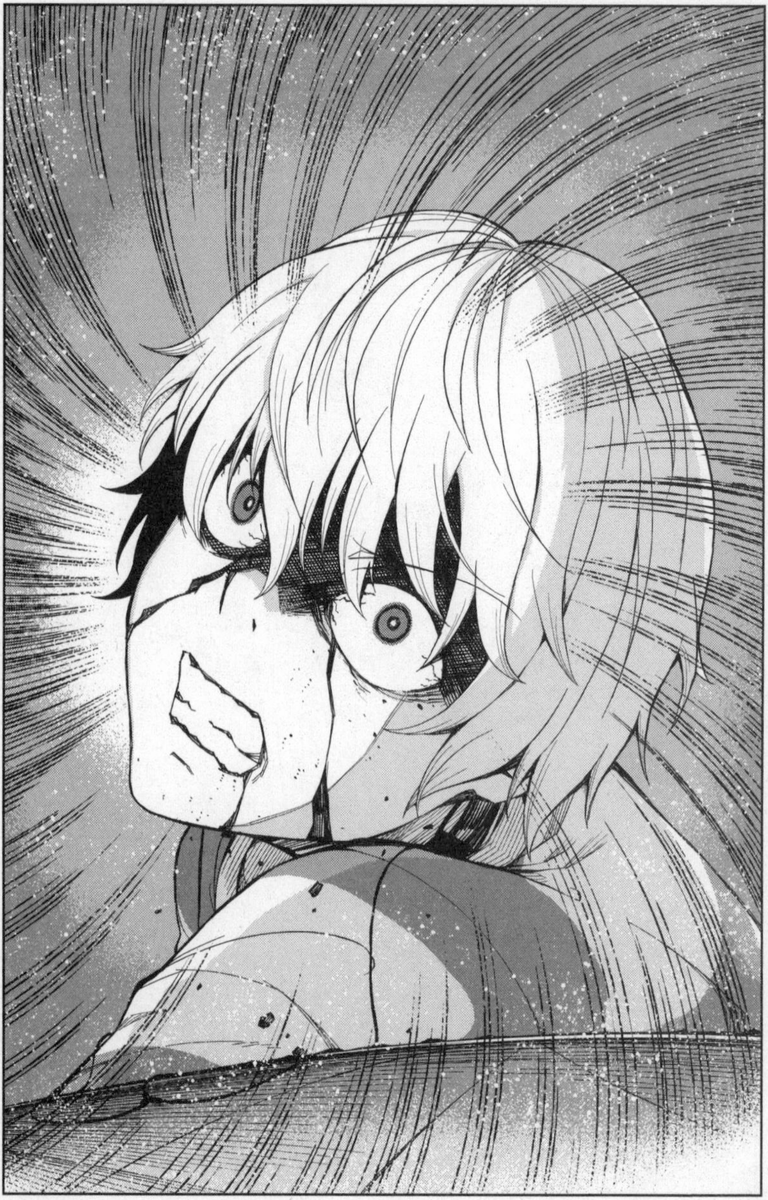

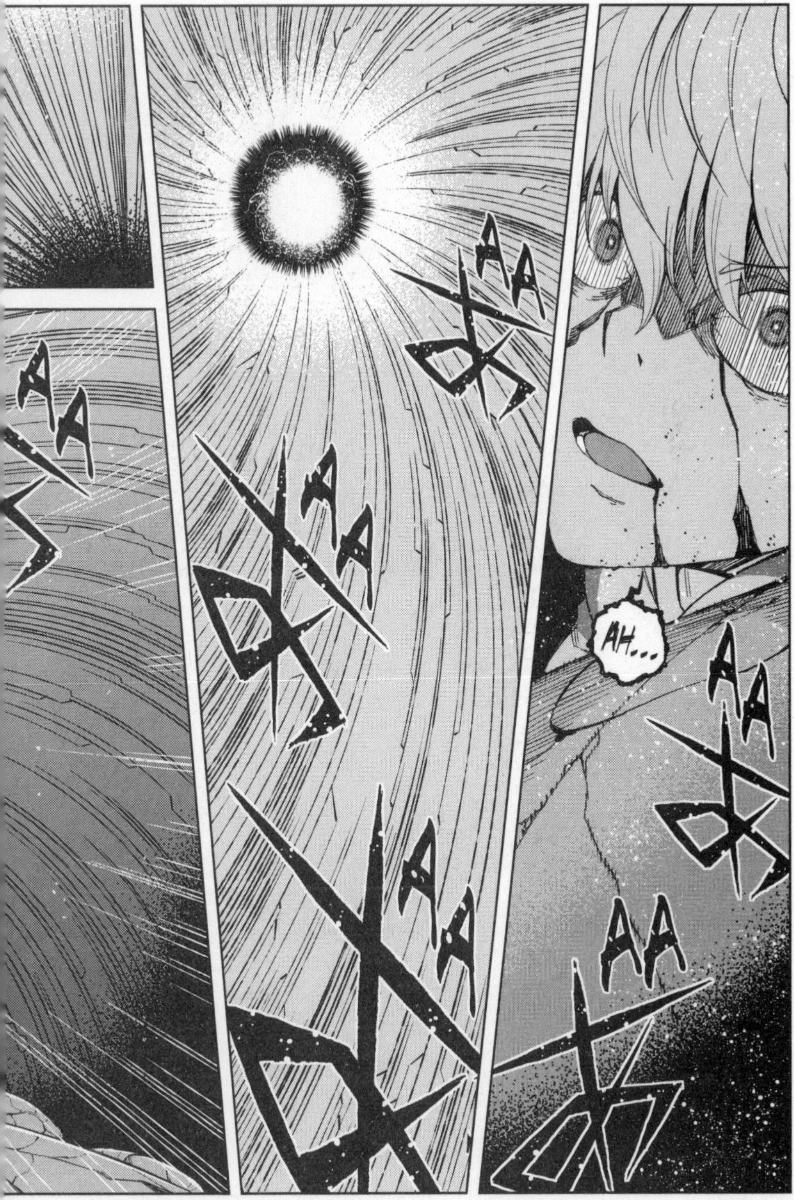

AH...
AA
AA
AA
AA
AA
AA

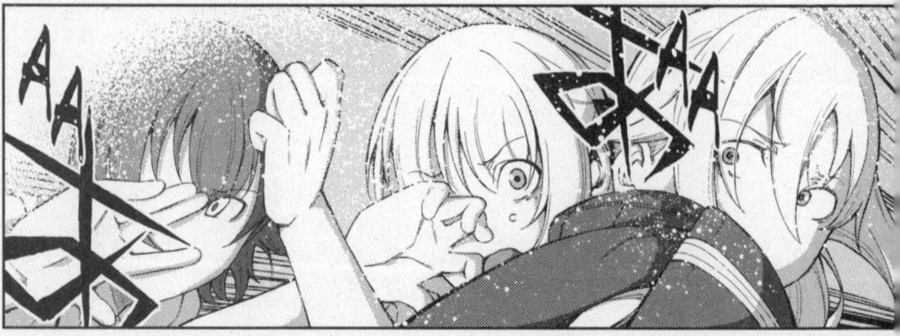
AAA
AA
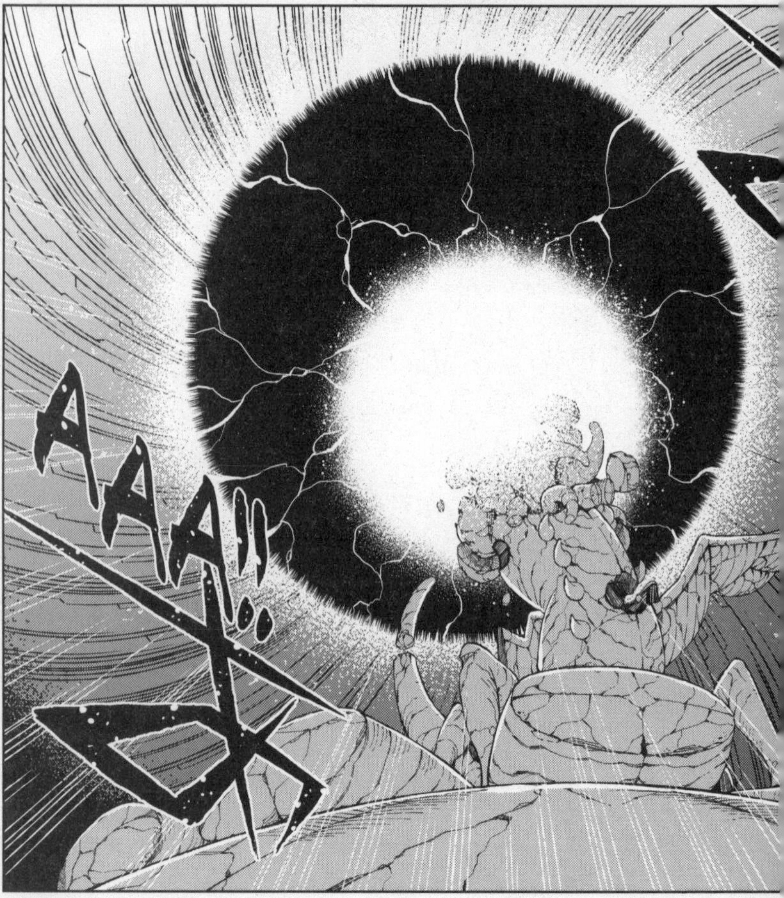
AAA!!

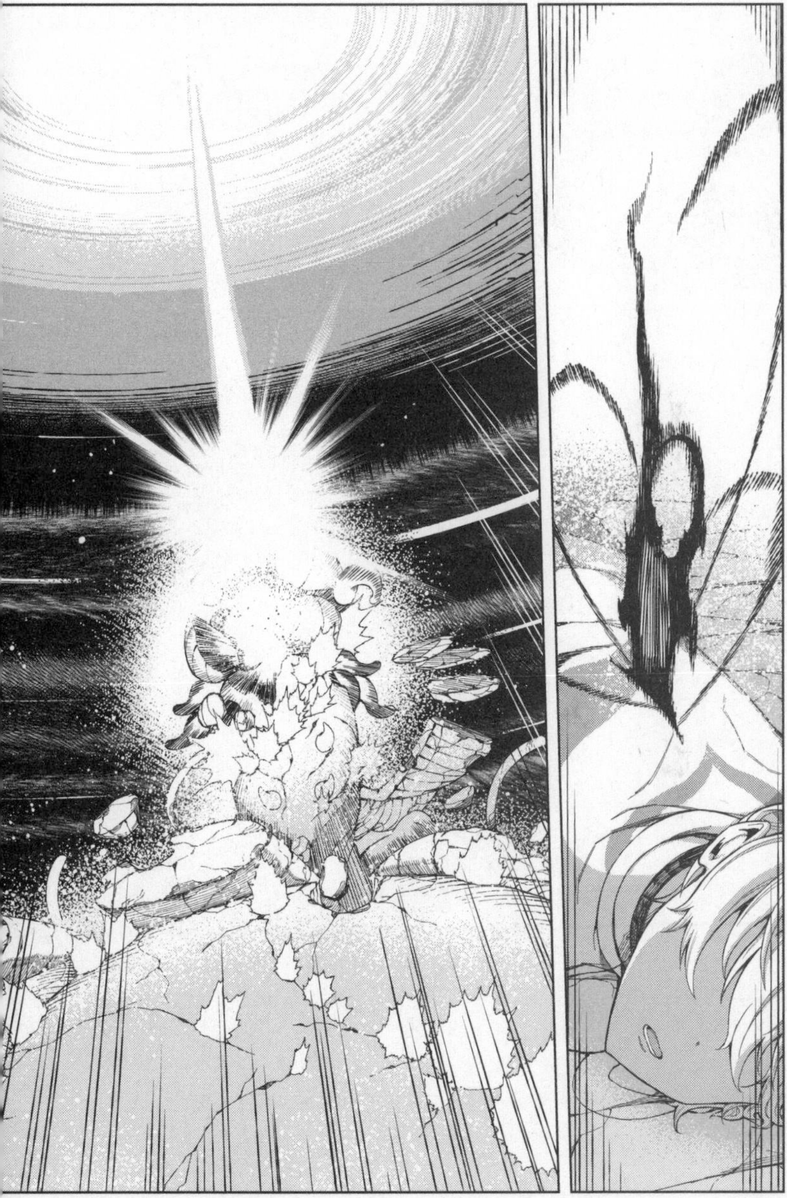

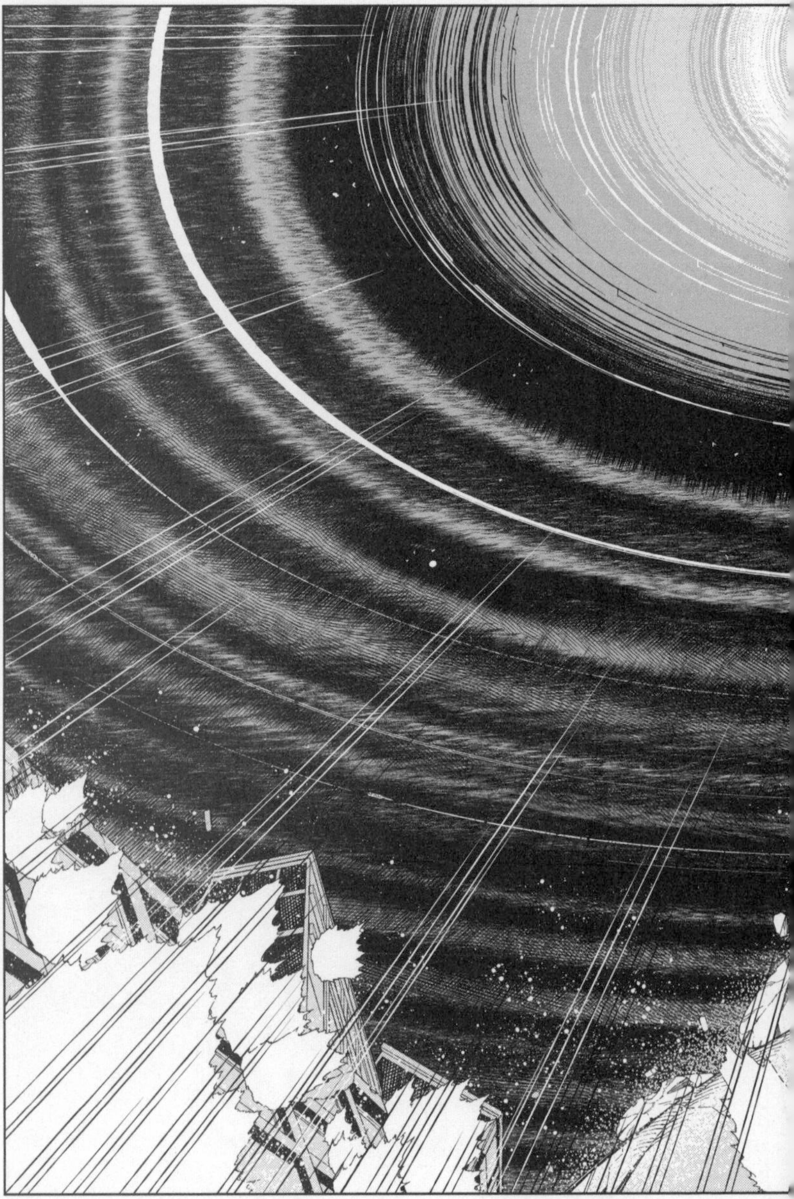

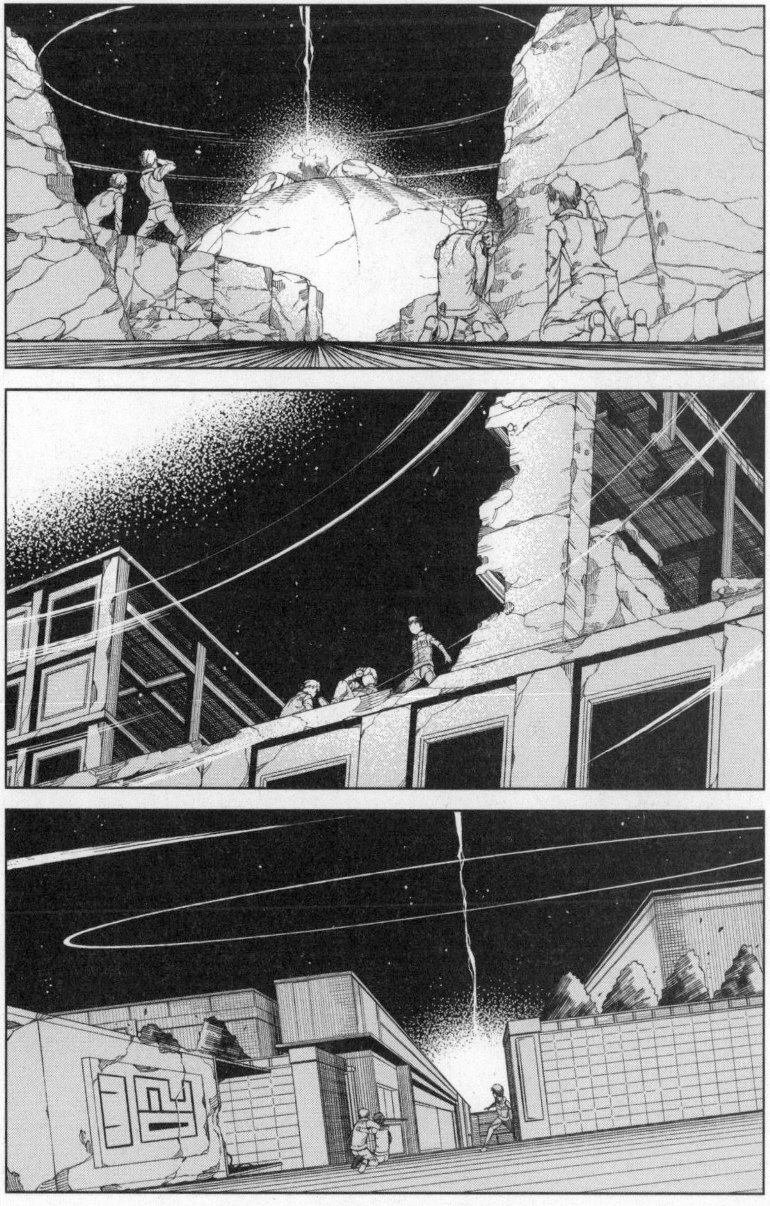

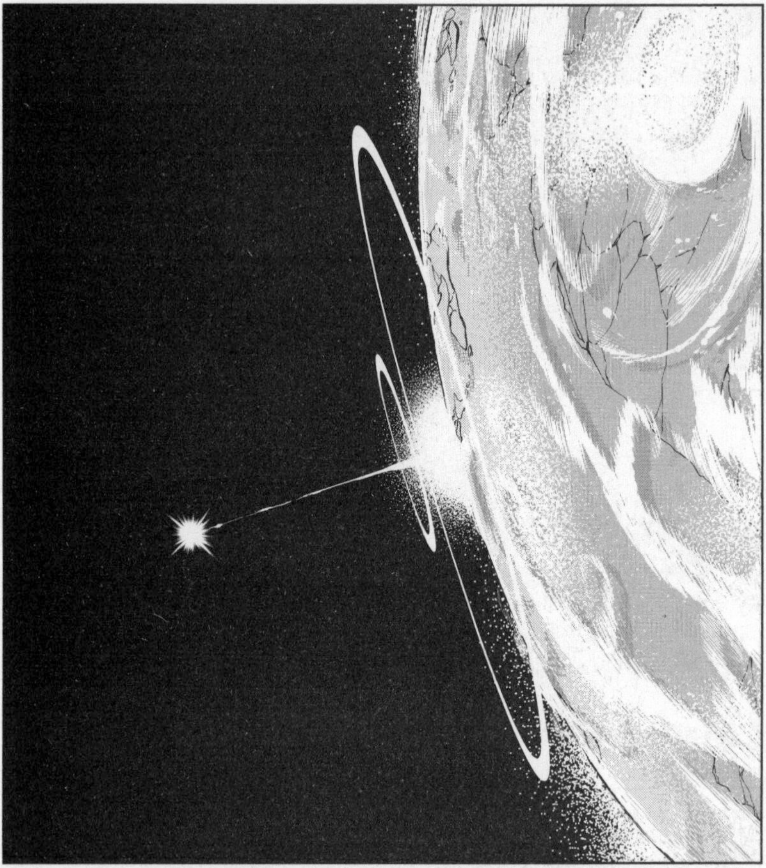
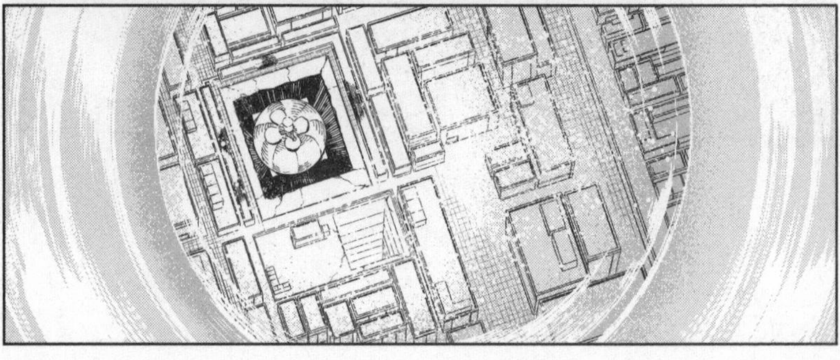

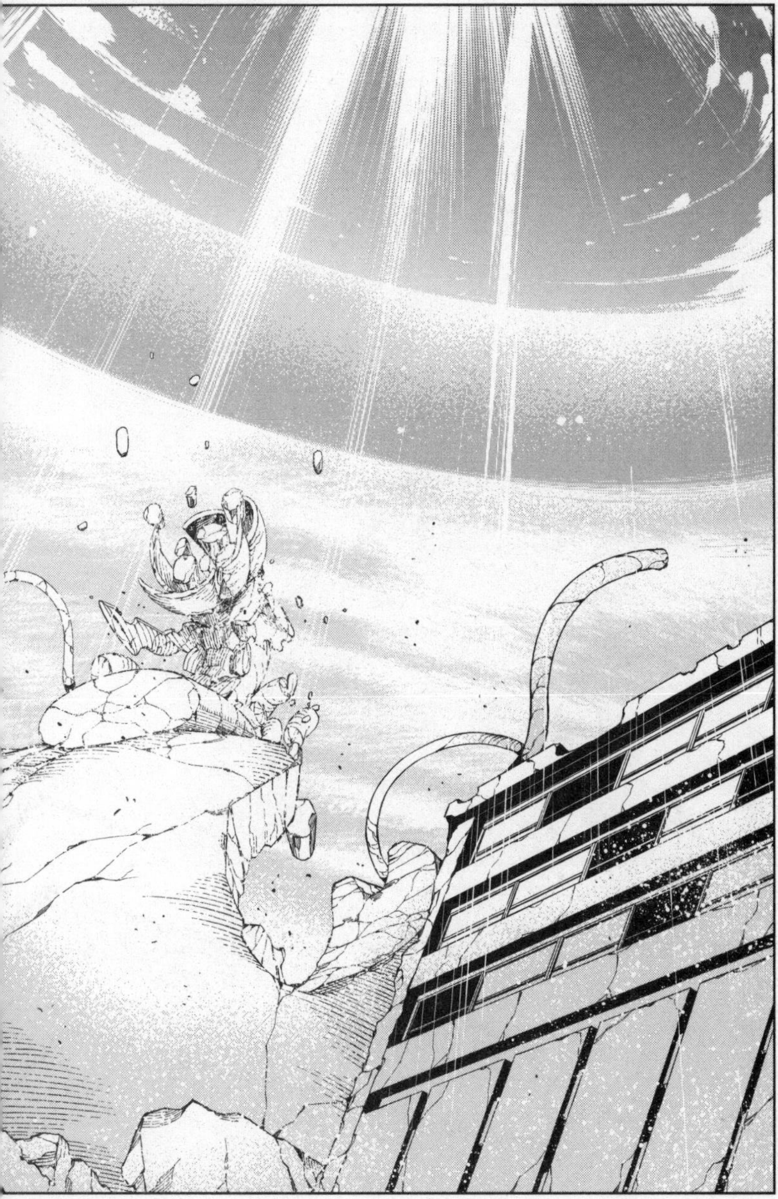

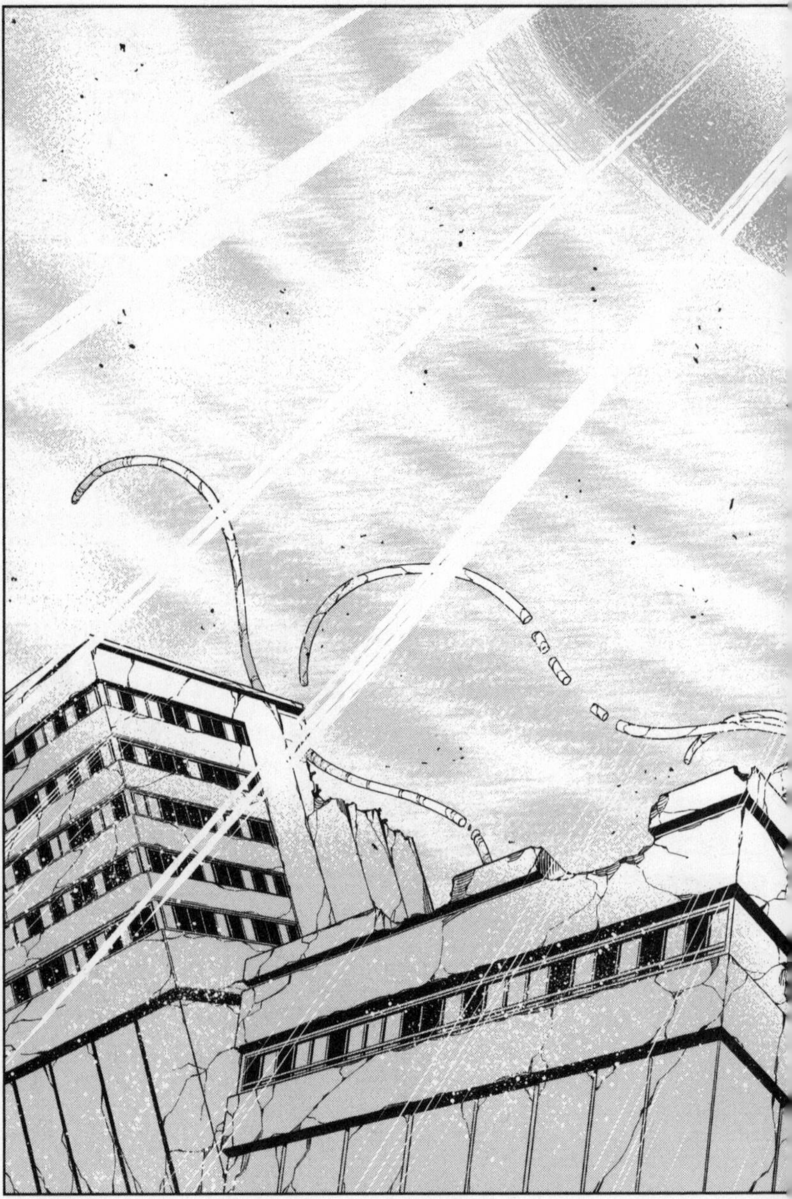

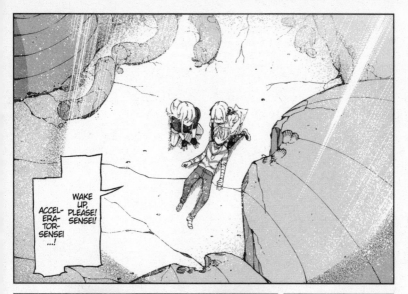

WAKE UP, PLEASE! SENSEI!

ACCEL-ERA-TOR-SENSEI! ...

PLEASE, I'M BEGGING YOU! OPEN YOUR EYES!

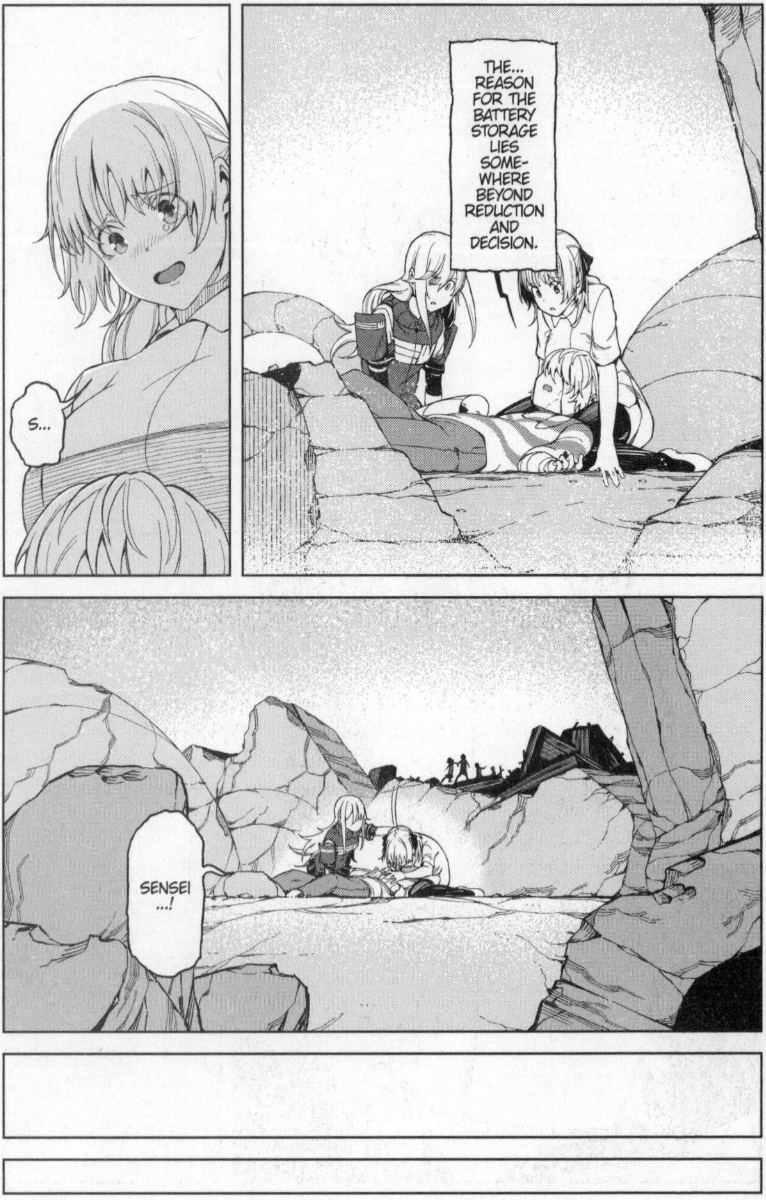
THE... REASON FOR THE BATTERY STORAGE LIES SOME-WHERE BEYOND REDUCTION AND DECISION.
S...
SENSEI ...!

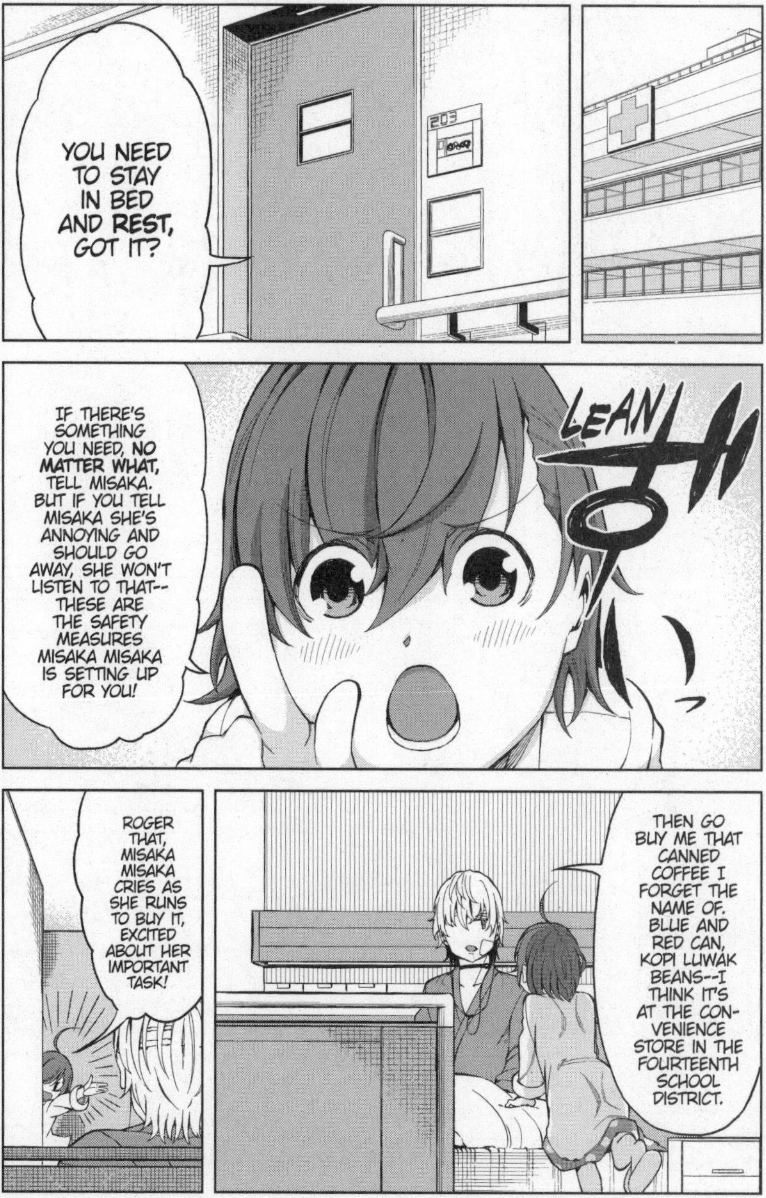
YOU NEED TO STAY IN BED AND REST, GOT IT?
LEAN
IF THERE'S SOMETHING YOU NEED, NO MATTER WHAT, TELL MISAKA. BUT IF YOU TELL MISAKA SHE'S ANNOYING AND SHOULD GO AWAY, SHE WON'T LISTEN TO THAT-- THESE ARE THE SAFETY MEASURES MISAKA MISAKA IS SETTING UP FOR YOU!
THEN GO BUY ME THAT CANNED COFFEE I FORGET THE NAME OF. BLUE AND RED CAN, KOPI LUWAK BEANS--I THINK IT'S AT THE CON-VENIENCE STORE IN THE FOURTEENTH SCHOOL DISTRICT.
ROGER THAT, MISAKA MISAKA CRIES AS SHE RUNS TO BUY IT, EXCITED ABOUT HER IMPORTANT TASK!

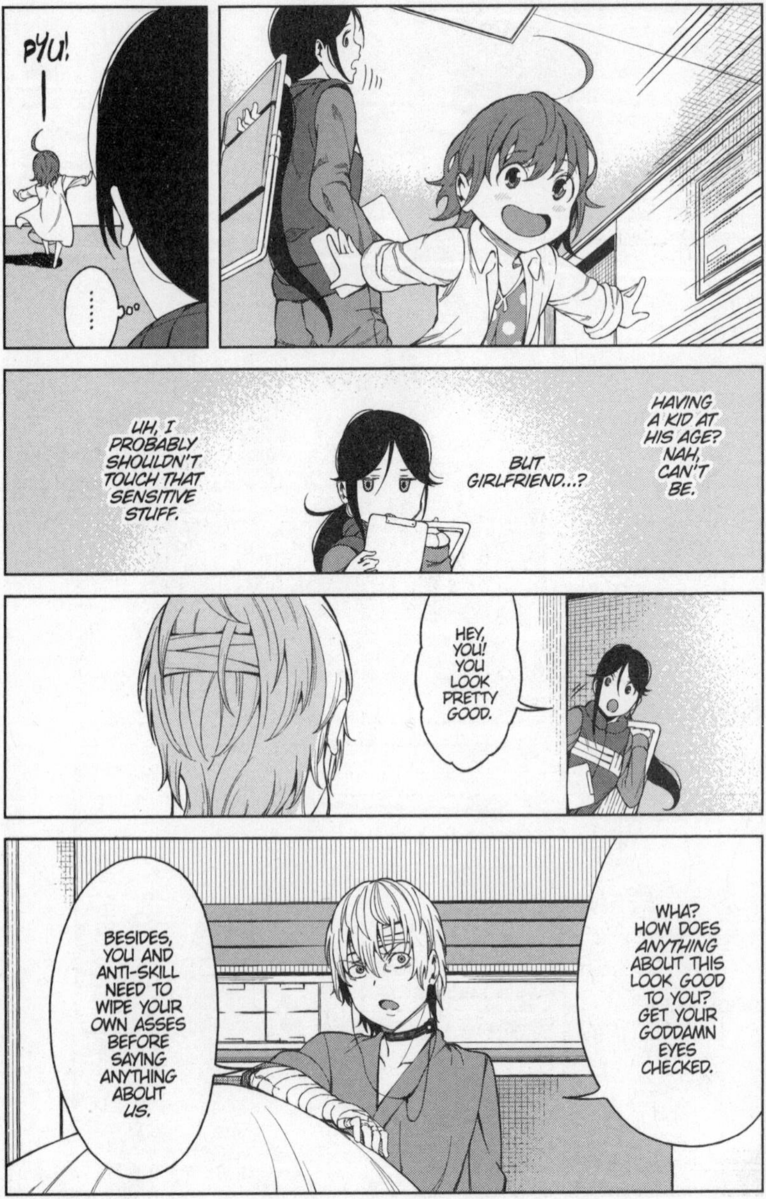
PYU!
!
......
HAVING A KID AT HIS AGE? NAH, CAN'T BE.
BUT GIRLFRIEND...?
UH, I PROBABLY SHOULDN'T TOUCH THAT SENSITIVE STUFF.
HEY, YOU! YOU LOOK PRETTY GOOD.
WHA? HOW DOES ANYTHING ABOUT THIS LOOK GOOD TO YOU? GET YOUR GODDAMN EYES CHECKED.
BESIDES, YOU AND ANTI-SKILL NEED TO WIPE YOUR OWN ASSES BEFORE SAYING ANYTHING ABOUT US.

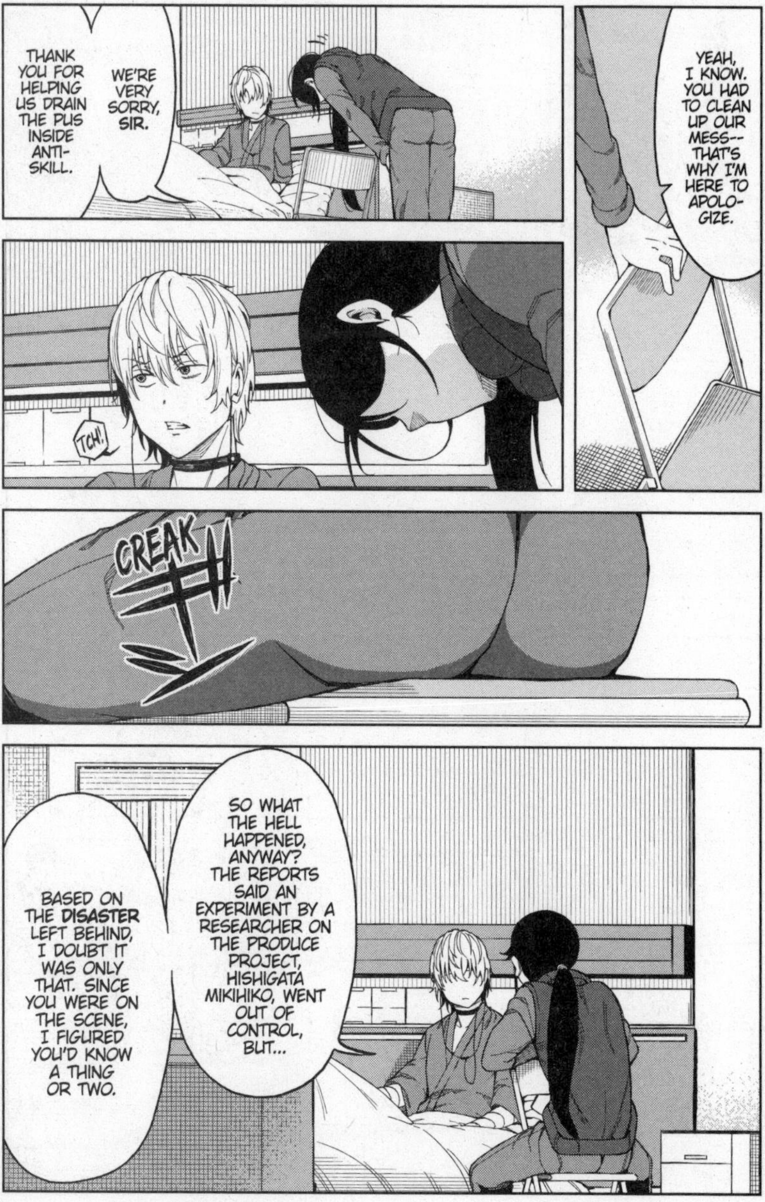
WE'RE VERY SORRY, SIR.
THANK YOU FOR HELPING US DRAIN THE PUS INSIDE ANTI-SKILL.
YEAH, I KNOW. YOU HAD TO CLEAN UP OUR MESS--THAT'S WHY I'M HERE TO APOLOGIZE.
TCH!
CREAK
SO WHAT THE HELL HAPPENED, ANYWAY? THE REPORTS SAID AN EXPERIMENT BY A RESEARCHER ON THE PRODUCE PROJECT, HISHIGATA MIKIHIKO, WENT OUT OF CONTROL, BUT...
BASED ON THE DISASTER LEFT BEHIND, I DOUBT IT WAS ONLY THAT. SINCE YOU WERE ON THE SCENE, I FIGURED YOU'D KNOW A THING OR TWO.

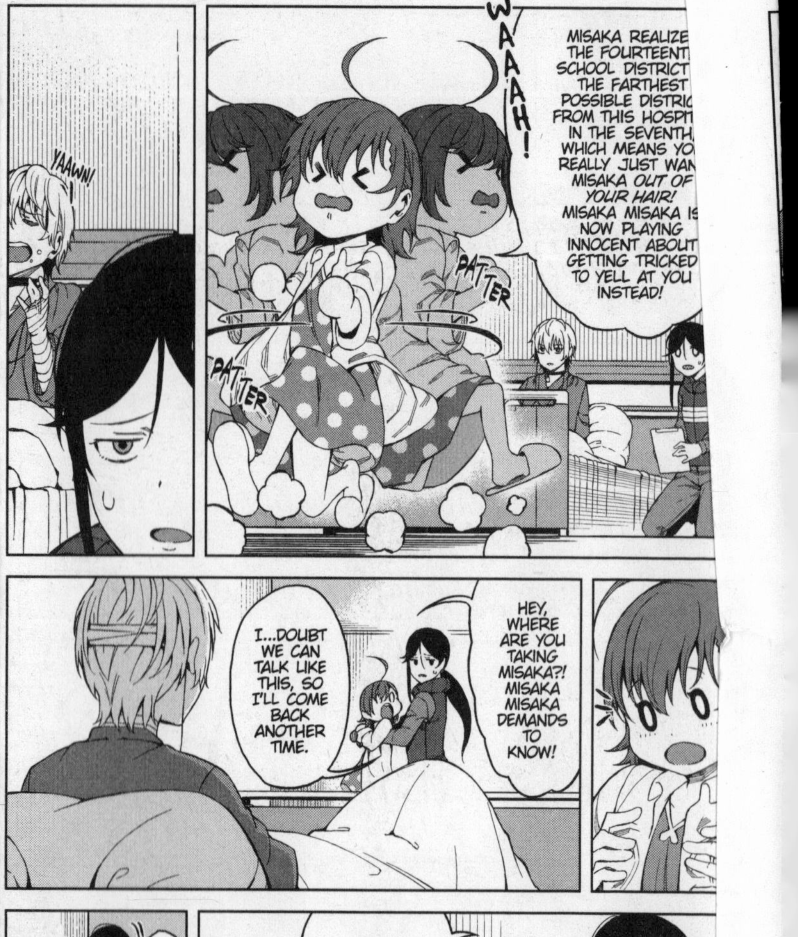
WAAAAH!
MISAKA REALIZE THE FOURTEENT SCHOOL DISTRICT THE FARTHEST POSSIBLE DISTRIC FROM THIS HOSPIT IN THE SEVENTH, WHICH MEANS YO REALLY JUST WAN MISAKA OUT OF YOUR HAIR! MISAKA MISAKA IS NOW PLAYING INNOCENT ABOUT GETTING TRICKED TO YELL AT YOU INSTEAD!
PATTER
PATTER
YAAWN!
I...DOUBT WE CAN TALK LIKE THIS, SO I'LL COME BACK ANOTHER TIME.
HEY, WHERE ARE YOU TAKING MISAKA?! MISAKA MISAKA DEMANDS TO KNOW!
HUH?! THIS IS KINDA LIKE WALKING ON AIR AND MIGHT BE FUN, MISAKA MISAKA SAYS AS SHE GETS THE MOST OUT OF THIS SITUATION!
RIGHT, RIGHT. BUT DON'T FLAIL SO MUCH YOU HURT YOURSELF.
LA-TER.
DON'T COME BACK.
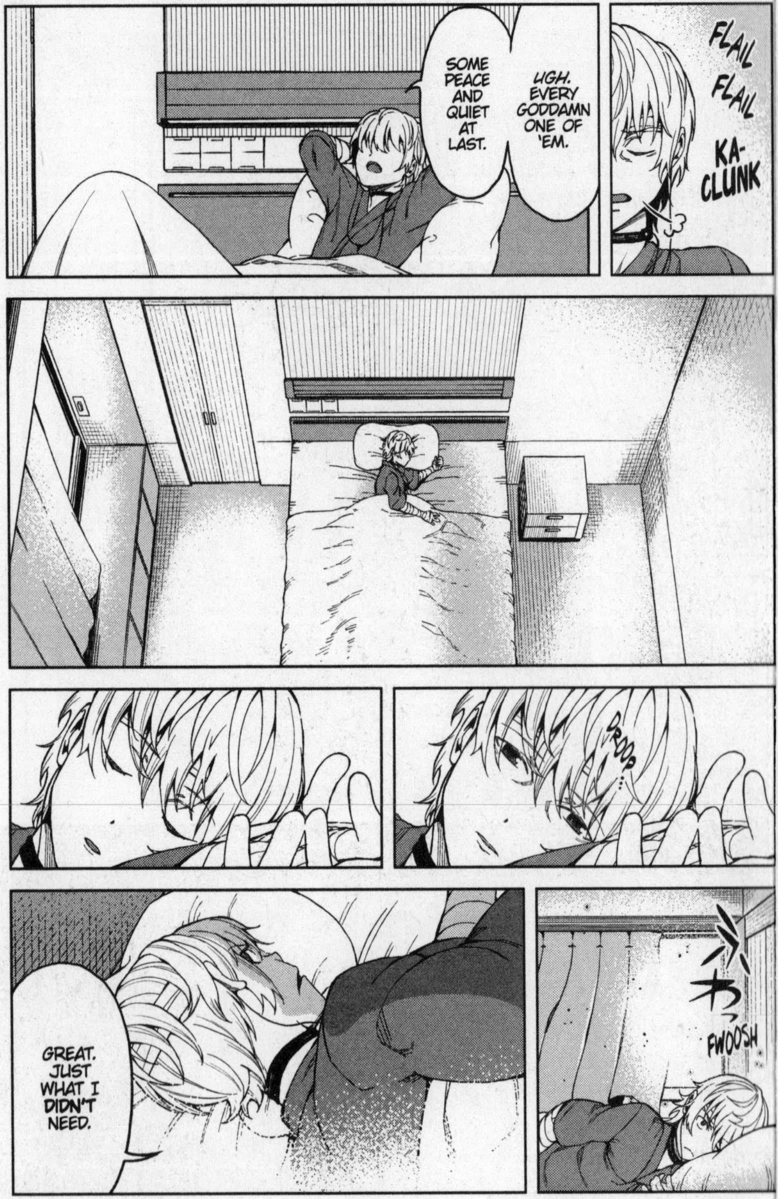
FLAIL
FLAIL
KA-CLUNK
UGH. EVERY GODDAMN ONE OF 'EM.
SOME PEACE AND QUIET AT LAST.
DROOP
FWOOSH
GREAT. JUST WHAT I DIDN'T NEED.

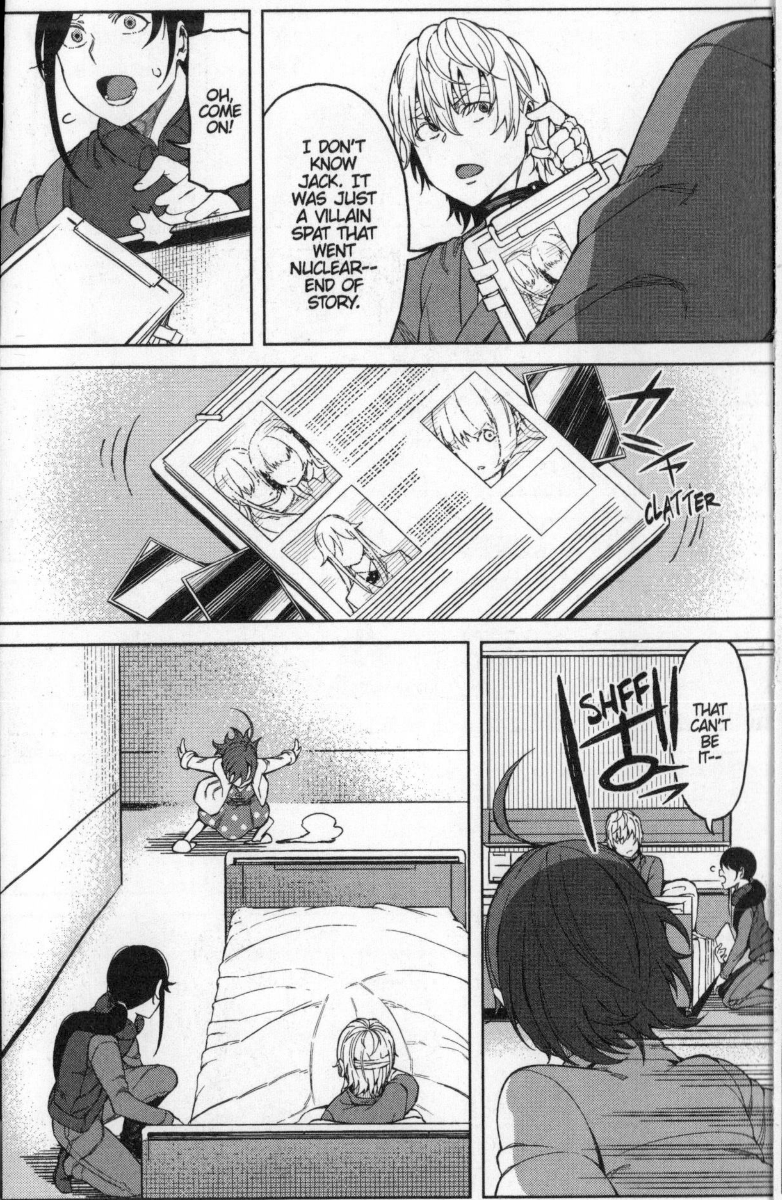
I DON'T KNOW JACK. IT WAS JUST A VILLAIN SPAT THAT WENT NUCLEAR--END OF STORY.
OH, COME ON!
CLATTER
SHFF
THAT CAN'T BE IT--
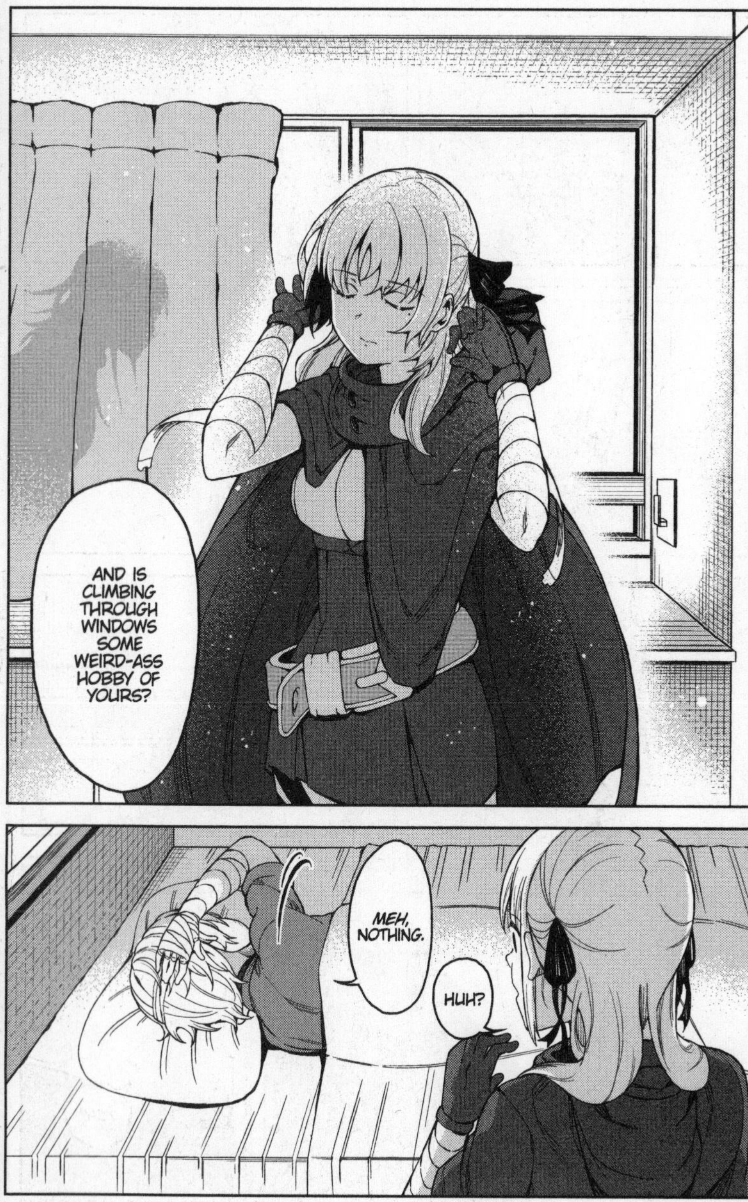
AND IS CLIMBING THROUGH WINDOWS SOME WEIRD-ASS HOBBY OF YOURS?
MEH, NOTHING.
HUH?

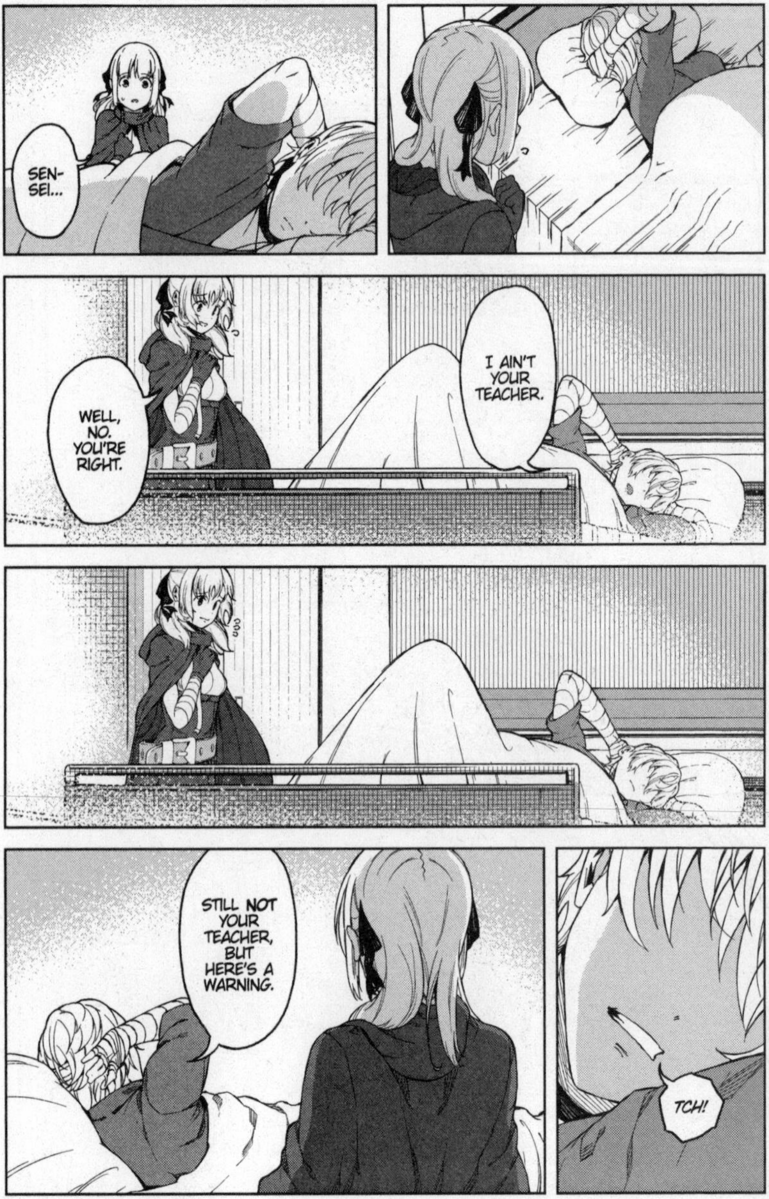
SEN-SEI...
I AIN'T YOUR TEACHER.
WELL, NO. YOU'RE RIGHT.
TCH!
STILL NOT YOUR TEACHER, BUT HERE'S A WARNING.

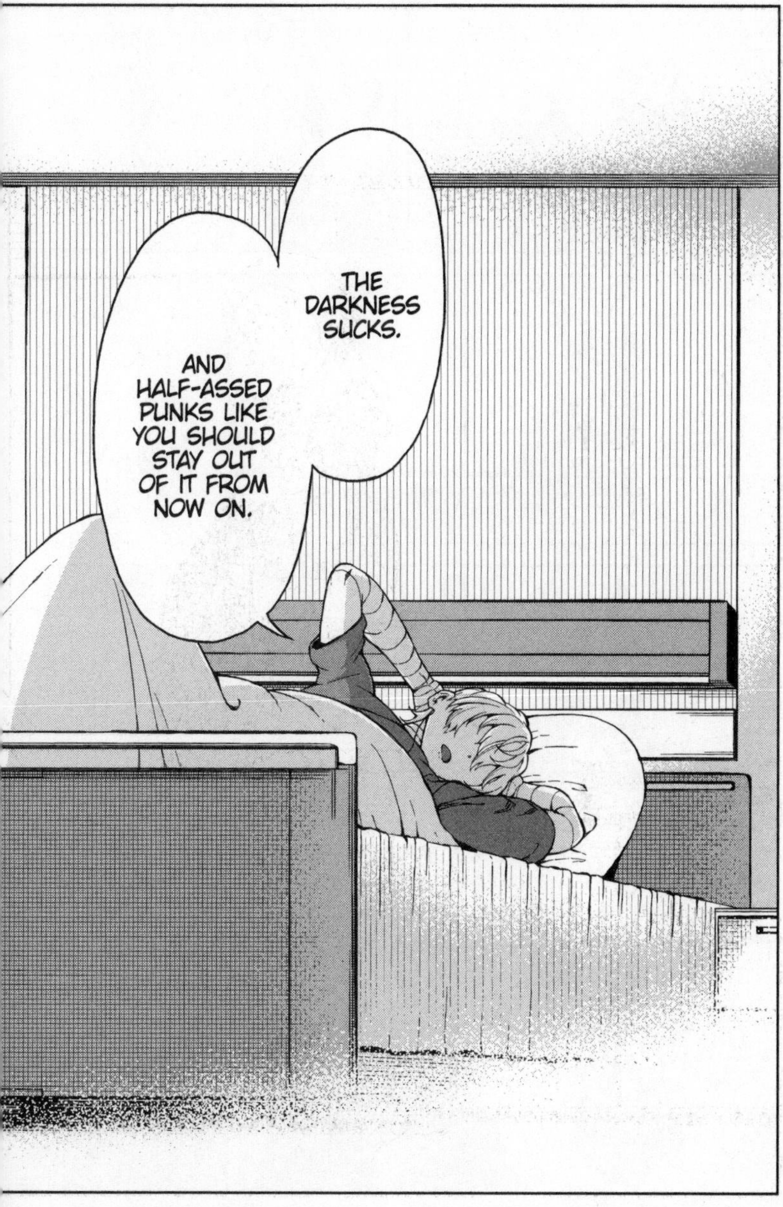
THE DARKNESS SUCKS.
AND HALF-ASSED PUNKS LIKE YOU SHOULD STAY OUT OF IT FROM NOW ON.

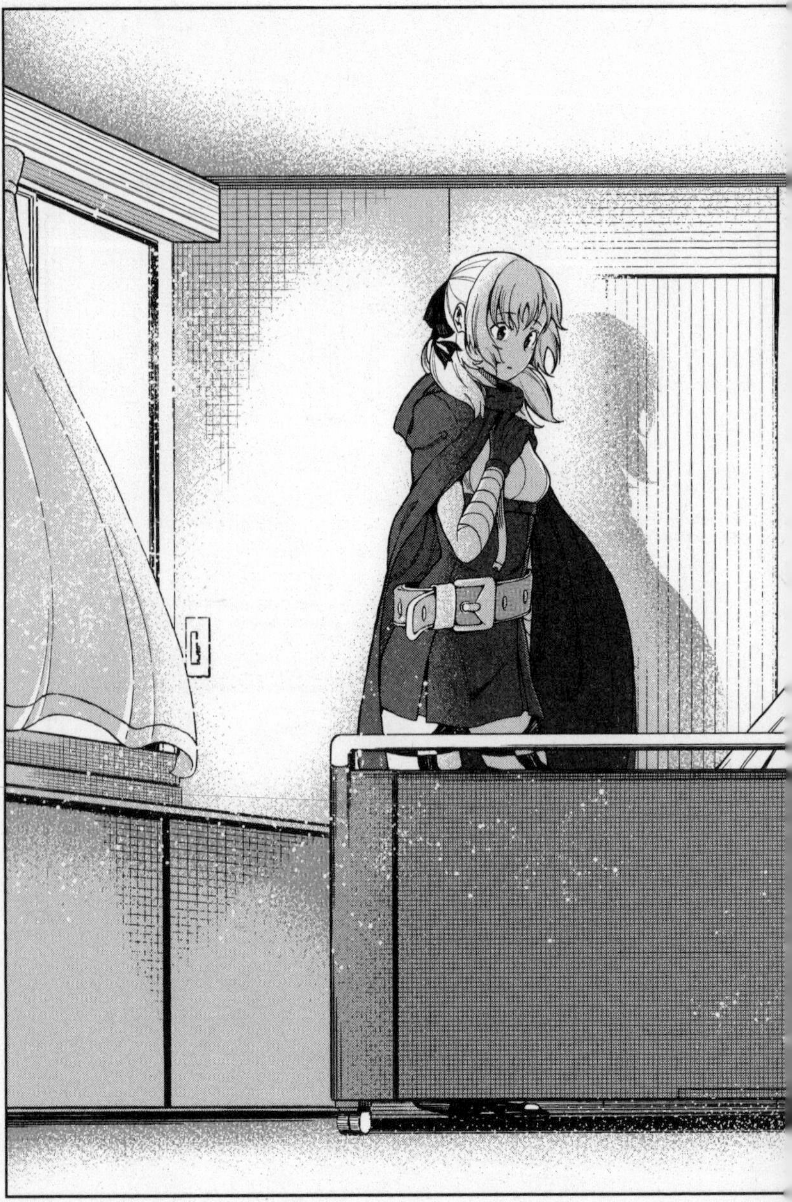

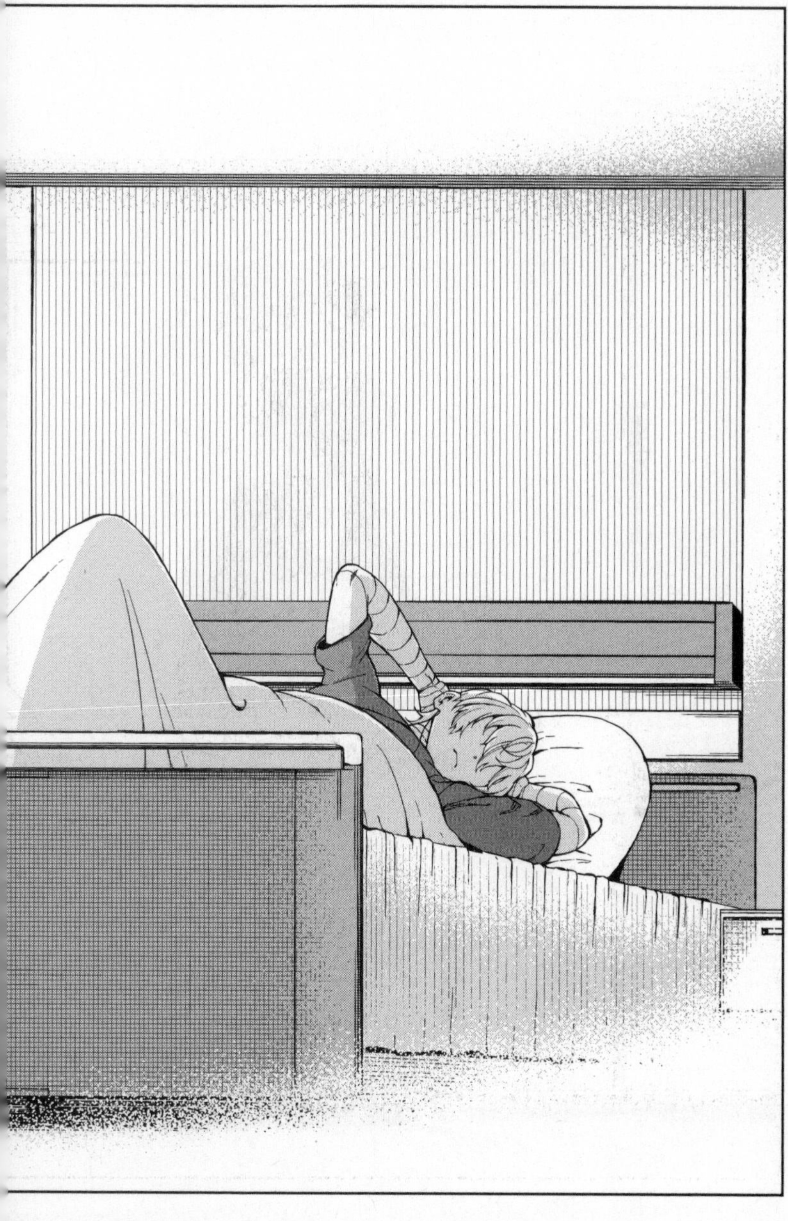

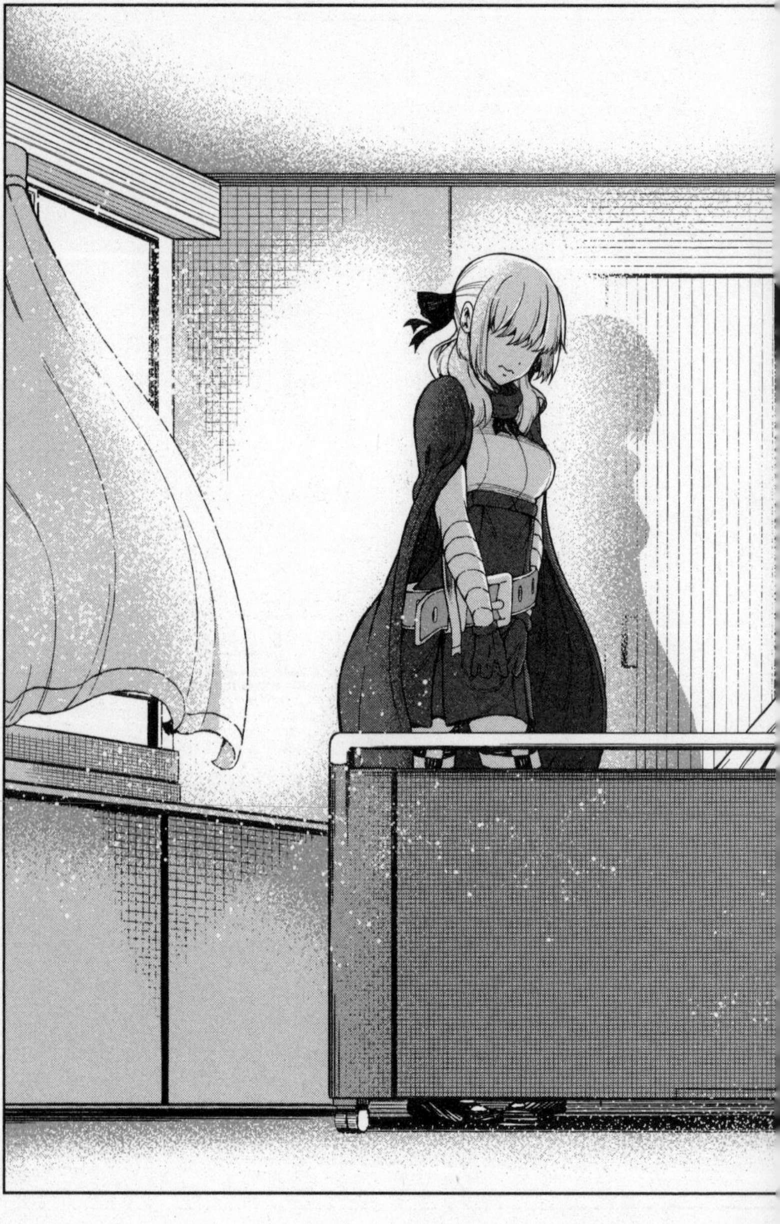

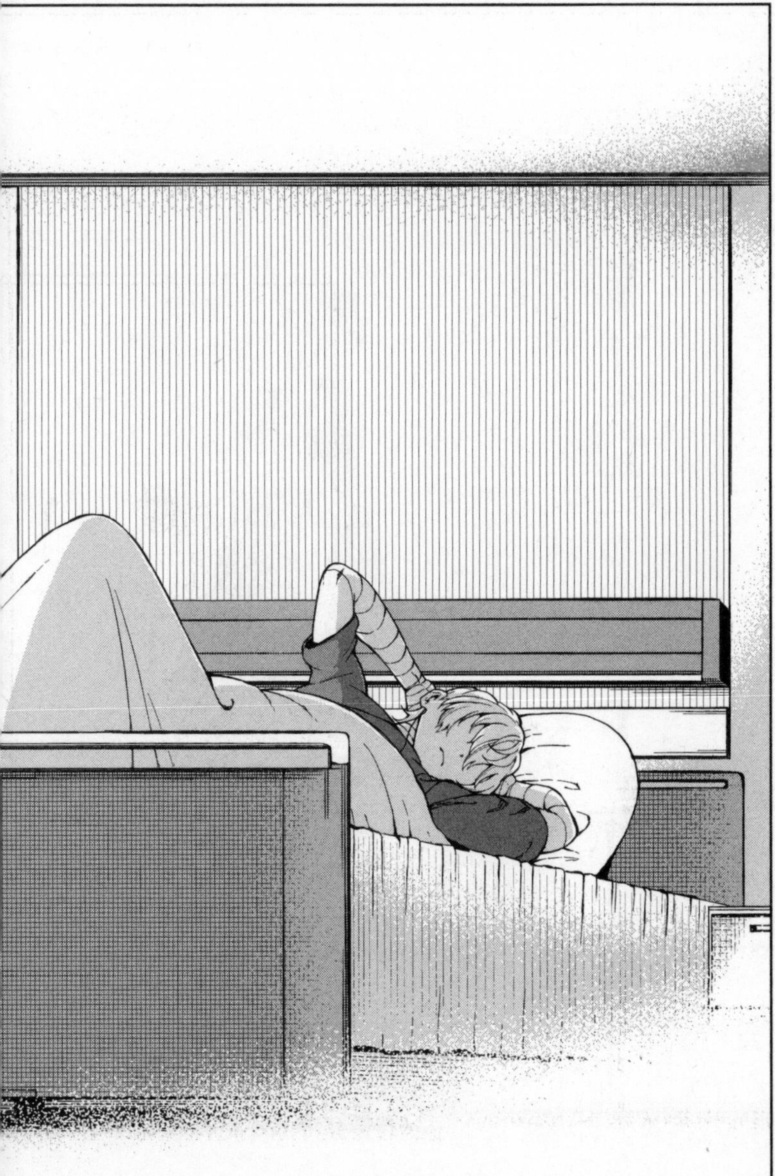

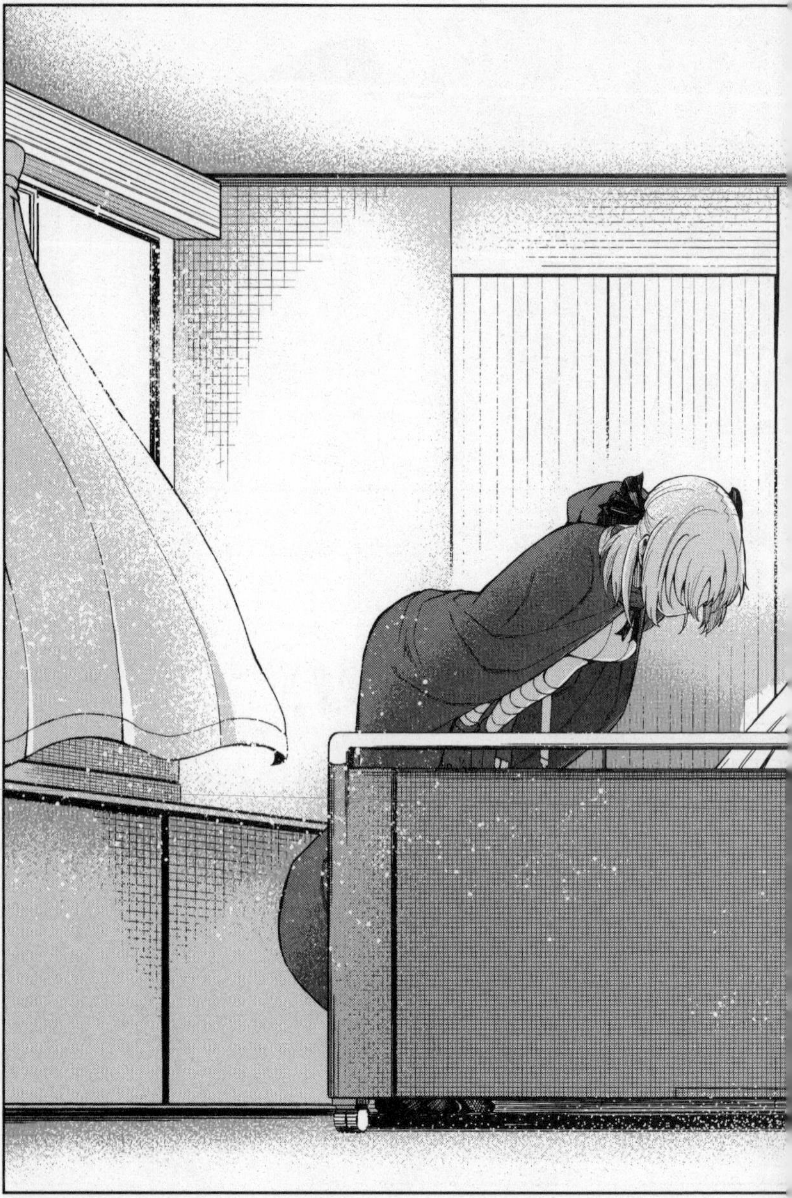

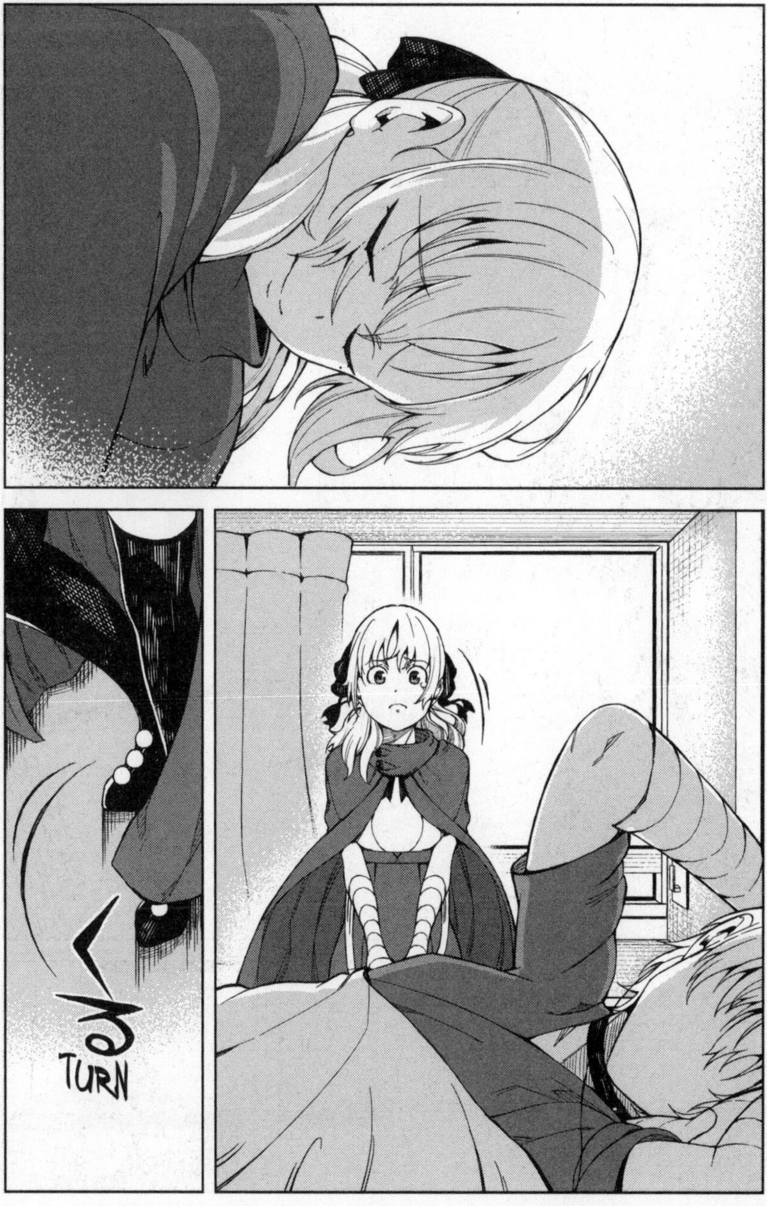
TURN

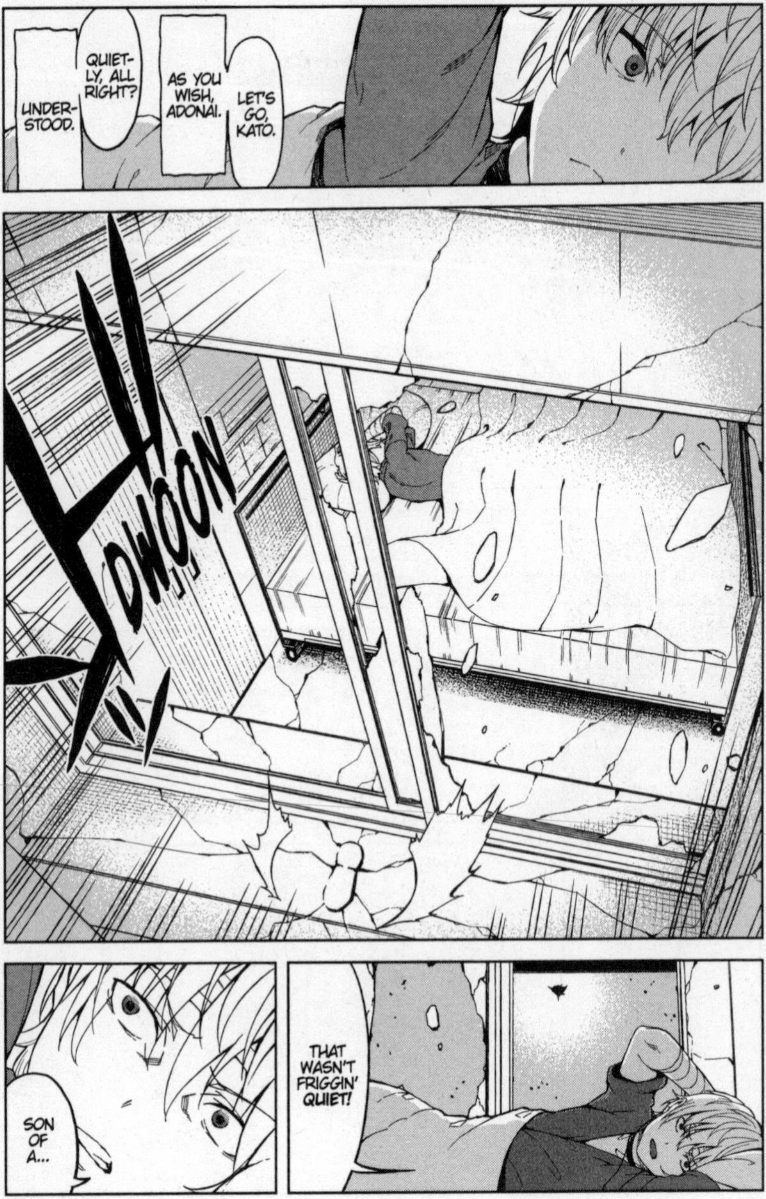
LET'S GO, KATO.
AS YOU WISH, ADONAI.
QUIETLY, ALL RIGHT?
UNDERSTOOD.
DWOON
THAT WASN'T FRIGGIN' QUIET!
SON OF A...

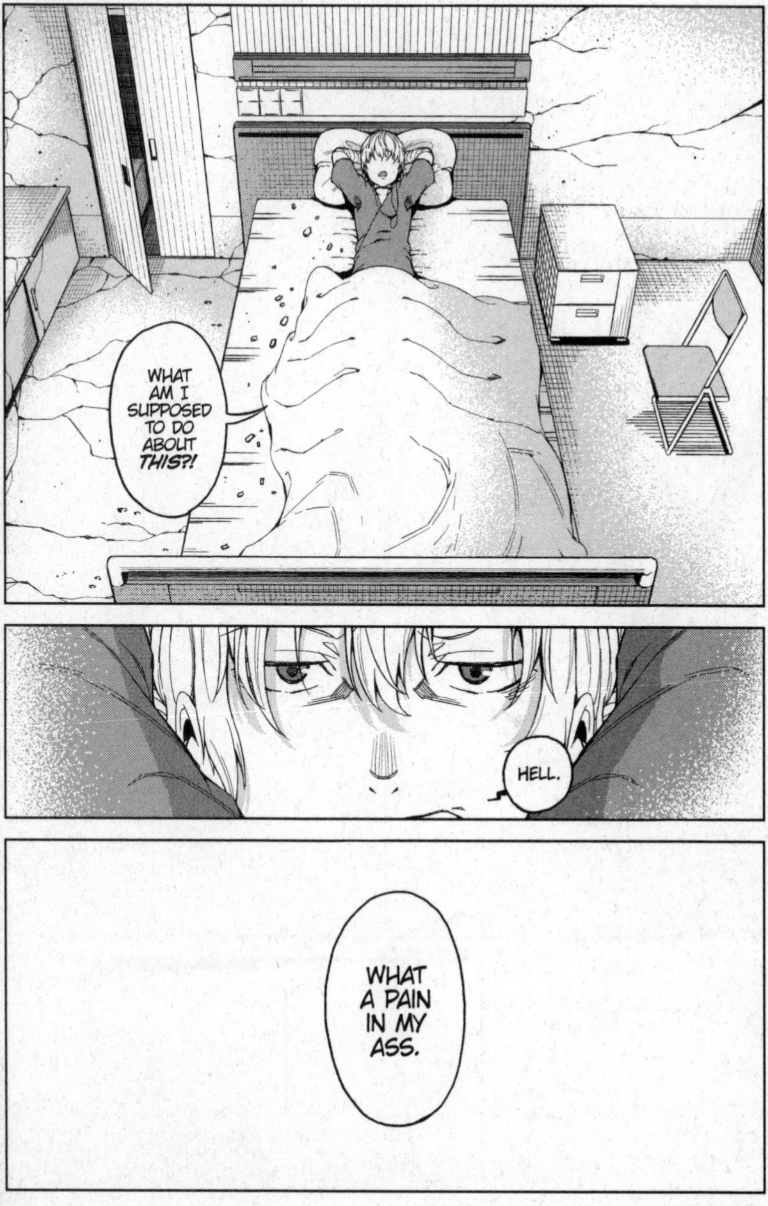
WHAT AM I SUPPOSED TO DO ABOUT *THIS?!*
HELL.
WHAT A PAIN IN MY ASS.

a certain
SCIENTIFIC
ACCELERATOR

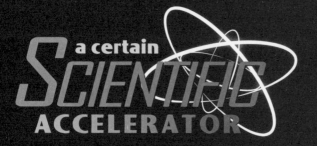

とある科学の一方通行

アクセラレータ

とある魔術の禁書目録外伝

CHAPTER 37

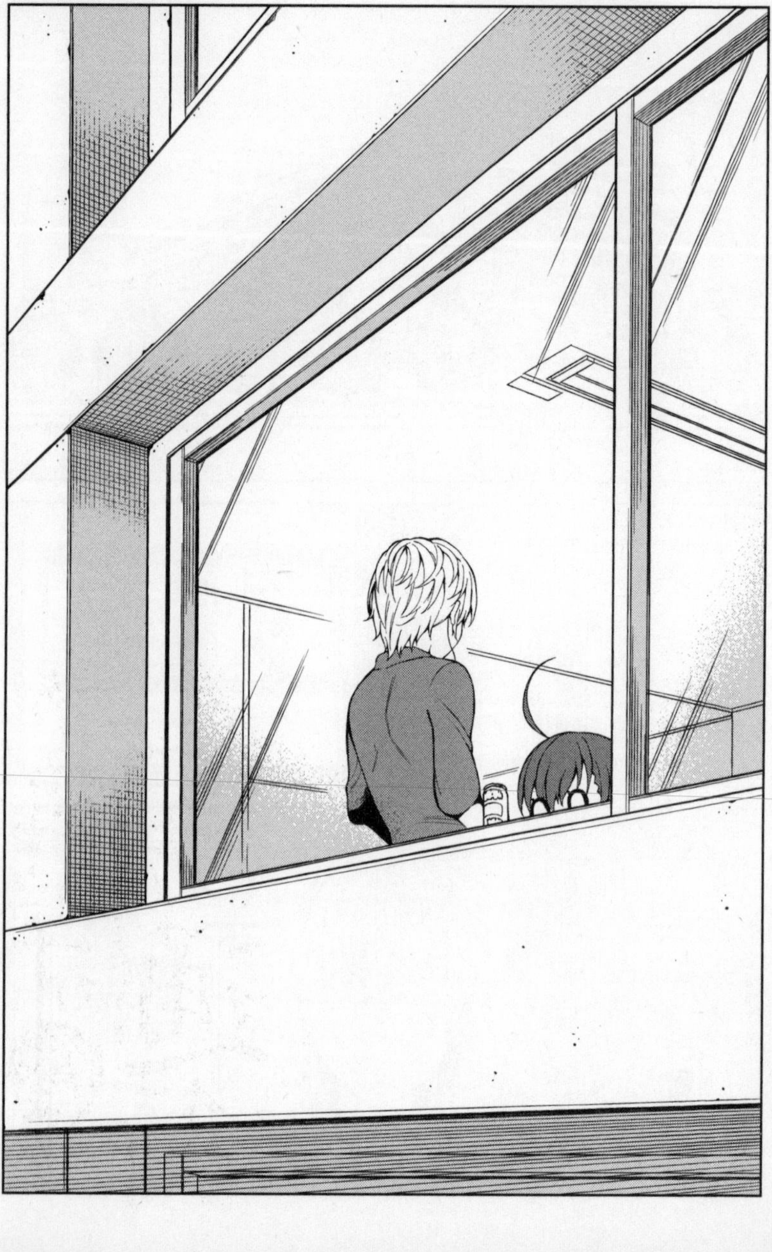

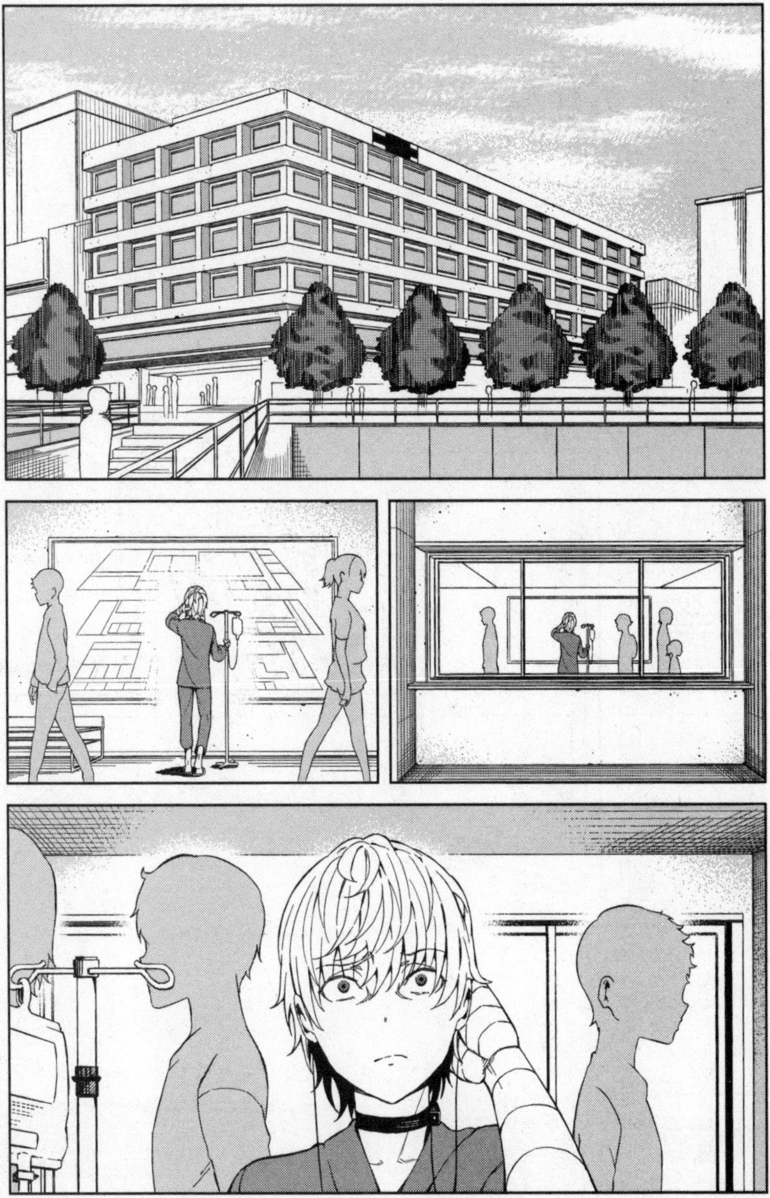

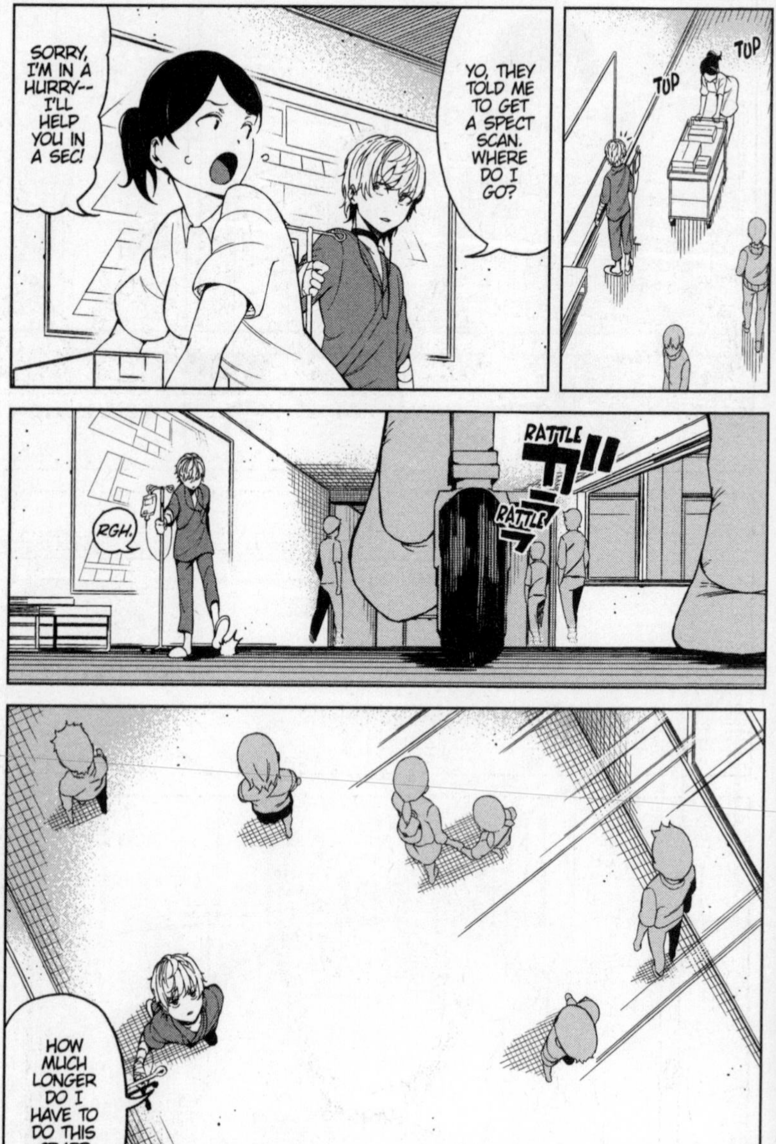
TUP
TUP
YO, THEY TOLD ME TO GET A SPECT SCAN. WHERE DO I GO?
SORRY, I'M IN A HURRY-- I'LL HELP YOU IN A SEC!
RATTLE
RATTLE
RGH.
HOW MUCH LONGER DO I HAVE TO DO THIS CRAP?

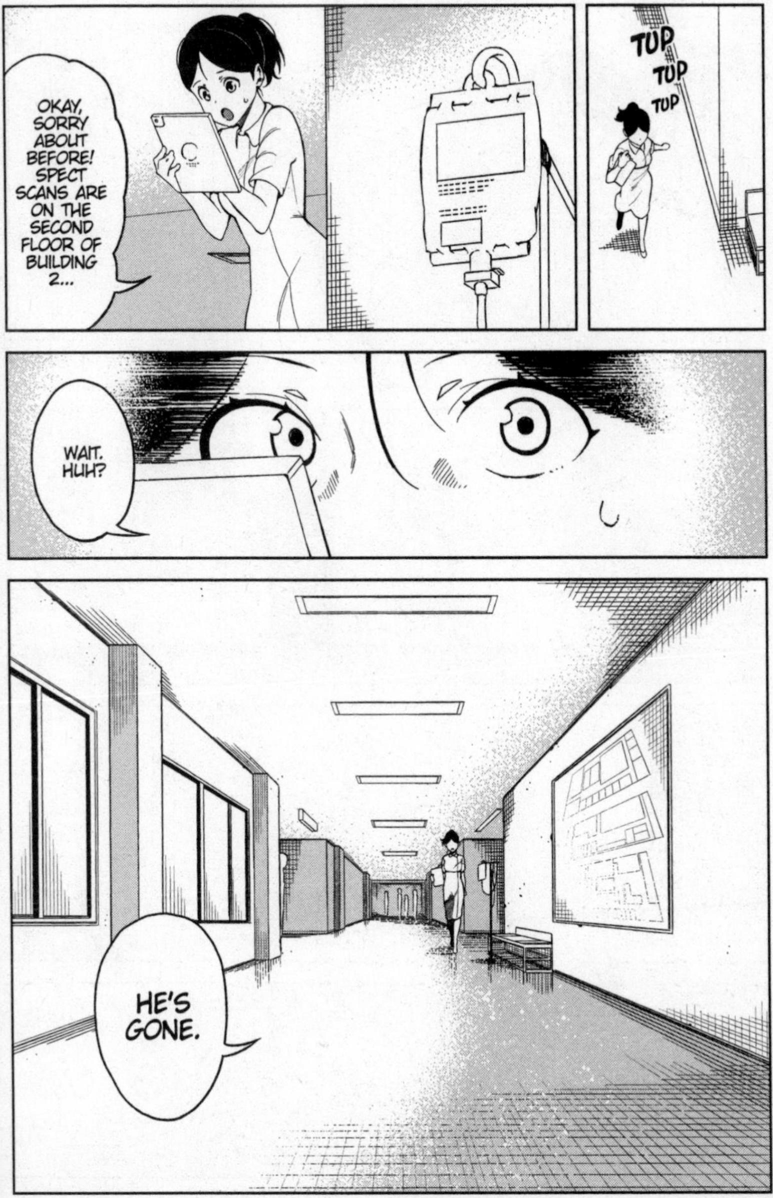
TUP
TUP
TUP
OKAY, SORRY ABOUT BEFORE! SPECT SCANS ARE ON THE SECOND FLOOR OF BUILDING 2...
WAIT. HUH?
HE'S GONE.

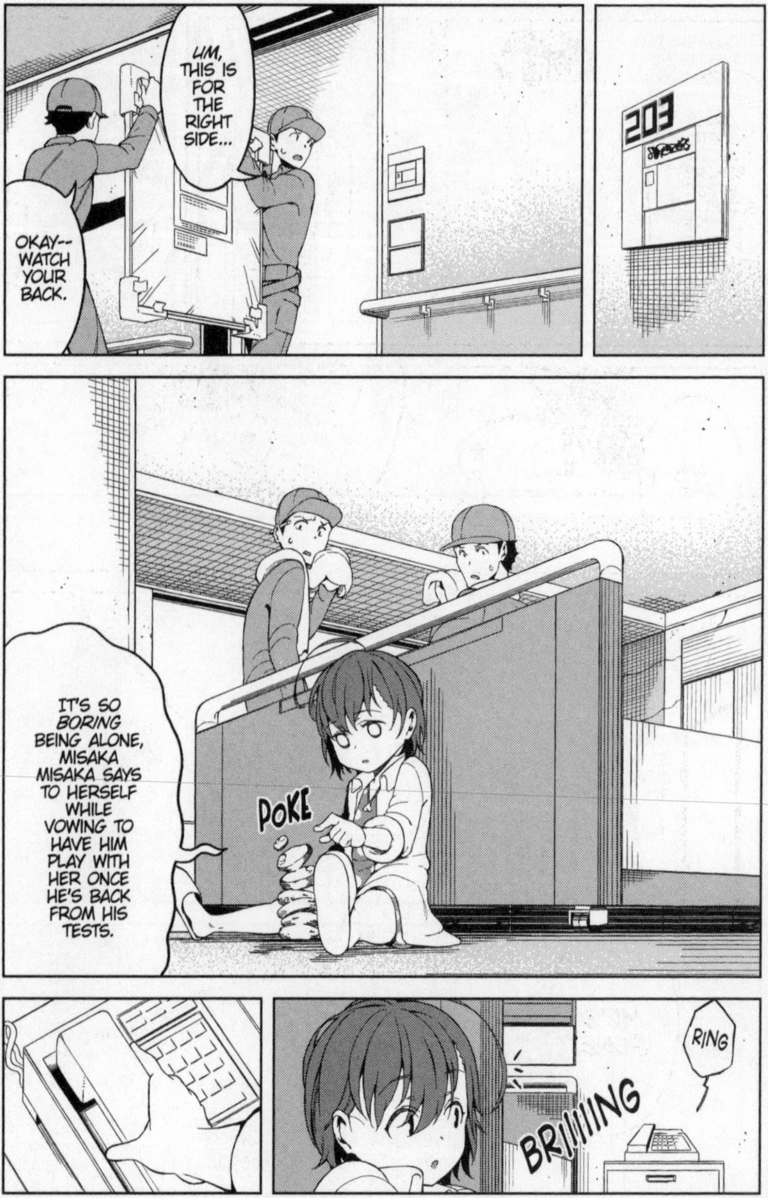
UM, THIS IS FOR THE RIGHT SIDE...
OKAY-- WATCH YOUR BACK.
IT'S SO *BORING* BEING ALONE, MISAKA MISAKA SAYS TO HERSELF WHILE VOWING TO HAVE HIM PLAY WITH HER ONCE HE'S BACK FROM HIS TESTS.
POKE
RING
BRIIIIING

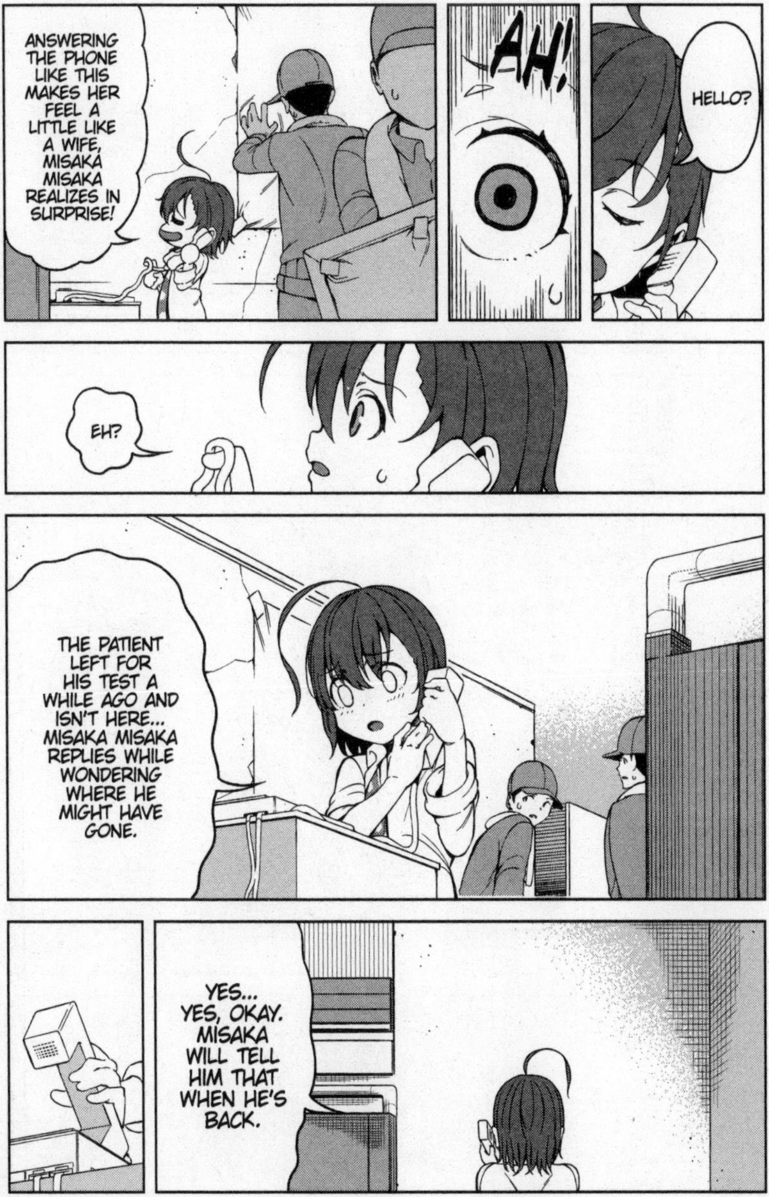
HELLO?
AH!
ANSWERING THE PHONE LIKE THIS MAKES HER FEEL A LITTLE LIKE A WIFE, MISAKA MISAKA REALIZES IN SURPRISE!
EH?
THE PATIENT LEFT FOR HIS TEST A WHILE AGO AND ISN'T HERE... MISAKA MISAKA REPLIES WHILE WONDERING WHERE HE MIGHT HAVE GONE.
YES... YES, OKAY. MISAKA WILL TELL HIM THAT WHEN HE'S BACK.

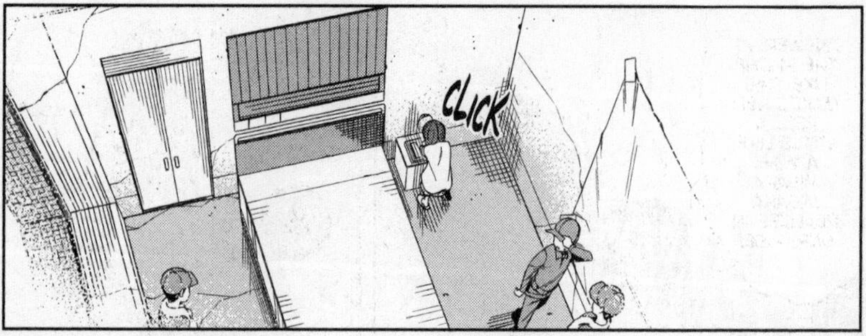
CLICK
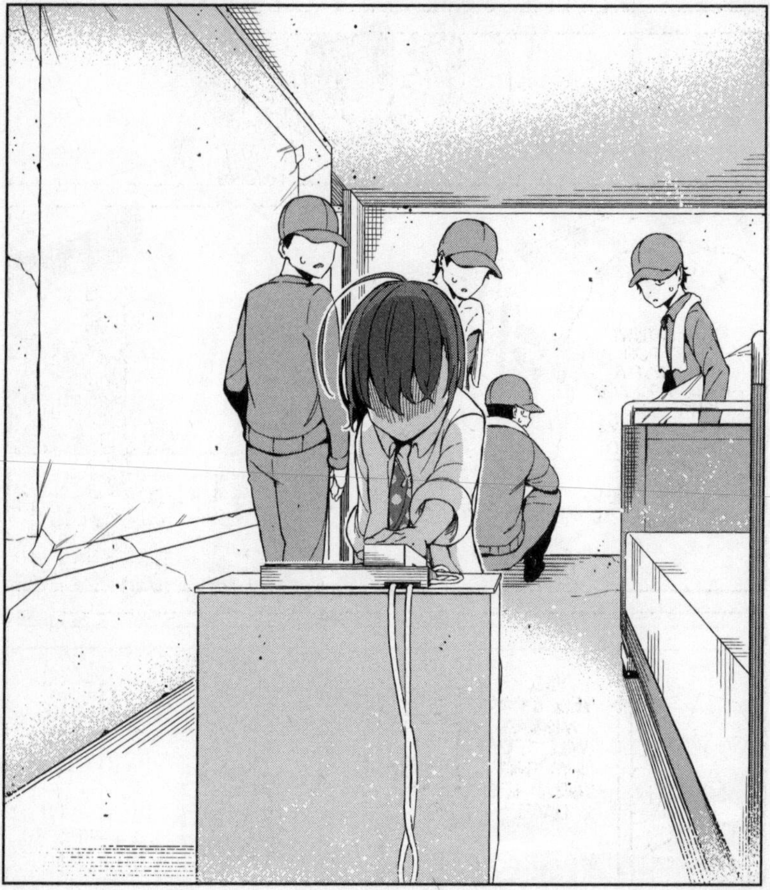

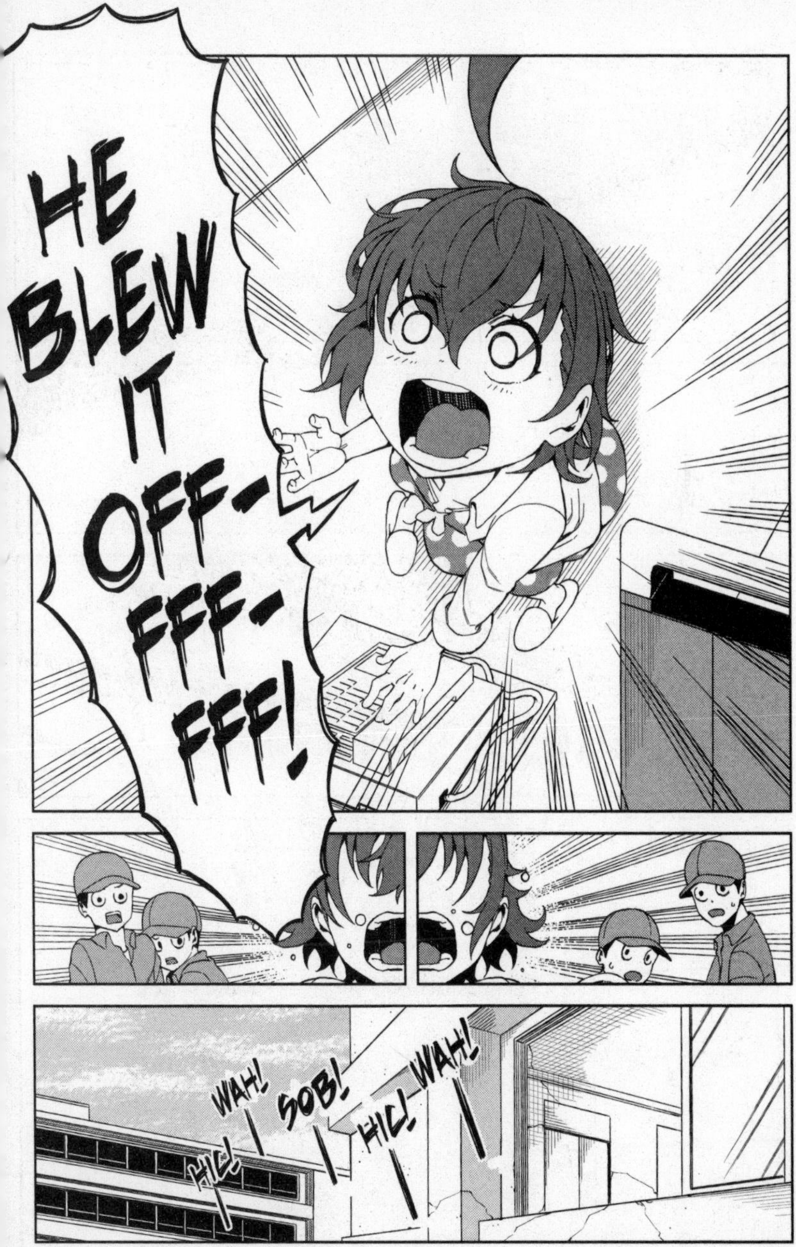
HE BLEW IT OFF-FFF-FFF!
WAH!
SOB!
WAH!
HIC!
HIC!
HIC!

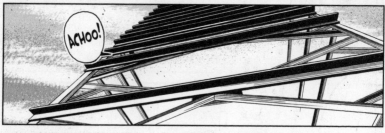

ACHOO!

SIP

NGH.

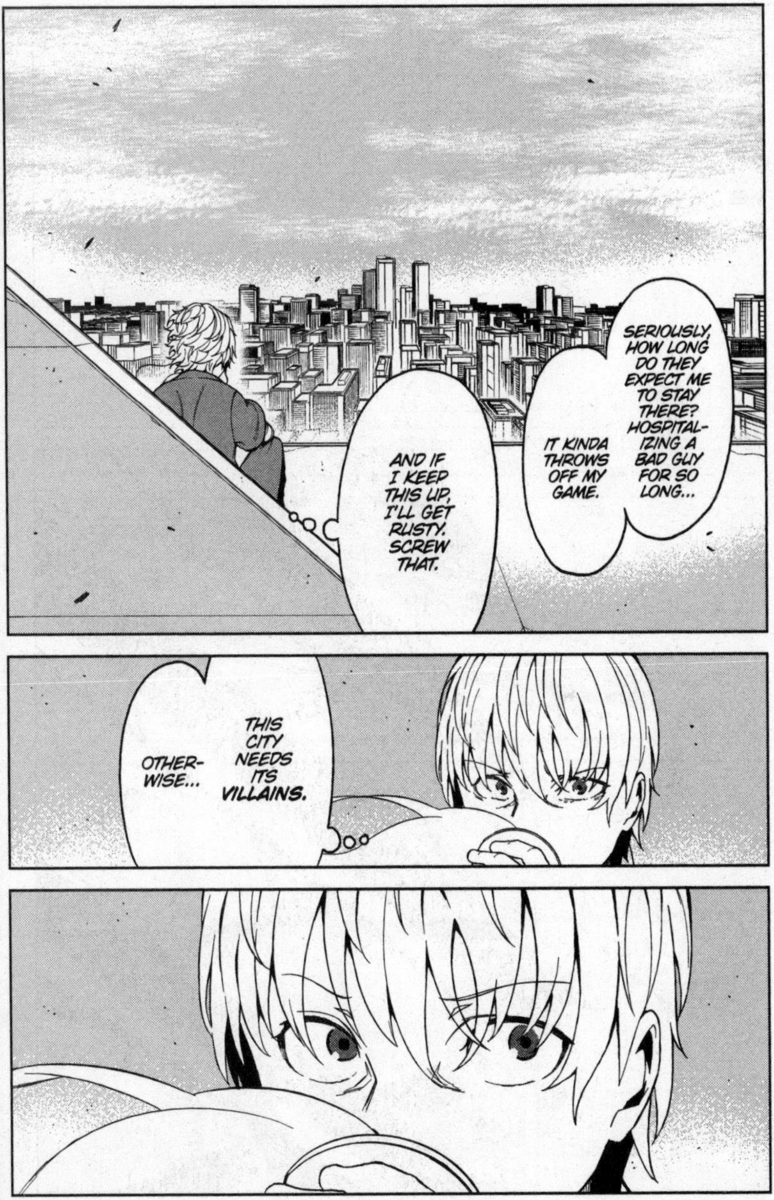
SERIOUSLY, HOW LONG DO THEY EXPECT ME TO STAY THERE? HOSPITALIZING A BAD GUY FOR SO LONG...
IT KINDA THROWS OFF MY GAME.
AND IF I KEEP THIS UP, I'LL GET RUSTY. SCREW THAT.
THIS CITY NEEDS ITS VILLAINS.
OTHERWISE...

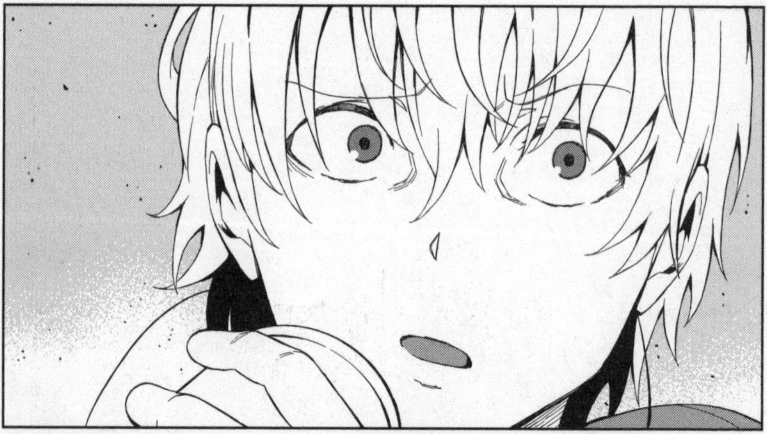

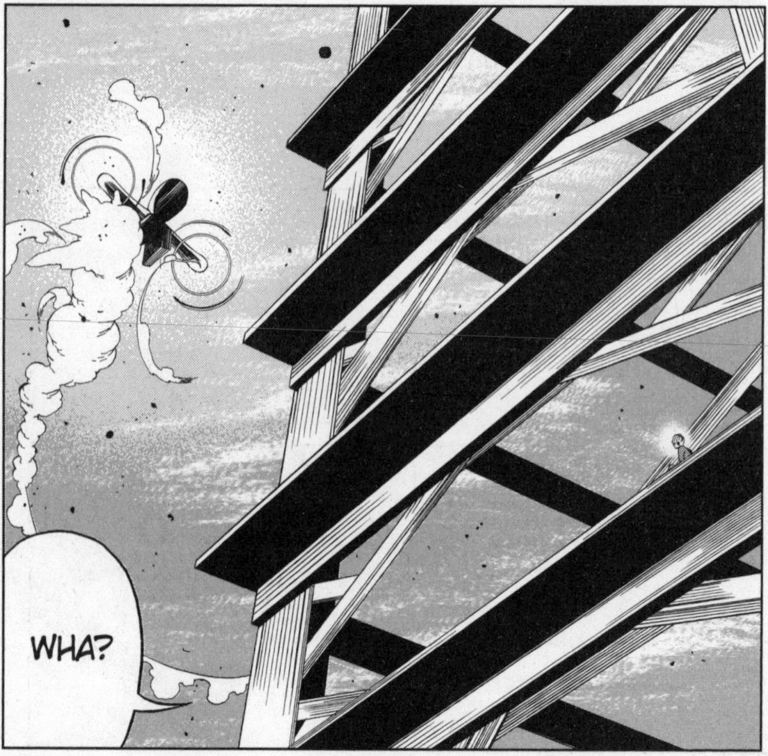
WHA?

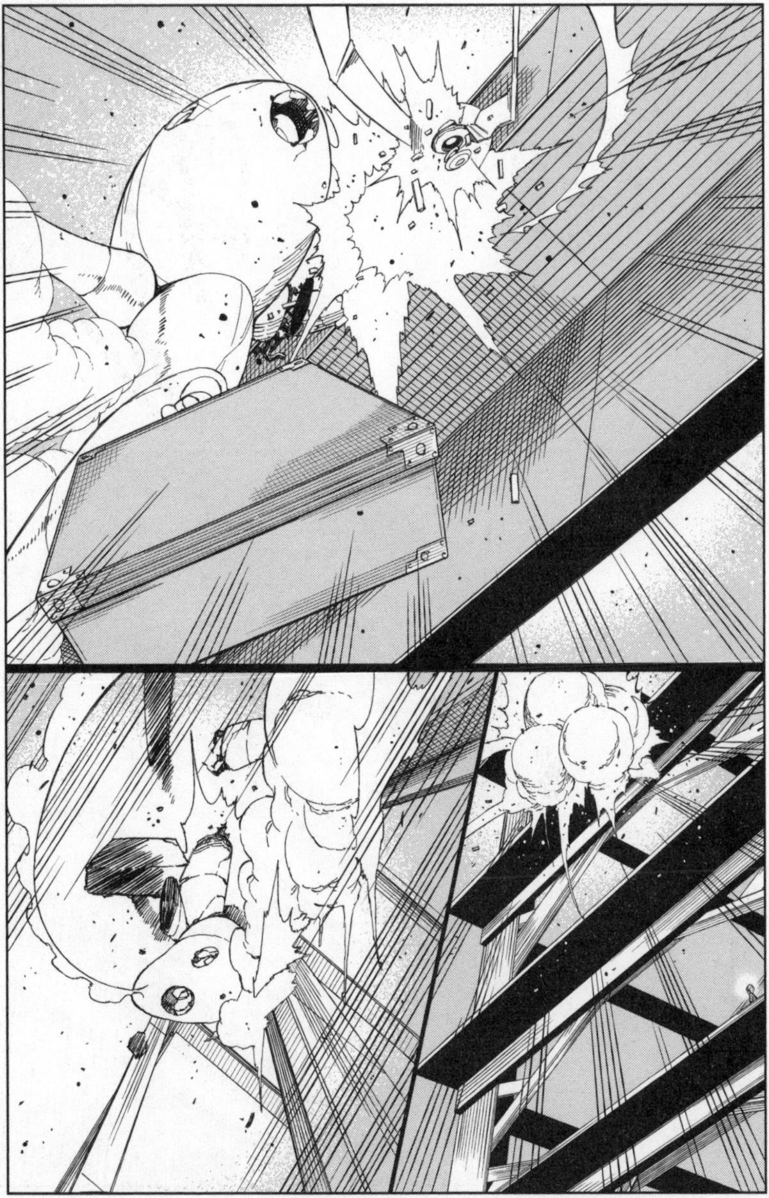

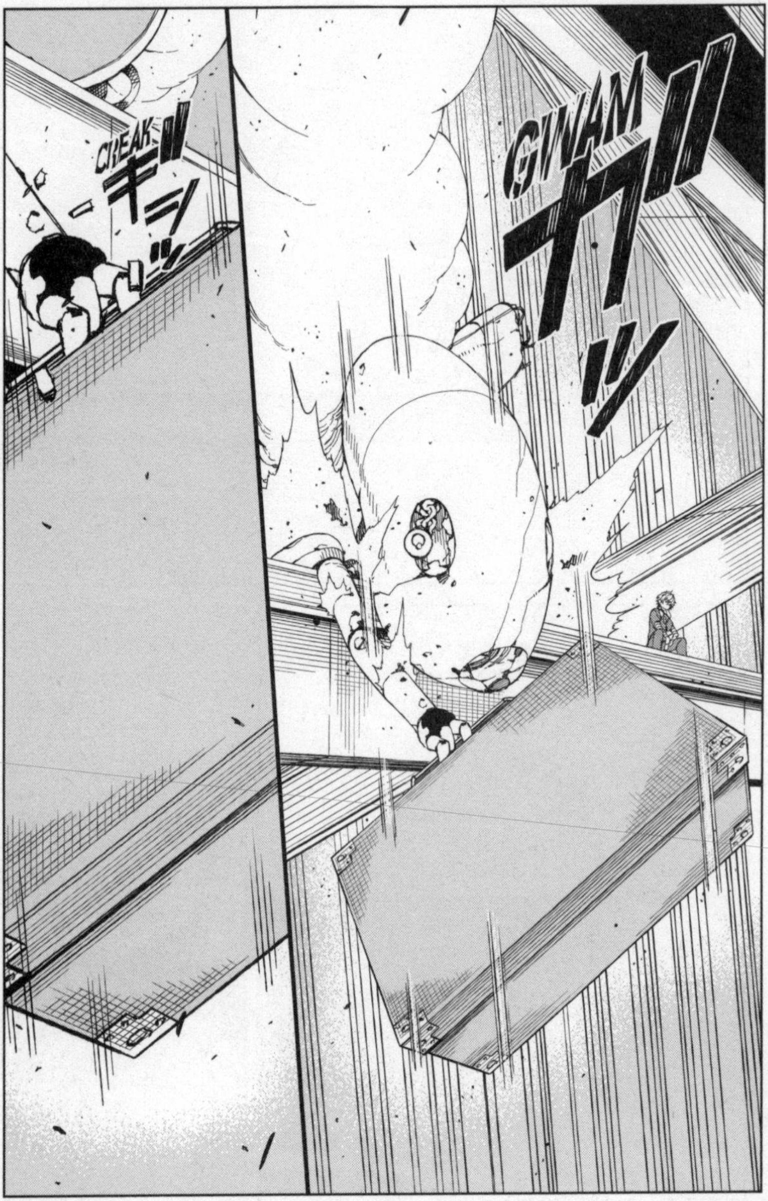
GWAN
CREAK

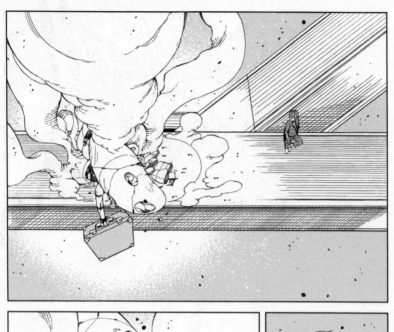

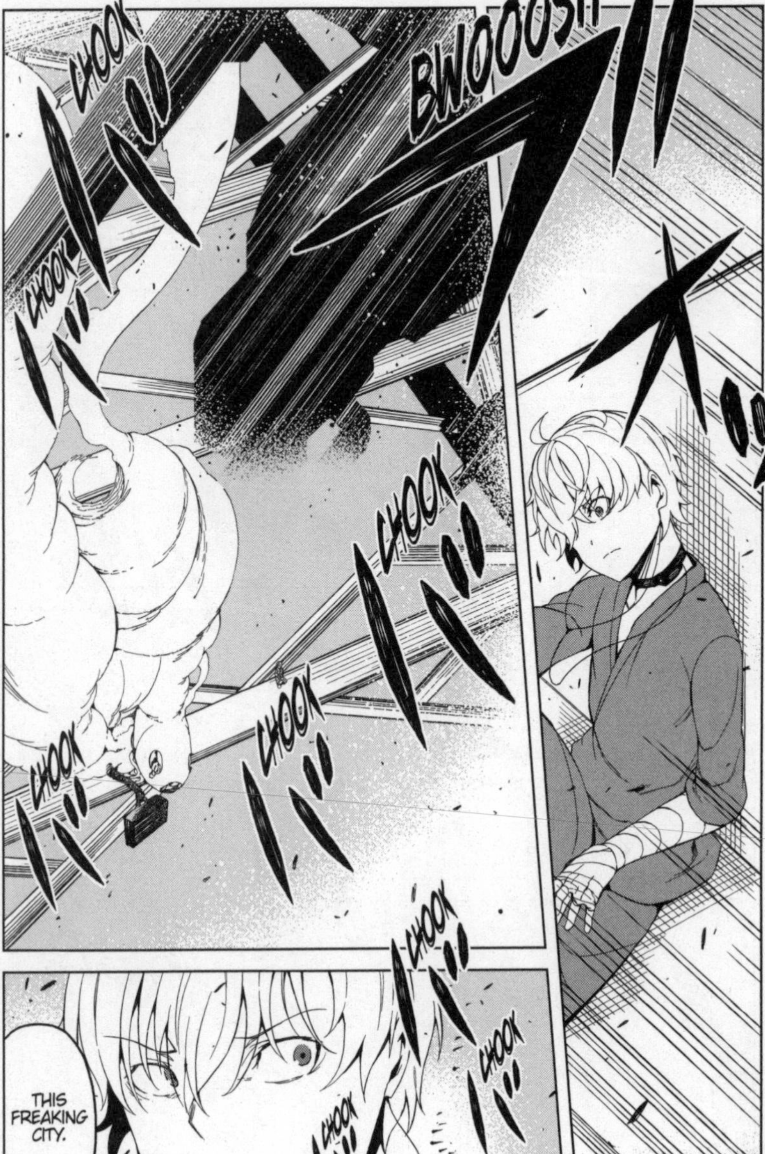
BWOOOSH
CHOOK
CHOOK
CHOOK
CHOOK
CHOOK
CHOOK
CHOOK
CHOOK
THIS FREAKING CITY.

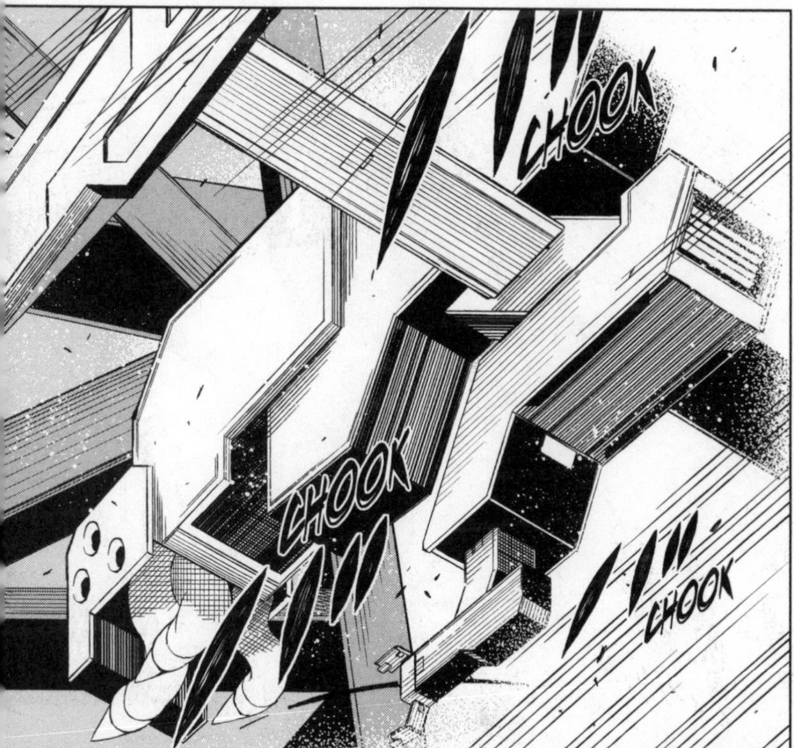
CHOOK
CHOOK
CHOOK

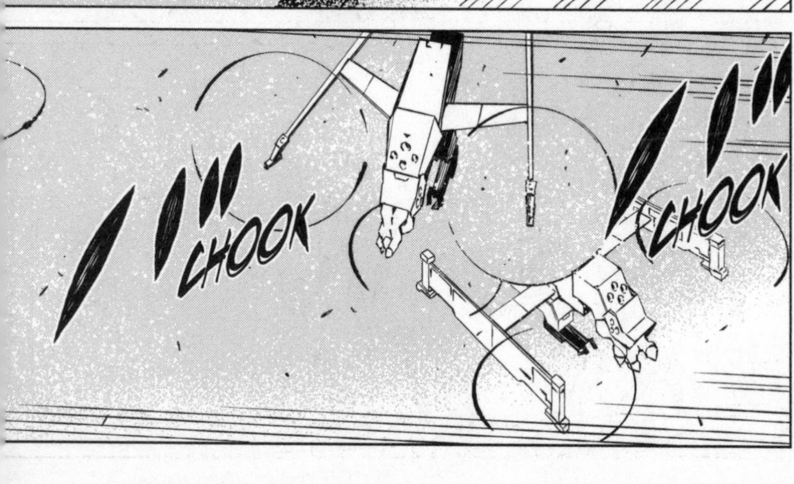
CHOOK
CHOOK

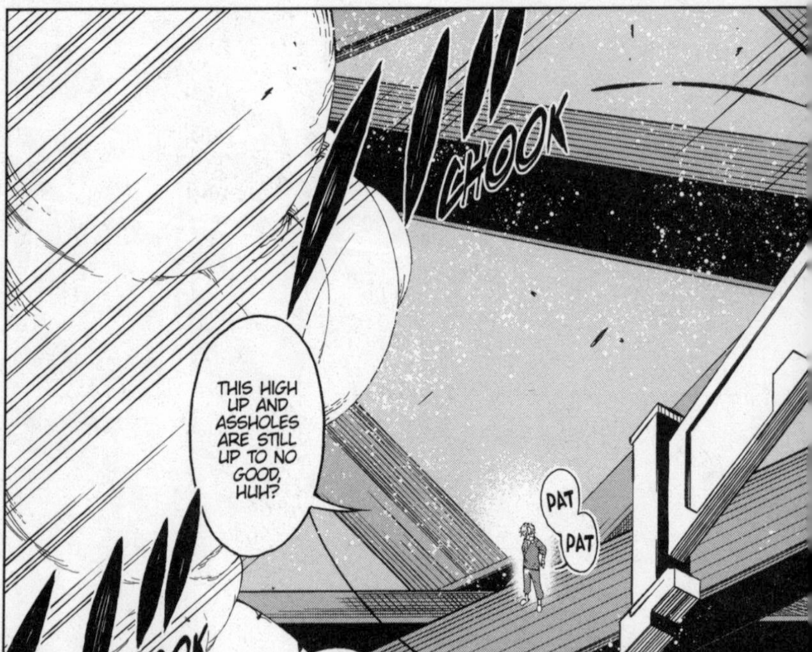
CHOOK
PAT PAT
THIS HIGH UP AND ASSHOLES ARE STILL UP TO NO GOOD, HUH?
CHOOK

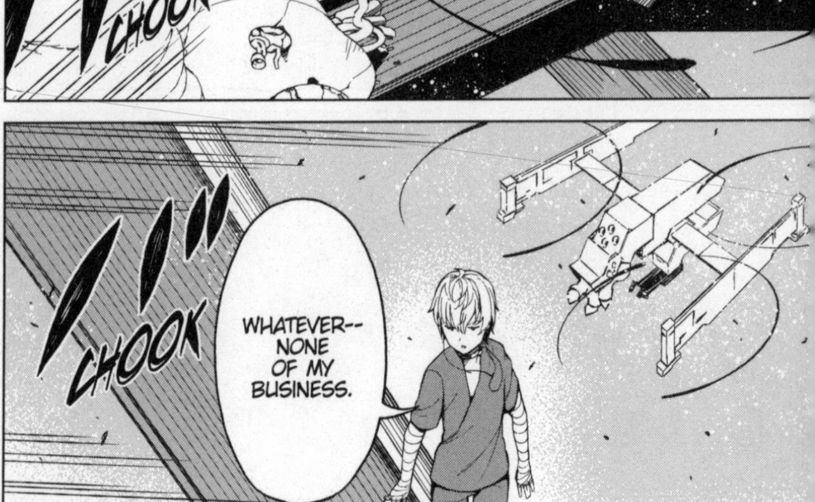
WHATEVER-- NONE OF MY BUSINESS.
CHOOK

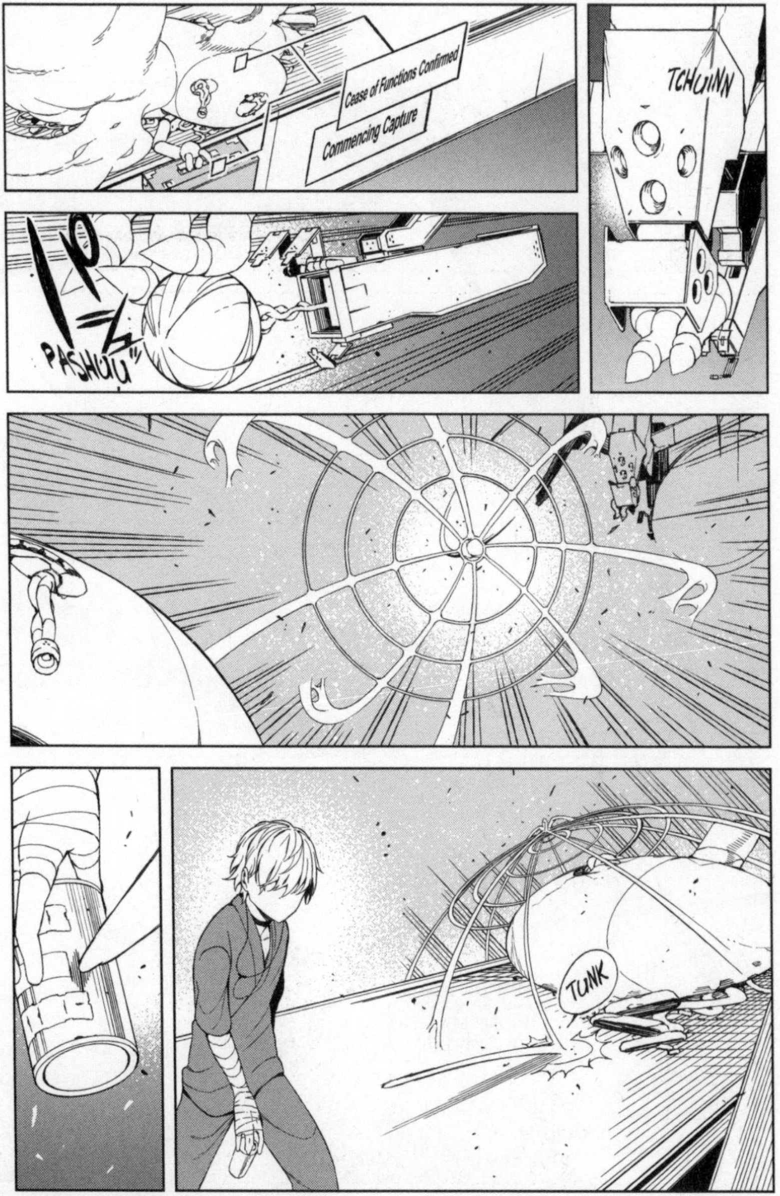
TCHUINN
Cease of Functions Confirmed
Commencing Capture
PASHUU
TUNK

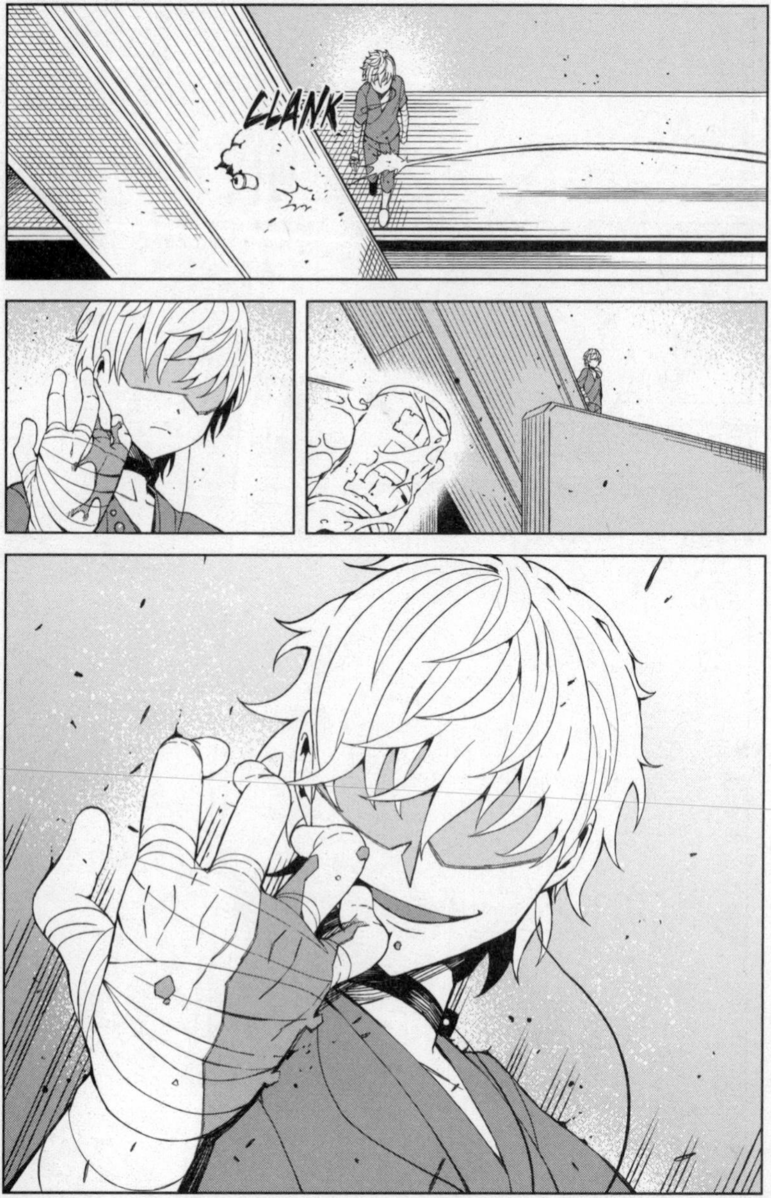
CLANK

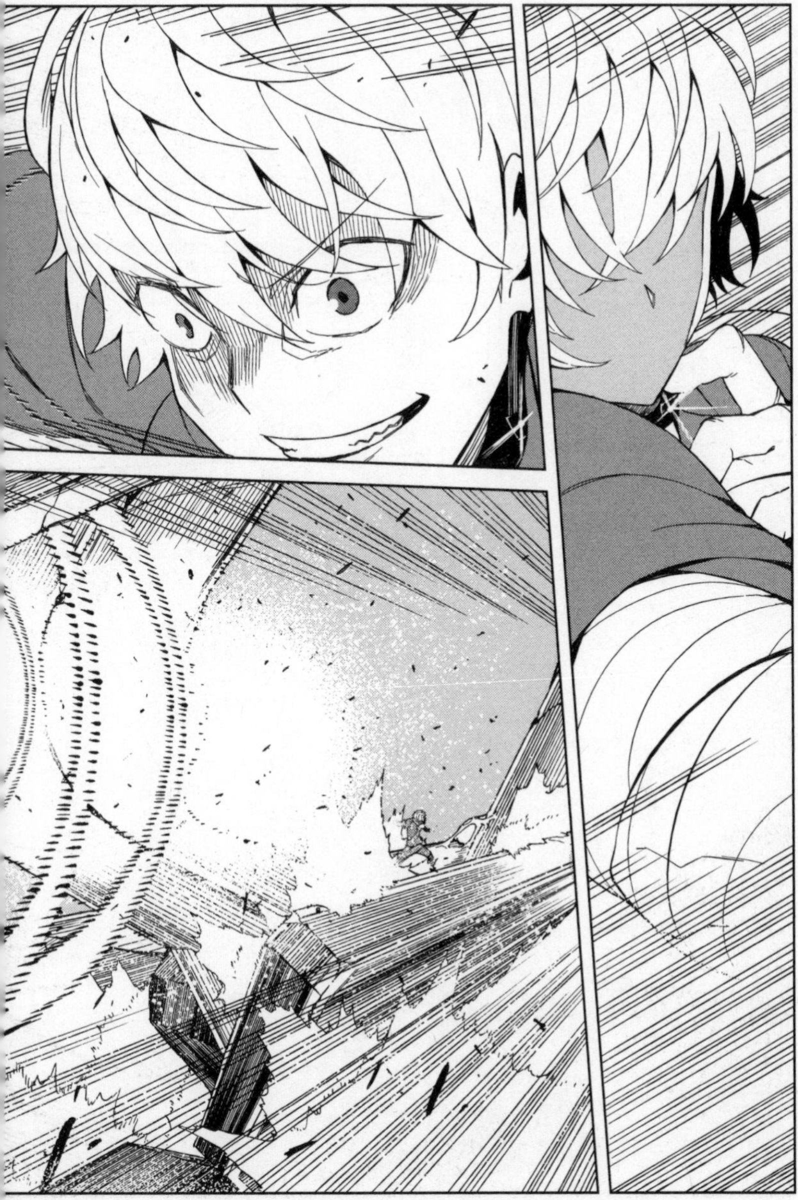

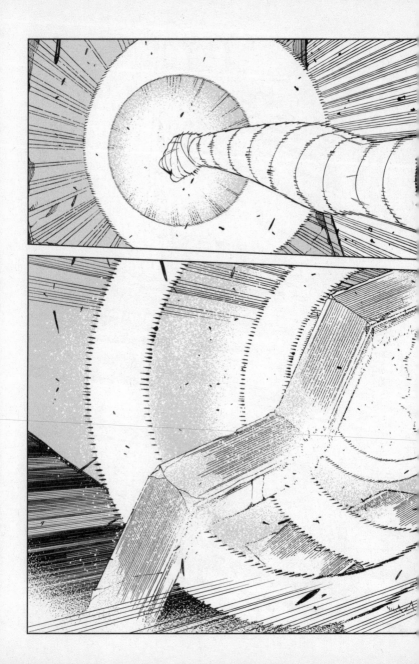

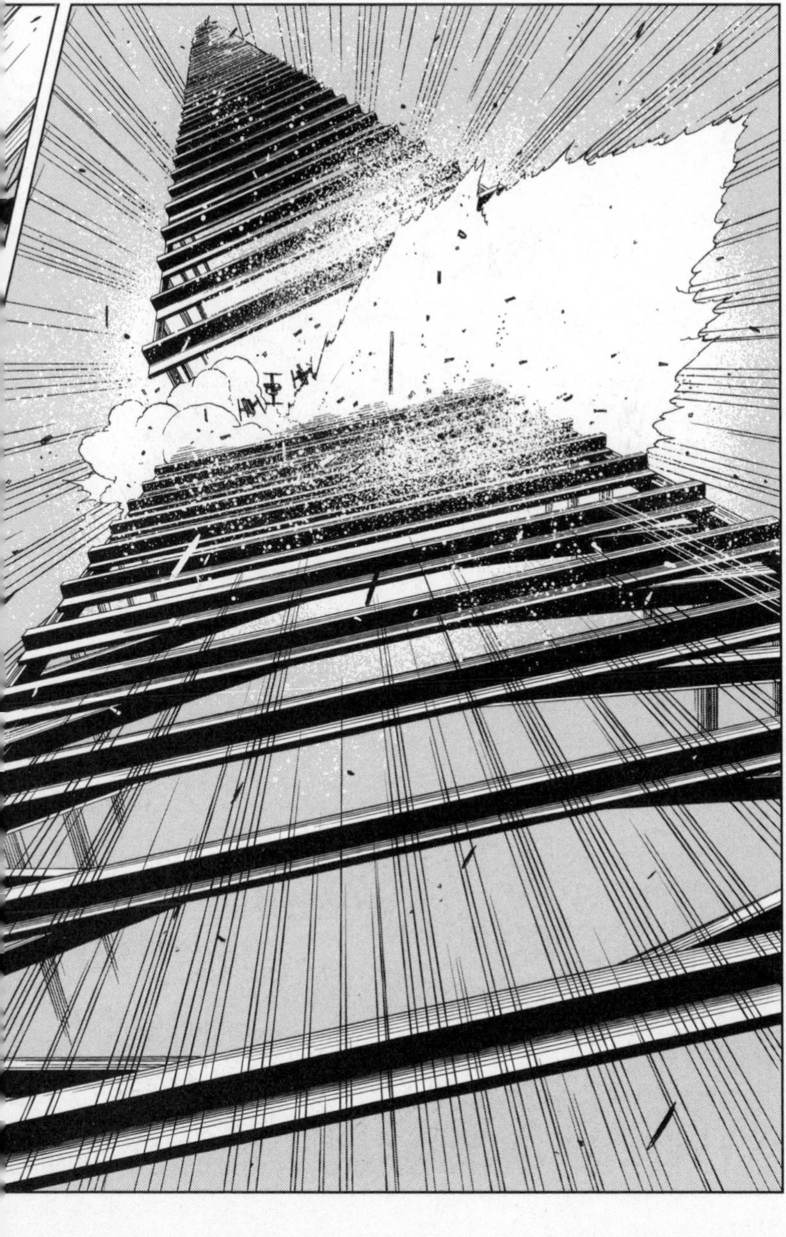

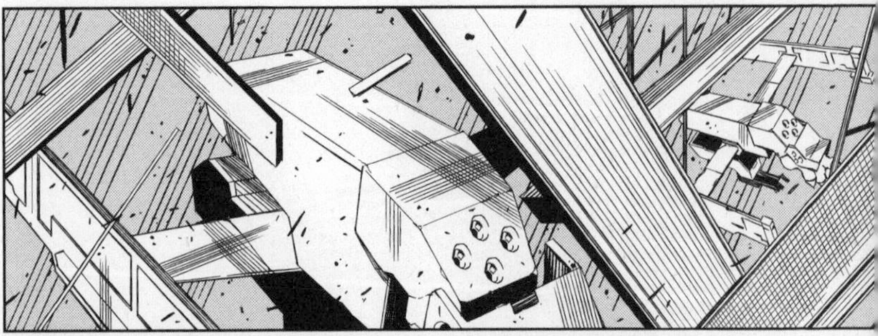
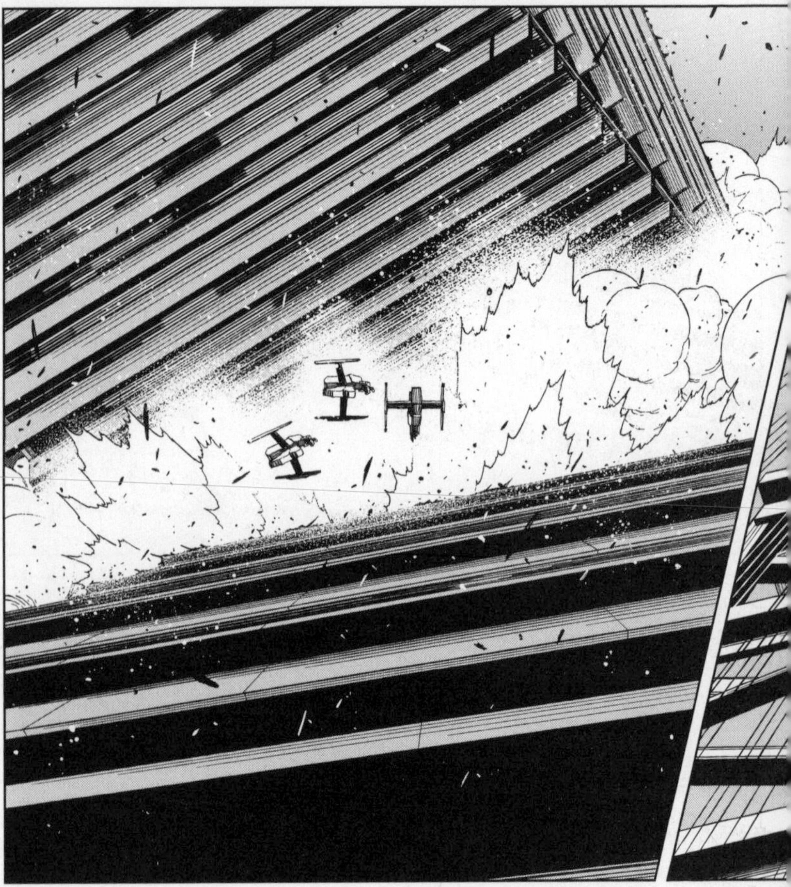

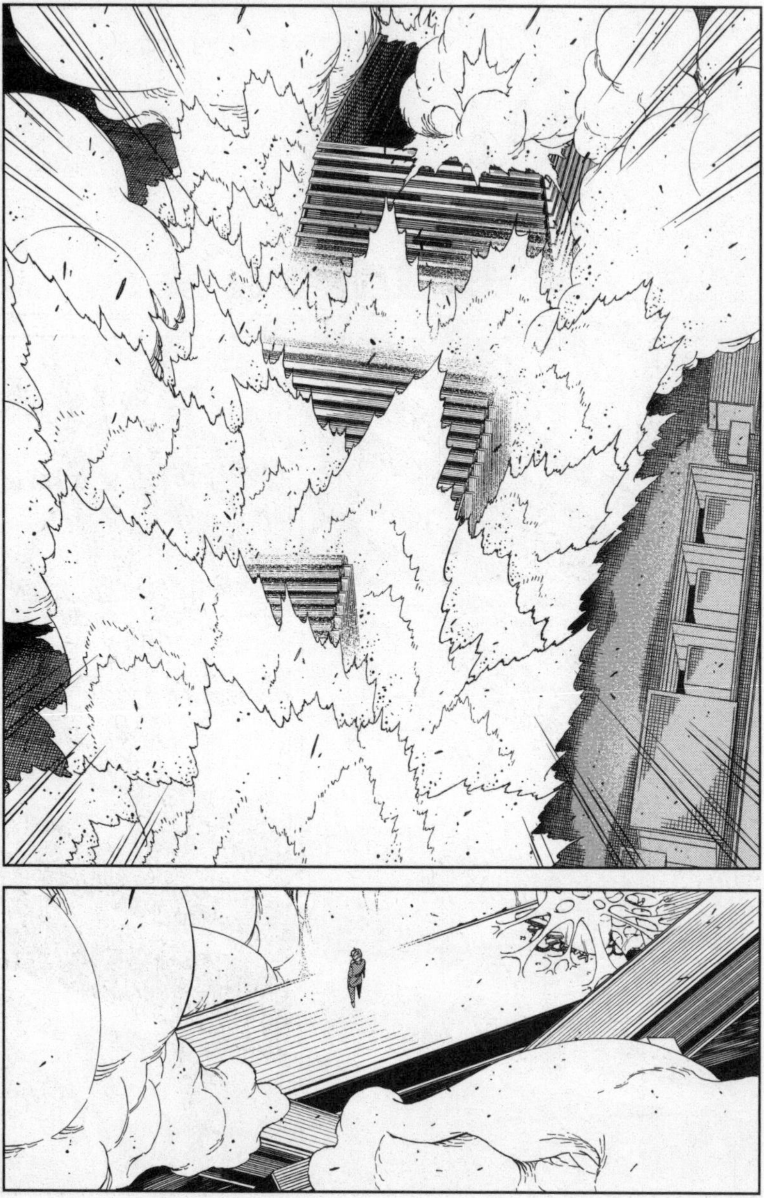

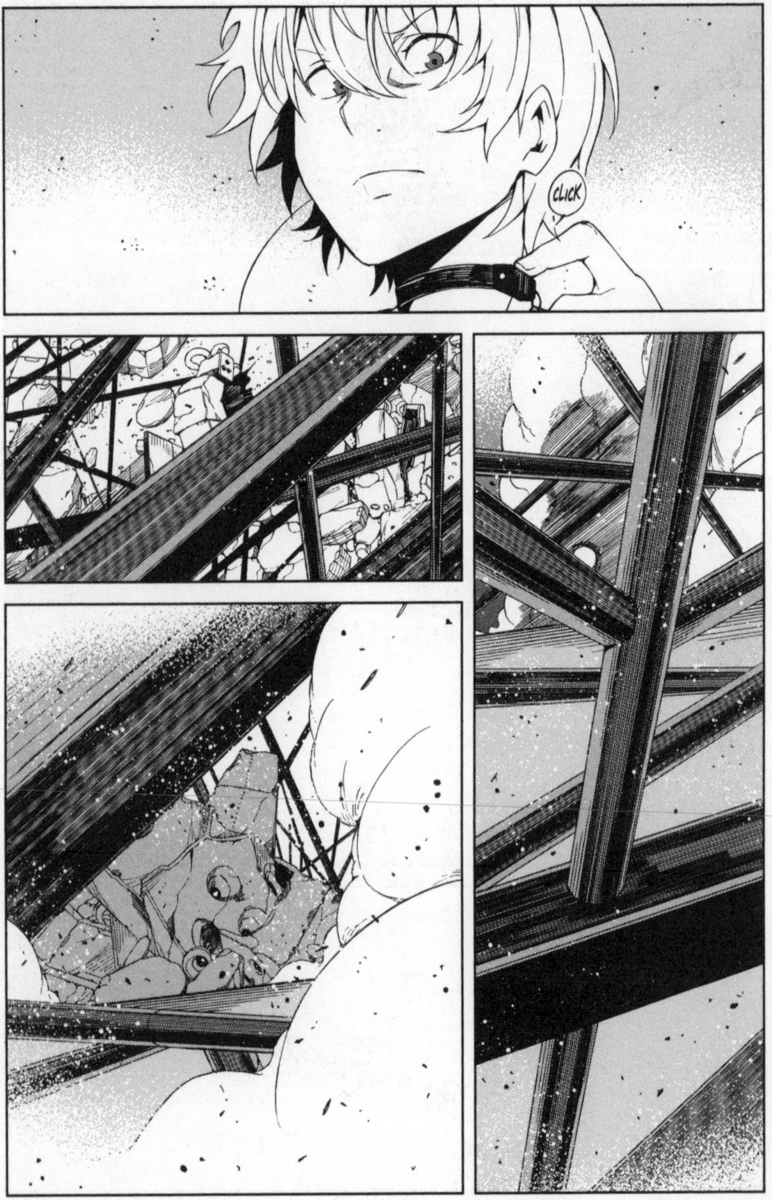
CLICK

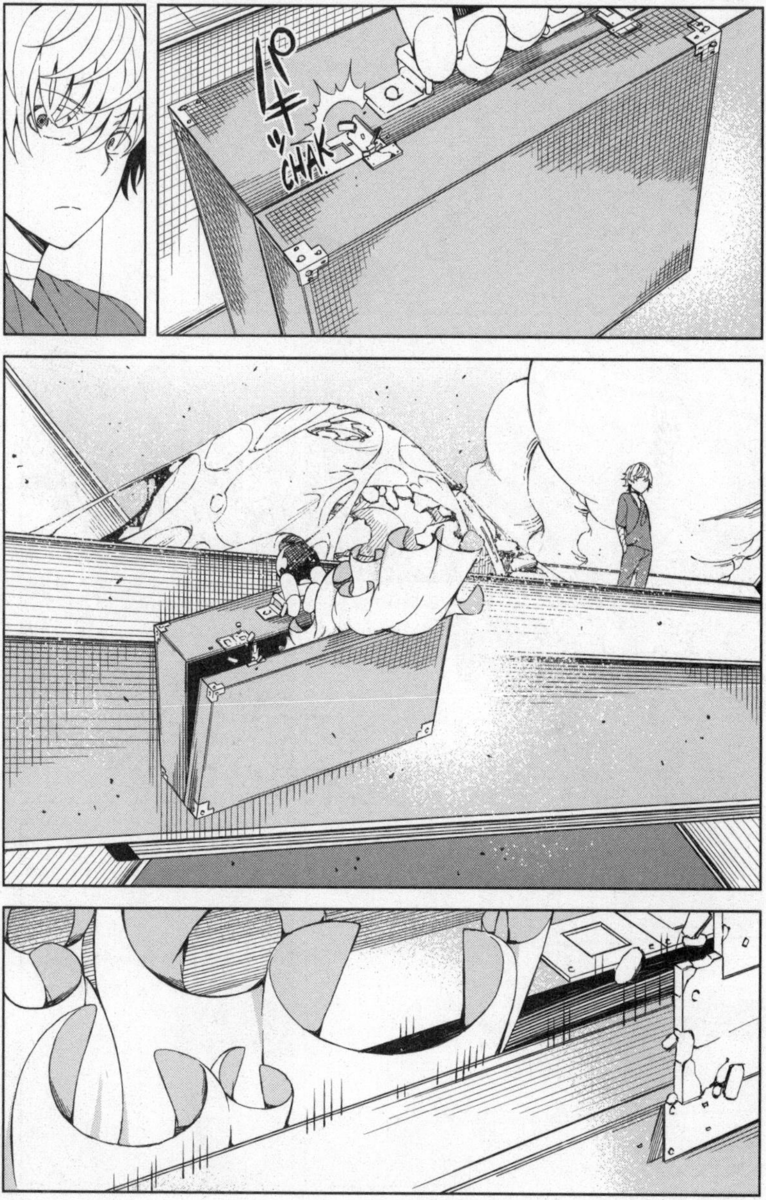
CHAK

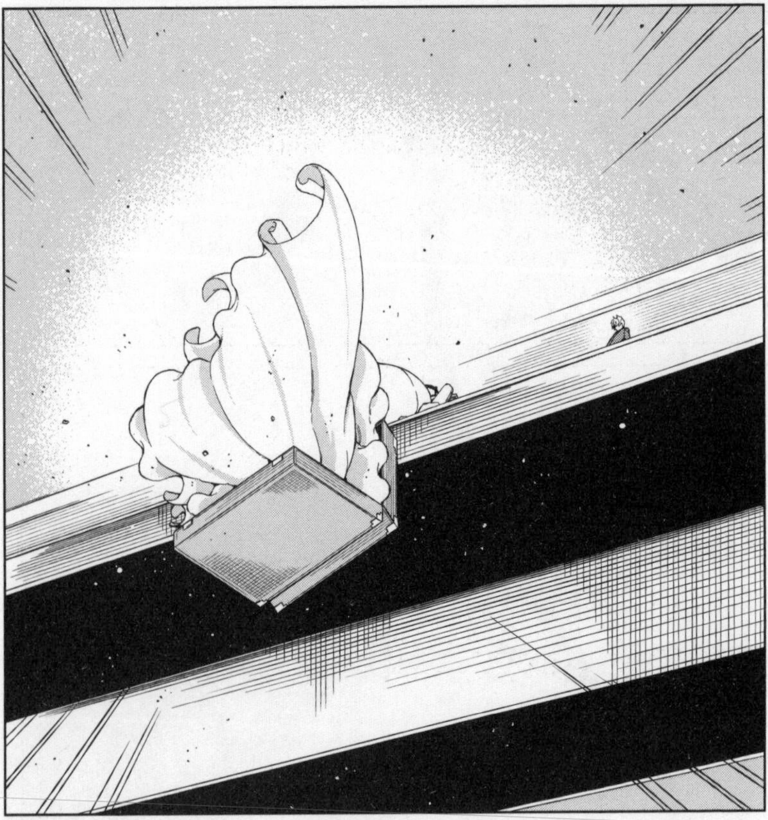
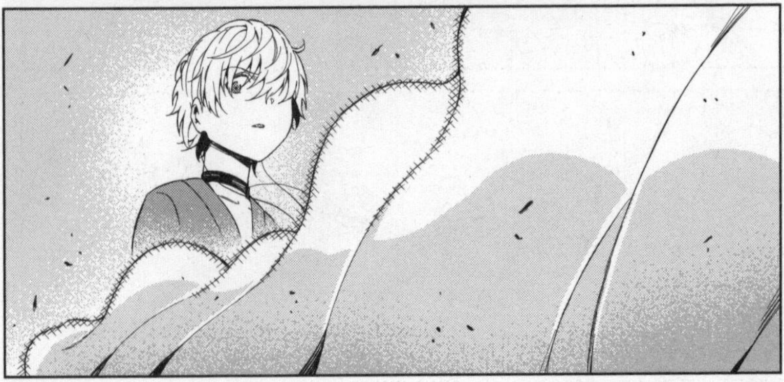

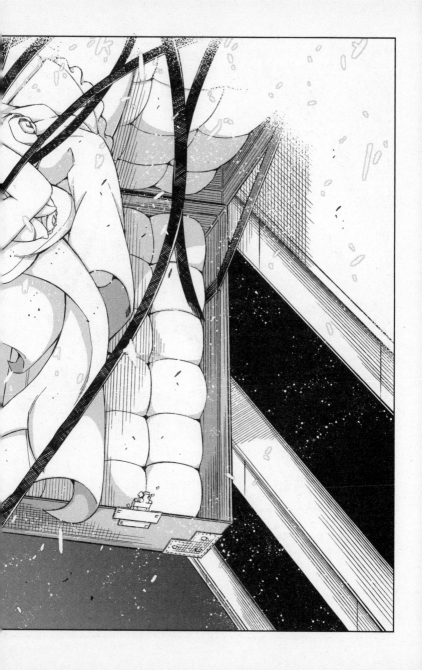

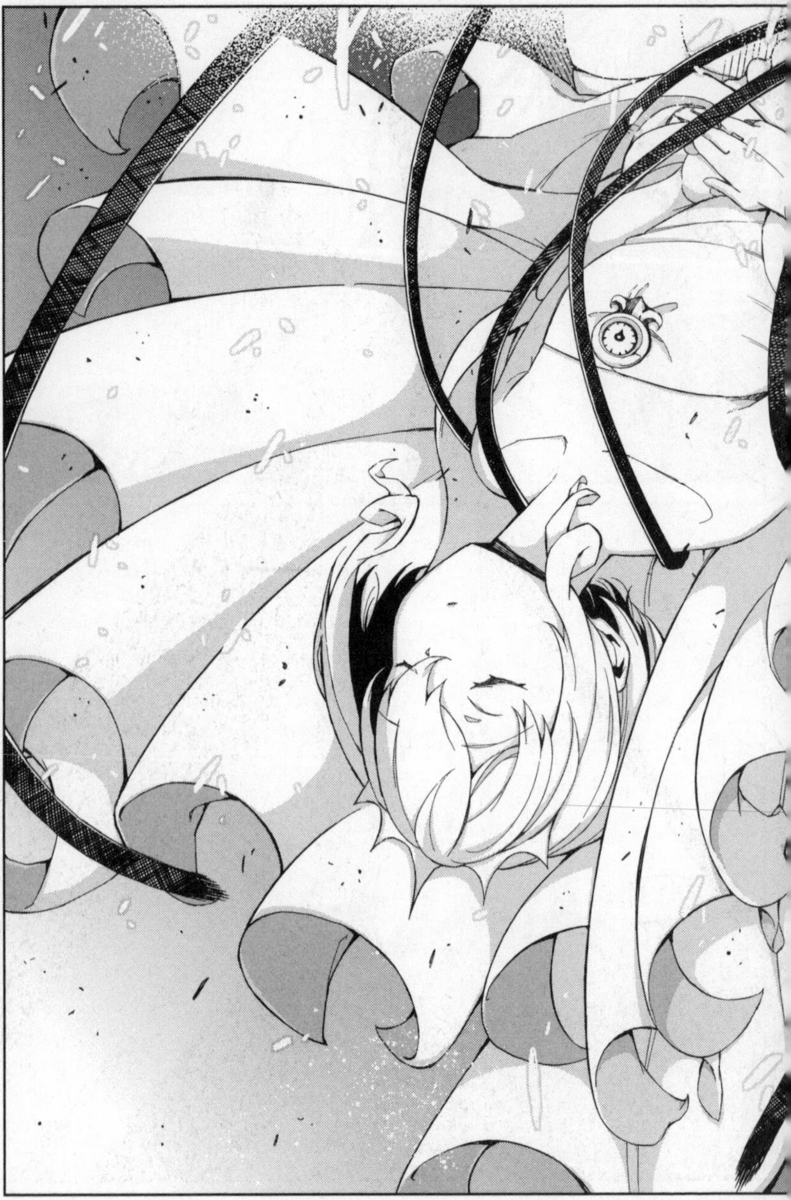

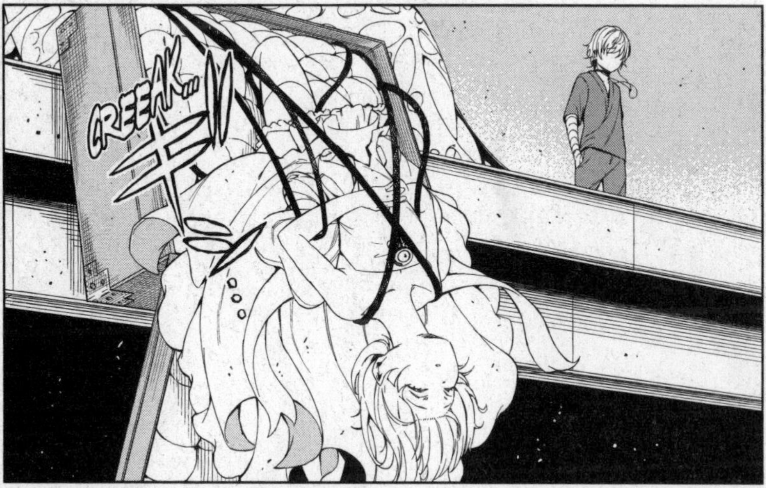
CREEAK...

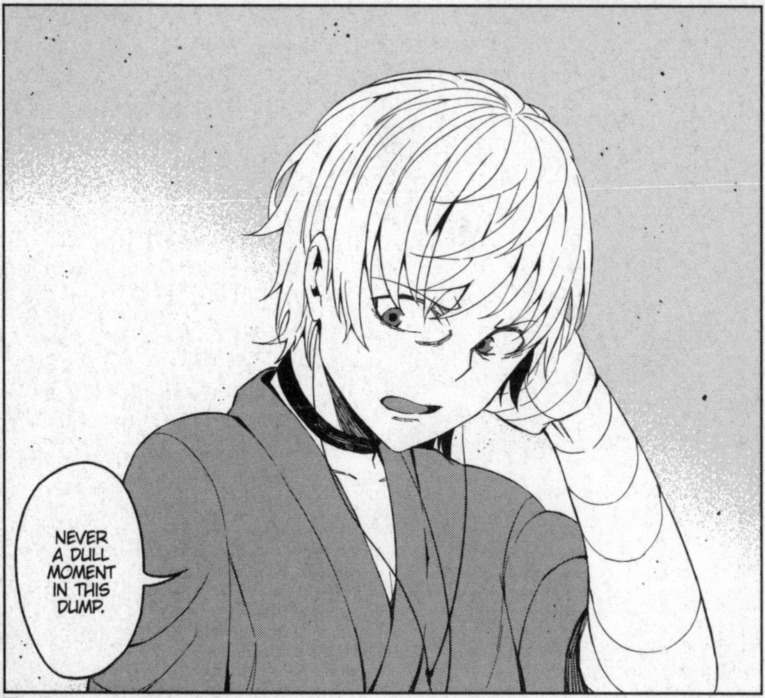
NEVER A DULL MOMENT IN THIS DUMP.

To be continued...

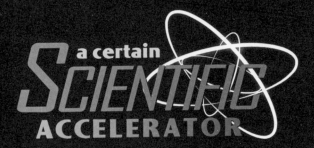

a certain
SCIENTIFIC
ACCELERATOR

PREVIEW OF NEXT VOLUME

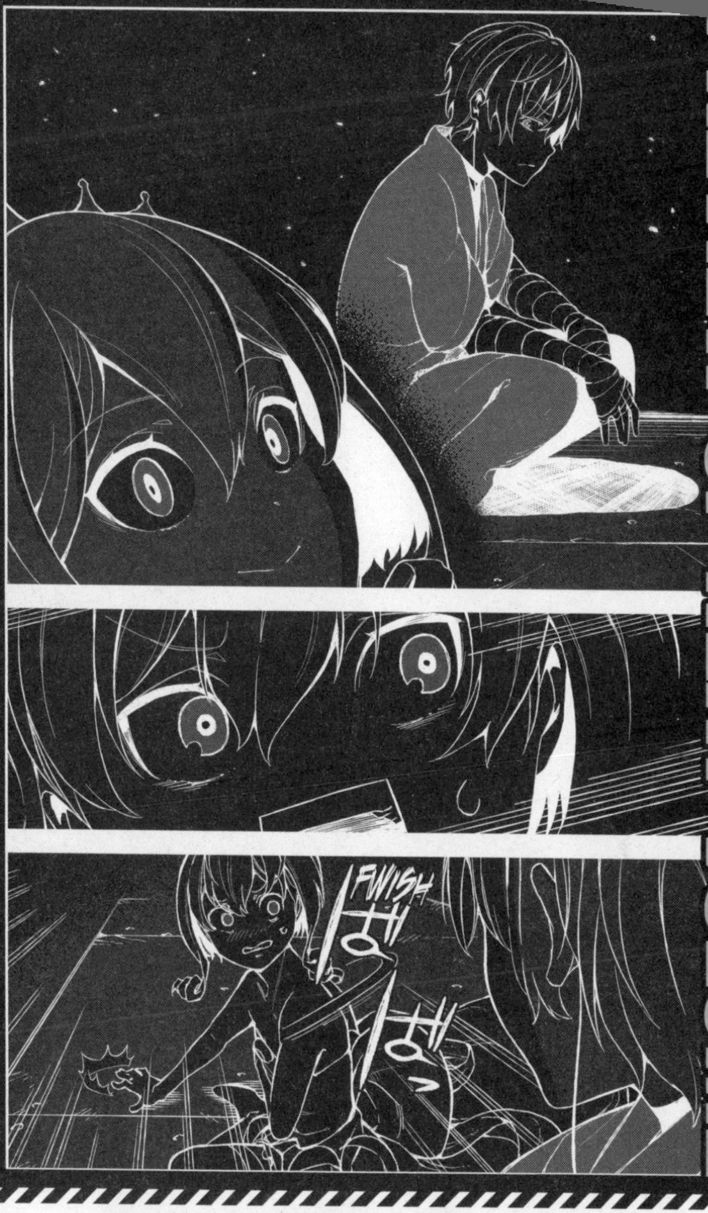
FWISH

Coming Soon!!

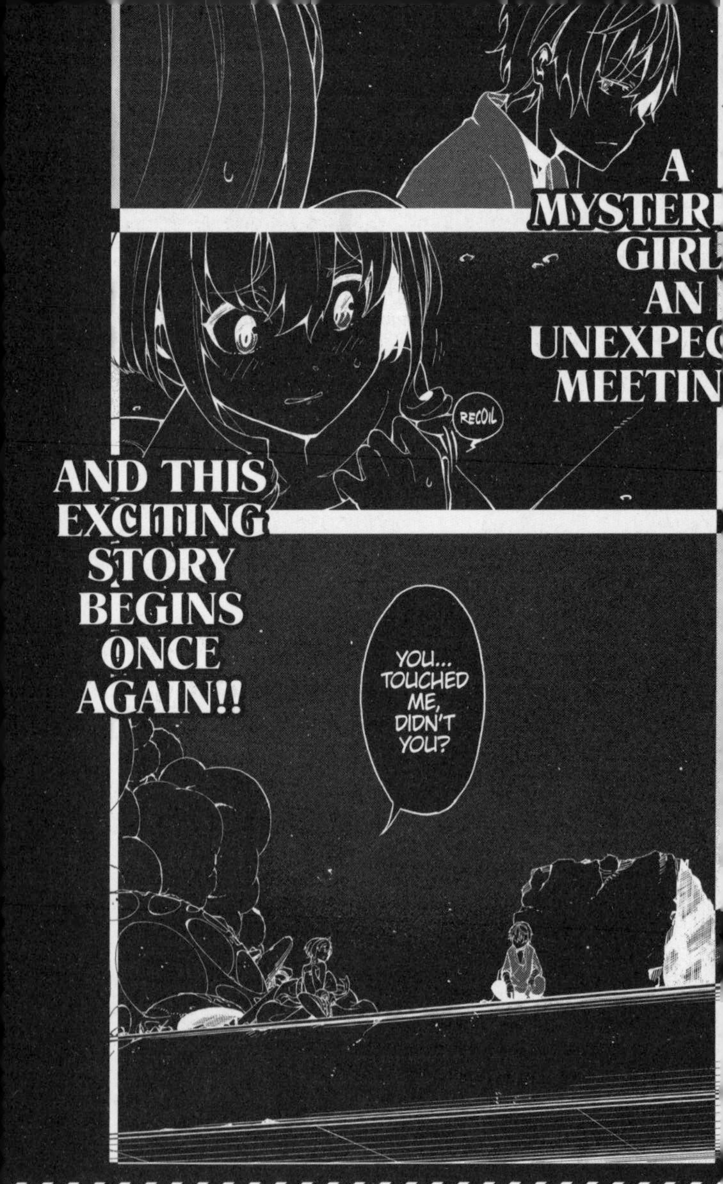
A MYSTER
GIRL
AN
UNEXPEC
MEETIN
RECOIL
AND THIS EXCITING STORY BEGINS ONCE AGAIN!!
YOU... TOUCHED ME, DIDN'T YOU?

A Certain Scientific Accelerat

a certain SCIENTIFIC ACCELERATOR
volume 7

story by **KAZUMA KAMACHI** / art by **ARATA YAMAJI**

TRANSLATION
Nan Rymer

ADAPTATION
Maggie Danger

LETTERING AND RETOUCH
Roland Amago
Bambi Eloriaga-Amago

COVER DESIGN
Nicky Lim

PROOFREADER
Shanti Whitesides
Janet Houck

ASSISTANT EDITOR
Jenn Grunigen

PRODUCTION ASSISTANT
CK Russell

PRODUCTION MANAGER
Lissa Pattillo

EDITOR-IN-CHIEF
Adam Arnold

PUBLISHER
Jason DeAngelis

Seven Seas books may be purchased in bulk for promotional, educational, or
business use. Please contact your local bookseller or the Macmillan Corporate
and Premium Sales Department at 1-800-221-7945, extension 5442, or by
e-mail at MacmillanSpecialMarkets@macmillan.com.

Seven Seas and the Seven Seas logo are trademarks of
Seven Seas Entertainment, LLC. All rights reserved.

ISBN: 978-1-626926-68-4

Printed in Canada

First Printing: January 2018

10 9 8 7 6 5 4 3 2 1

FOLLOW US ONLINE: *www.gomanga.com*

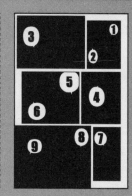

READING DIRECTIONS

This book reads from *right to left*, Japanese style.
If this is your first time reading manga, you start
reading from the top right panel on each page and
take it from there. If you get lost, just follow the
numbered diagram here. It may seem backwards at
first, but you'll get the hang of it! Have fun!!